Administering Early Childhood Settings

THE CANADIAN PERSPECTIVE

2nd Edition

Administering Early Childhood Settings

THE CANADIAN PERSPECTIVE

2nd Edition

Marilynn Yeates, St. Lawrence College, Kingston
Donna McKenna, Conestoga College, Kitchener
Carolyn Warberg, Centennial College, Toronto
Karen Chandler, George Brown College, Toronto

Maxwell Macmillan Canada

Published in Canada by
Maxwell Macmillan Canada Inc.
1200 Eglinton Avenue East, Suite 200
Don Mills, Ontario
M3C 3N1

Canadian Cataloguing in Publication Data

Main entry under title:

Administering early childhood settings : the
    Canadian perspective

2nd ed.
Includes bibliographical references and index.
ISBN 0-02-954205-7

1. Day care centers - Canada. 2. Early childhood
education - Canada. I. Yeates, Marilynn.

HV861.C2A36 1994   362.7'12   C94-930738-6

Printed on acid-free paper

Design, including cover: Brian Lehen • Graphic Design
All photographs including cover (except page 72) by Nikki Abraham
Photographs on page 72 by Donna McKenna
Editor: Sean Armstrong
Production Co-ordinator: Stephanie Cox
Printed and bound in Canada

123456789 / 987654

PREFACE TO THE SECOND EDITION

This book is designed to help student-teachers gain an understanding of what is often thought of as "the other side of child care"—the administrative, advocacy and professional responsibilities required of you as an early childhood educator.

As students, you spend most of your time refining your skills with children, their parents and the centre team. In this book we challenge you to also consider the administrative aspects of child care, since they affect the quality of that care and the effectiveness of programs. Further, we hope you will broaden your knowledge to include the development of child care as a profession. We believe knowledge of both these areas is essential to understanding the big picture.

One of the greatest difficulties our profession faces is the continuing struggle for recognition. This struggle is reflected in the confusion over nomenclature—the names we call ourselves and the names that others know us by. When you use words like *doctor*, *lawyer*, *nurse*, *teacher*, you generally have a set of images about what that profession does and what it stands for. The field of early childhood education suffers from a lack of clear terminology. We use terms ourselves as different as *early childhood educator*, *teacher*, *caregiver*, *child care worker*, *day care staff*, and *child care provider*. Others know us by these terms and more—sometimes we even still hear "babysitter." One of our current tasks as a profession is to reach agreement on what we are going to call ourselves. This book generally uses the terms *teacher* or *educator*, and *administrator* or *supervisor*.

A second difficulty we face is how to advocate for changes affecting our future as a profession. Child care is a national issue, of increasing complexity and importance. What responsibility do the different levels of government have to guarantee child care that is high quality, affordable and accessible to all? Should child care become a universal free service—and if so, who should pay? Who is going to make sure that child care remains a high priority with our politicians? Our everyday experience in the field teaches us what children and families need. How to provide it, and who pays for it, are the questions we need to consider.

Instructors who are familiar with *Administering Early Childhood Settings: The Canadian Perspective* will notice many improvements in this second edition.

- Since the first edition came out, much has happened—or failed to happen—in the field of early childhood education. This second edition takes account of these developments, and each chapter has been revised to reflect new research and current concerns. The titles of several have been changed, to reflect their increased scope.

- Each chapter has been carefully rewritten, to include new material and make the discussion as clear as possible. Each now begins with a list of the major topics that are covered, and these topics correspond to the main headings within the chapter.
- The discussion has been greatly expanded in several key areas, such as "The role of government," "Physical environments" and "Staffing."
- Chapter 7, "Leadership: Styles and Challenges," is entirely new, reflecting the importance of this topic in professional development in the field.
- Many new appendices have been added, with sample forms and surveys.
- The comprehensive bibliography is new.
- Clarity and accessibility are improved by the new look.

People entering the profession in the 1990s need acquaintance with the entire field of early childhood education. The quality of care you can give the children you care for will be greatly affected by the setting, which is greatly affected by the issues covered in this book.

We dedicate this book to you, today's students—the future of early childhood education. We challenge you to become informed about all aspects of our profession.

Acknowledgements

Many reviewers contributed their time and expertise to the development of the second edition. The authors and the publisher would like to thank the following people:

Lynda Brown, Donway Co-operative Nursery School, Don Mills, Ontario
Maureen Feeney, Vancouver Community College, Langara, B.C.
Elaine Ferguson, Child Care Connection Nova Scotia, Halifax, N.S.
Harriet Field, Mount St. Vincent University, Halifax, N.S.
Paul Fralick, Mohawk College, Hamilton, Ontario
Martha Friendly, University of Toronto, Toronto, Ontario
Sandra Griffin, University of Victoria, Victoria, B.C.
Joan Kunderman, Red River Community College, Winnipeg, Manitoba
Jane Lowe, Durham College, Oshawa, Ontario
Judy Pollard, Selkirk College, Castlegar, B.C.
Brenda Pollock, Vanier College, Ville St. Laurent, Quebec
Cheri Szereszewski, Assoc. of E. C. E. of Ontario, Richmond Hill, Ontario
Alice Taylor, Holland College, Charlottetown, P.E.I.

CONTENTS

High Quality Child Care— A Definition

A high quality early childhood program meets children's needs and interests at each developmental stage. This chapter identifies and discusses some of the issues affecting quality, under these headings:

◆　The expanding child care system
◆　What is quality child care?
◆　Indicators of quality child care
◆　Indicators of quality: The child's environment
◆　Indicators of quality: Caregiver characteristics
◆　Indicators of quality: Contextual factors
◆　Methods of achieving quality.

"Two out of every three mothers working"

"Part-time work seen as future trend"

"Management, union agree to discuss job sharing"

"Food prices continue to fluctuate, says Statscan"

These headlines point to some of the reasons why child care has moved from being a private concern to a public issue in the past few years. As the economy continues to change rapidly, business and industry have begun to recognize that the quality and availability of child care affect the well-being of their employees, and contribute positively to their job performance.

Early childhood programs that nurture, protect and educate young children affect not only the children themselves, but beyond them their families, communities and the larger society. The social and economic benefits reach into every segment of Canadian society—parents are free to work or attend school, while children receive the best nurturing and early childhood education possible.

THE EXPANDING CHILD CARE SYSTEM

Canadian children live in a world that is often very different from the one their parents were raised in. There are more single-parent families, and most families with two parents also need two wage earners. The typical Canadian mother works outside the home, usually at a full-time job. Often she returns to work soon after the birth of a child—the latest census figures indicate that significant numbers of mothers of young children are employed outside the home. Most single parents are women, and women's wages are generally lower, so many single parents raise their families on incomes below the poverty level.

These developments make the provision of quality child care a major challenge of the 1990s. The need is shown in the statistics: for 1992, the latest year for which full statistics were available, Health and Welfare Canada reported there were 1 749 319 children with a lone parent or two parents working or studying full-time, and 350 680 regulated child care spaces. These figures argue a great unmet need for child care, and show why families, child care advocates and women's groups have been pressing, over a number of years, for the development of a national child care policy.

As early as 1970, the Royal Commission on the Status of Women identified the child care crisis in its report. The Commission pointed out that parents required supplementary child care to allow them to meet both work and parental responsibilities, and emphasized that society had a role in contributing to the development of these services.

Recognizing the benefits to Canadian families and the larger society, the federal government announced a national child care policy in late 1987. This policy planned to double the number of then existing licensed spaces by 1994, to 400 000, a number many experts felt was still too low. This plan was never put into effect—all plans to proceed with a national child care program were cancelled by the federal government in April 1989, after it had won the 1988 federal election. Chapter 2 discusses in more detail the history of child care policy and the unmet demand for regulated child care.

Parents who seek child care outside their homes should be able to choose from a variety of options, since family needs and preferences can vary substantially. In the formal system, families would be able to select from options that include regulated home day care/family day homes, group care and parent-child resource centres. These services should meet the needs of infants, toddlers, preschool and school-age children, providing full- or part-time care on a regular or flexible basis. Multicultural sensitivity should be a given, and children with special needs should be integrated.

Many families who choose to look after their children at home may require flexible work schedules to allow this. For example, one parent may work part-time, or on a night shift, providing care for the child during the daytime hours when the other parent is working. Other families prefer to make private arrangements, but need access to information and referral services to accomplish this. Many families cannot afford the high cost of care.

In reality, this range of services is not available in most communities across Canada. Families have been left to struggle on their own, balancing work demands with their children's needs. The supply of child care is inadequate, especially for school-age children and infants. Virtually no child care exists in some areas of the country, and where there is adequate supply, quality is uneven. Where a full range of child care services exists, many parents are barred by the high cost.

Many Canadians feel there must be more, and better, child care. Progress is needed to increase the total number of spaces, but there cannot be a large-scale creation of spaces without a general agreement on standards that must be met. Standards must be established that reflect the kind of high quality care Canadian children need.

To understand the place of such standards, we need to look at the question of what defines quality. What are the components of high quality care? How do these elements interact? How can parents assess which caregiving situation is right for their child? Answers to these questions will guide the efforts of practitioners and spur action to upgrade the quality of our nation's child care.

WHAT IS QUALITY CHILD CARE?

Quality has become a central topic of study among early childhood educators and developmental psychologists, and no single issue related to child care is as complex, controversial or important. Over the past twenty years, we have moved beyond debates about whether child care helps or harms development, or which types of child care are best. The question today is, "How can we make child care better?"

A program can be analyzed through several perspectives:

- its services to working parents
- its enhancement of children's development
- its position within a range of family support services.

These are not mutually exclusive—all three should be goals in any child care setting. But each provides a different way of analyzing a centre's operation, and together they show the diversity of issues related to high quality child care.

From the parent's perspective, the child should be safe, adequately fed, active, and happy. The service must be reliable, affordable, consistent with the family's values, and similar to the kind of care the parents themselves would provide. Other factors important to parents include flexible scheduling, a location convenient to home or work, provision of care for more than one child in the family, and occasional care when children are sick.

The second perspective emphasizes the child's development. The professionals directly involved in providing child care stand most directly behind this view, although of course parents are also vitally concerned with their child's development. Good child care meets children's needs and stimulates their interests at each developmental stage. For example, infants need good physical care, continuing love and affection, and opportunities for interaction, exploration and sensory stimulation.

The third viewpoint acknowledges that quality child care cannot be provided in isolation, but must be part of a broader range of services to children and families. Parents may need services which provide support, counselling and referrals. For example, families that have children with special needs benefit from this co-ordinated service. In a comprehensive family support services approach, staff may be drawn from the fields of health, education and social work.

Each perspective highlights part of what is involved in quality care, and needs to be considered by caregivers, parents, advocates, and policymakers. The different emphasis provided by each illustrates how complex the issue of quality is. The *ecological approach* provides a way of thinking about the overall question.

The Ecological Model of Child Care

Ecology is the study of how organisms interact with their environment. Researchers in the child care field increasingly use such a broad perspective in assessing child care environments. An ecological approach to understanding child care looks at the interaction among children, parents and early childhood educators, and their relationship with the environments in which they work and live.

An ecological look at child care considers not only how to structure environments to foster children's growth, but also how these environments interact with influences outside the centre. Often efforts to improve child care have seen each program as a self-contained classroom, and so concentrated on internal factors, doing things like buying new equipment or adjusting curriculum. But experienced practitioners have come to understand that the impact of such changes will be limited, if a centre fails to consider the wider environment within which its programs take place.

Bronfenbrenner (1979) provides a framework for looking at child care programs in his ecological model of human development. He thinks in terms of four levels, each embedded within the next (see Figure 1-1). Bronfenbrenner's model provides a way of moving beyond the immediate setting, to consider in turn the layers of influence acting on the developing child, along with the impact of child care upon family, community and society.

FIGURE 1-1
Bronfenbrenner's Ecological System

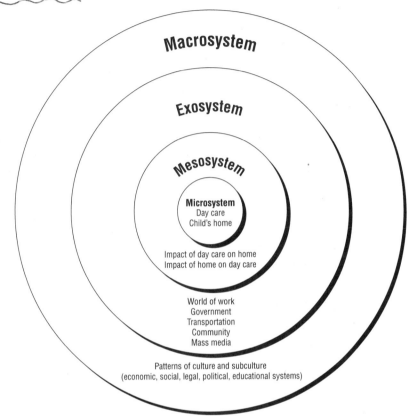

At the centre, the *microsystem* (*micro* = small) is centred on the developing child herself within her immediate settings—the child care program, a school classroom, a family child care, or her own home.

The second circle is the *mesosystem* (*meso* = middle), where different microsystems interact. For example, the relationship of the child care environment with the home would be considered here. These interactions will be influenced by how different adults perceive the child, and by child-rearing beliefs.

Outside this is the *exosystem* (*exo* = outside), which represents the social structures, both formal and informal, which influence the settings the child experiences. In this dimension, one must consider the roles and influences of various government agencies and policies in child care, the local economy, transportation, the mass media, the workplace, and the immediate community.

All these sets of relationships are located in a *macrosystem* (*macro* = great). It includes patterns of culture, such as the economic, educational, legal, and political systems. These would include attitudes towards the family and the role of motherhood, and community definitions of appropriate environments for young children. The macrosystem defines what is possible: for example, a society which believes children belong to their parents, rather than to society at large, will greatly restrict government involvement in child care.

All these systems are in play when we address the question of quality.

INDICATORS OF QUALITY CHILD CARE

Quality is best understood as a blend of desirable factors. Adult-child ratio, group size, caregiver education and experience, curriculum, physical environment, quality of adult-child interactions, adult work environment, level of parent involvement—all are aspects of quality.

Research has identified a number of these discrete indicators of quality (the term *indicator* is frequently used in the professional literature to refer to the individual characteristics of a program). It is becoming apparent that many of these indicators are interrelated, and that their mutual impact ultimately affects the child's well-being. Deborah Phillips' *Quality in child care: What does research tell us?* provides an overview of significant research into the factors affecting quality. Another review is provided by Doherty's book *Quality matters in child care* (1994), which looks at more than a hundred research studies conducted in the past ten years in Canada, the United States, Europe, and elsewhere, identifying a common core of caregiver behaviours and program characteristics associated with positive outcomes for children in both the short and long term.

Both the Canadian Child Care Federation (1991) and the U.S. National Association for the Education of Young Children (1984) define quality child care as child care which:

- supports and assists the child's physical, emotional, social, and intellectual well-being and development, and
- supports the family in its child-rearing role.

Research indicates child care quality can be discussed in terms of *structural quality* or *process quality*. *Structural quality* generally refers to variables that can be regulated, including adult-child ratio, group size, and the education and training of caregivers. *Process quality* refers to interactions, the provision of developmentally appropriate activities, and warm, nurturing, sensitive caregiving.

Process quality is difficult to regulate. For example, most people would agree that a teacher should be sensitive to the children in his or her care. But it is difficult to imagine how a supervisor could assure sensitivity during hiring, or through job performance evaluation.

However, structural quality and process quality are related, and structural quality can be regulated. While it would be difficult to measure a teacher's sensitivity, research suggests that teachers with more years of formal education are, as a group, more sensitive (Whitebrook et al. 1990). Therefore, a requirement of formal education may be intended to ensure that teachers are more likely to be sensitive.

Careful and systematic research on child care programs is relatively new; the bulk of it has appeared since 1970. The National Day Care Study (1979) conducted in the United States has had a profound impact on legislation both there and in Canada. This study identified group size and specialized caregiver training as significant elements of child care quality in centre-based programs for preschoolers, with staff-child ratios a further crucial element in infant and toddler care.

While research has helped answer many questions, others remain unanswered. Those interested in the improvement of quality in child care services must consider the program's relationship with the external environment, and the exploration of this relationship helps provide a research agenda for the 1990s.

Licensing and regulatory systems that are well-designed and effectively administered can help assure the provision of early childhood programs that will nurture, protect and educate young children. Regulation by itself does not ensure quality: it is designed to prevent programs from harming children, rather than promote programs that enhance development. But if regulation does not ensure quality, it is an important factor safeguarding it. The responsibility for regulation rests with each province and territory. Child care services are patchwork, provided by a variety of agencies and auspices, with minimum regulation.

Through the next sections, the following indicators of quality child care will be examined:

The child's environment

- adult-child ratio
- group size
- curriculum
- physical environment
- interactions.

Caregiver characteristics

- education and experience
- stability and job satisfaction.

Contextual factors

- funding, auspice, licencing standards
- relationships with the external environment
- parent involvement.

INDICATORS OF QUALITY: THE CHILD'S ENVIRONMENT

Adult–Child Ratio

One of the most important indicators of quality is the ratio of caregivers to children. A program should have sufficient numbers of trained staff to meet the needs of the children and promote their physical, social, emotional, and cognitive development. Each caregiver should engage in a stimulating and sensitive fashion with a limited number of children.

Children in settings with a low child-staff ratio are more likely to receive appropriate caregiving and experience more developmentally appropriate activities. Higher ratios (more children to each staff member) are associated with a lower standard of care, because staff are less able to provide each child with the necessary amount of individual attention.

Research indicates that optimal ratios vary with the age of the child. Reduced ratios appear to be especially important for infants and toddlers: ratios higher than 1:4 for children under three have been observed to result in increases in child apathy and distress. For older children, the more children per adult, the more time staff need to spend managing and controlling activities, and the less time they have to interact with children.

Group Size

For children older than the toddler stage but under five, adult-child ratios may be less significant than group size (see Figure 1-2). The total number of children within each group is clearly linked to program quality. Where groups are smaller, caregivers spend more time interacting with children and less time simply watching them.

The determination of maximum group size should reflect the developmental needs of children, along with practical considerations such as the demands on the caregiver's time. In smaller groups, children are more verbal, more involved in activities and less aggressive, and they make the greatest gains in standardized tests of learning and vocabulary. Group size should be evaluated and defined to facilitate adult-child interaction, individualized attention for children, and constructive activity among them.

Maximum group size should be determined by the distribution of ages within the group, the activity, and the inclusion of children with special needs. The group must be small enough to permit caregivers to manage both individual and group activities effectively. This will encourage the appropriate development of independence, self-assertion, problem-solving, co-operation, and friendliness.

Health officials also recommend group-limiting strategies—that is, keeping small groups of children consistently together—to reduce the spread of infection in child care settings.

FIGURE 1-2
Staff-Child Ratios Within Group Size

Age of children*	Group Size									
	6	8	10	12	14	16	18	20	22	24
Infants (birth-12 months)	1:3	1:4								
Toddlers (12-24 months)	1:3	1:4	1:5	1:4						
Two-year-olds (24-36 months)		1:4	1:5	1:6**						
Two- and three-year-olds			1:5	1:6	1:7**					
Three-year-olds					1:7	1:8	1:9	1:10**		
Four-years-olds						1:8	1:9	1:10**		
Four- and five-year-olds						1:8	1:9	1:10**		
Five-year-olds						1:8	1:9	1:10		
Six- to eight-year-olds (school age)								1:10	1:11	1:12

* Multi-age grouping is both permissible and desirable. When no infants are included, the staff-child ratio and group size requirements shall be based on the age of the majority of the children in the group. When infants are included, ratios and group sizes for infants must be maintained.

** Smaller group sizes and lower staff-child ratios are optimal. Larger group sizes and higher staff-child ratios are acceptable only in cases where staff are highly qualified.

Source: Canadian Child Care Federation, *Definition of high quality child care* (1991)

Curriculum

Young children learn from all their experiences. In high quality early childhood programs, teachers trained in child development use their skills of observation and assessment to plan appropriate experiences. Curriculum includes such items as program goals, planned activities, the daily schedule, and the availability of materials and equipment. It should facilitate the development of the whole child.

Children need a wide choice of developmentally appropriate activities and opportunities to explore their own interests. They need adequate amounts of uninterrupted time to persist in self-chosen tasks and activities. Multiculturalism, in conjunction with an anti-bias curriculum, must be an integral and continuous part of the program, just as it is part of Canadian society. Children can be encouraged to share aspects of their culture and lifestyle, and their parents can also contribute to the program.

Different curriculum approaches emphasize different aspects of child development. In general, research shows that highly structured programs emphasizing cognitive and language development are particularly effective with disadvantaged children. In programs structured by adults, children show less independence and initiative, but do better on intelligence and achievement tests. Children in open or child-centred programs are observed to be more independent and persistent. Children in moderately structured programs appear to fare best overall, demonstrating gains in creativity and self-esteem as well as cognition and achievement.

Whatever the approach, a program's success is related to how clearly its philosophy is defined. Curriculum is discussed at length in Chapter 4, "Developing Curriculum—The Supervisor's Role."

Physical Environment

Whether indoors or outdoors, the environment affects the behaviour and development of both adults and children. It should provide opportunities for exploration and learning. Physical environment affects the level of involvement of children, and the quality of interaction between adults and children.

In examining the impact of the environment, one must consider:

- both indoor and outdoor space
- the overall size, design and layout of space
- the availability of materials and equipment
- the health and safety needs of children.

Child care environments must ensure a minimum number of square metres per child. Studies have found that as the number of children in a space increases, so do aggressiveness, destructiveness and apathetic behaviour.

Equipment requirements are more difficult to quantify, since many types of equipment contribute to the objective of high quality care. Equipment should be age-appropriate, and designed to develop skills at various age levels. Materials should be available in sufficient quantities to allow choices by children and avoid unnecessary competition.

The environment must be safe and healthy. Staff in quality early childhood programs educate children concerning safe and healthy practices, and act to prevent illness and accidents. Further considerations around the physical environment are discussed in Chapter 5, "Physical Environments."

Interactions

The quality of interaction between adults and children determines program quality more than anything else. Adults provide affection and support—they comfort children when they cry and reassure them when they are fearful. Optimal development is enhanced by relationships with adults that are positive, supportive and individualized. Adults support developing independence by helping when needed, while allowing children to do what they are capable of and want to do for themselves.

Young children also develop through peer interaction, and here adult intervention is again crucial. The schedule should provide many opportunities for children to play with and beside other children. Teachers support children's beginning friendships.

Interactions between children and staff should provide opportunities for children to develop an understanding of self and others, and therefore all interactions should be characterized by respect, affection, freedom from bias, and humour.

From a child's point of view, child care is a joint enterprise of parents and caregivers. This fact is recognized in some studies that examine the joint efforts of home and child care environments on child development. There is some concern about caregiver/parent relations here—Galinsky (1988) revealed that many caregivers harbour negative attitudes about the parents of children in their care. Galinsky further revealed that these attitudes vary with the caregiver's perceptions of the quality of parental child-rearing, parental education and marital status, and whether the parents are using subsidized care. This research points to a key area needing to be studied further, and indicates a need for additional caregiver education on how to meet a variety of parental needs.

Quality of interaction is interrelated with other factors we have discussed: ratio of adults to children, caregiver education, continuity in relationship, group size, and program size. In her summary of research, Doherty (1994) suggests ratio has a direct influence on the child's experience of caregiver responsiveness, or lack of it, and this ultimately affects the child's well-being and development. This aspect of a program can be assessed using instruments such as the *Early childhood environment rating scale* (Harms and Clifford 1980, 1989, 1990).

Further issues around quality of interaction are discussed in Chapter 6, "Staffing—The Key to Quality."

INDICATORS OF QUALITY: CAREGIVER CHARACTERISTICS

Education and Experience

The teacher is the most important factor in the quality of child care. Among the important variables that affect a teacher's performance are the amount and kind of formal education, experience in child care, and length of service.

Formal education and specialized training in child development appear to favourably influence the caregiver's ability to engage in developmentally appropriate behaviour with children (Whitebrook et al. 1990). Research has found that appropriate staff training in child development contributes to positive outcomes for children in areas such as increased social interaction with adults, the development of prosocial behaviours, and improved language and cognitive development. Appropriate training for staff is linked to more social interaction between caregiver and children, more cooperation and task persistence among children, and less apathetic unengaged behaviour among children.

The amount of teacher preparation, both preservice and in-service, significantly predicts program quality, which in turn is linked with more positive child outcomes, especially in terms of language and representational skills—critical areas for school success. Caregivers with more training have less authoritarian styles and slightly more knowledge about child development.

In contrast, experience alone appears to have little association with positive child outcomes. By itself, caregiver experience is not a predictor of effective caregiving, and in the absence of other factors has been linked to less cognitive and social stimulation among children, and more apathy among infants. To emphasize this point: in child care as in other fields, experience is valuable. But experience alone, without other supporting factors, does not appear to necessarily make an effective caregiver.

Teachers should be trained in the requirements of children with special needs, and given an awareness of the social and political forces affecting early childhood programs. They must possess the knowledge, skill and competency to interact sensitively and successfully not only with the children they care for, but also with adults. A number of studies (Almy 1975; Feeny 1985) have probed beyond training to examine the significance of personal characteristics of staff such as motivation, communication skills and enjoyment of children. One study suggests that important teacher qualifications are rooted in basic personal qualities.

Stability and Job Satisfaction

A further very important connection between staffing and quality is stability. Increased stability in child care arrangements is linked with positive child outcomes in both the short and long term. Caregiver stability is particularly important for infants and toddlers, because they are in the process of forming attachment relationships. It is also an increasingly serious problem, with annual teacher turnover rates in the field of 26 per cent, and estimated to be even higher in family day care.

Stability is only one of several ways that caregiver job satisfaction among caregivers affects child behaviour and development. Studies indicate that salary is the best predictor of job satisfaction: higher salaries are associated with higher job commitment that views child care as a career. Whitebrook et al. (1990) also found that teachers earning salaries at the higher end of the range worked in centres with better quality. In the study *Caring for a living* (1993), Karyo et al. found that the nature of the work and relationships with co-workers were listed as the most satisfying aspects of working in child care.

Caregivers who are satisfied with their job are more likely to provide encouragement and guidance to children. Caregivers who are dissatisfied tend to be restrictive and controlling. The concerted efforts of professional groups, government and caregivers are needed to ensure a more stable and effective child care system that meets the personal and professional needs of caregivers.

To improve job satisfaction, the field must:

- improve salaries
- increase teacher involvement in decision-making
- ensure that caregivers receive their breaks and lunch hours
- raise the status of the early childhood profession
- provide opportunities for continuing education and professional development.

INDICATORS OF QUALITY: CONTEXTUAL FACTORS

Funding, Auspice, Licensing Standards

Quality is affected by many contextual factors, such as funding, auspice, standards, and regulations.

As staff and many parents know, funding comes primarily from parent fees. Child care is a labour intensive service, with cost depending on the child/staff ratio and the wages and benefits paid to the staff. As we have seen, quality requires favourable ratio and group sizes, adequate supplies of appropriate equipment and materials, and reasonable compensation. All these require adequate funding.

The term *auspice* is used to describe the way in which a program is operated. In Canada, such auspices include municipal, non-profit and commercial programs, and the availability of each possibility varies widely across the country. These different configurations are discussed in Chapter 2, "The Role of Government." Auspice influences quality through its effect on wages, working conditions and job satisfaction. In fact, the auspice of a centre is often the strongest predictor of quality.

Studies clearly support the conclusion that high quality child care is more likely to be found in non-profit than commercial auspices. Teaching staff in a non-profit centre generally have higher levels of formal education and more specialized training in child development, and the setting usually has better staff-children ratios and teacher consistency. This is not to deny the existence of high quality for-profit programs, or poor quality non-profit programs. Some think non-profit centres are higher in quality because they receive more government funding.

Experts and advocates are agreed on what needs to be done to provide a national system of child care, but this agreement has not been shared by government. Some critics of child care regulation have suggested that the establishment of national regulatory standards will not lead to higher quality child care. They argue that no one can regulate a warm, loving caregiver and that regulations lead to institutionalized care. The findings suggest otherwise. When centres voluntarily met regulatory standards, teachers were more sensitive and able, and children benefited.

Relationships with the External Environment

Any effort to improve the quality of child care programs needs to direct some attention to developing and maintaining good relationships with external parties. Early childhood programs benefit from cultivating good relationships with community people such as legislators, bankers, doctors, licensing officers, merchants, and community leaders. Children benefit when they learn about the community as a vital component of their curriculum. Field trips, visits from a police officer, or trips to the market are a few of the ways for children to be involved in their community.

Community interaction should include:

- awareness and appropriate use of community resources
- communication and interaction with elementary schools
- sensitivity to changing community needs

‹• co-operative projects within the community, such as multi-generational projects and public education endeavours.

Child care is a vital part of any community. Chapter 11, "Community, Resources and Advocacy," examines this aspect of quality further.

Parent Involvement

A program must recognize the importance of families and develop strategies to work effectively with them. Parent involvement can cover a range of activities, from a simple newsletter for parents to active partnerships between parents and staff.

Parents and staff should communicate about child-rearing practices such as discipline and routines, in order to minimize potential conflicts and confusion for the children. Studies suggest that open and regular communication between caregiver and parent has a very significant impact on quality. This is especially so where the parent is observant and informed, and perhaps serves as a member of the program's board of directors or advisory group, participating in the evaluation of the program. Chapter 10, "Parents and Programs—A Vital Partnership," provides more examples of how to involve parents in early childhood programs.

Child care is a collaborative endeavour, with children moving back and forth between home and program. Future research needs to examine the combined effects of the child's experience in child care and at home.

METHODS OF ACHIEVING QUALITY

The mechanisms that can be used to maintain quality fall into three general categories:
- regulatory methods
- voluntary standards
- other non-regulatory methods.

An effective licensing and regulatory system can be the cornerstone of any national effort to assure quality in early childhood programs. Licensing provides the necessary foundation upon which all other efforts are built. Government licensing requirements tend solely to address structural indicators such as staff-child ratios, even though process dimensions may be more important for quality. Nonetheless, regulatory requirements based on the findings of research increase the probability that all children in licensed settings will receive higher quality care.

Quality levels higher than the minimum required for licensing may be established by making such standards a condition of funding, or by requiring that staff meet certain levels. A funding agency can define the level of quality it is prepared to purchase. For example, a municipal government may require a centre in which it is purchasing subsidy spaces to meet higher standards than those set by the provincial government. These additional standards will in effect raise the level of quality care.

Two additional measures focus on enhancing the quality of child care through the development of professional standards of practice. This can be done at both the program and the individual level. *Accreditation* is a process by which standards are set by a recognized body. An example is the accreditation standard set by the U.S. National Association for the Education of Young Children. Accredited programs are identified as meeting high standards of practice. Accreditation is usually a voluntary process, although it could be required of a program by its funding body.

The second method takes the form of *certification* of qualified individuals. Specialized training in early childhood education is essential for people to become competent teachers. Certification ensures that individuals have completed specific training programs, and demonstrated specific competencies in working with children.

Staff can improve the quality of a program through public education, membership in professional organizations, and consultation with other professionals. Other important methods for encouraging quality include program evaluation, staff training, parent education, and the provision of various types of support for the caregiver.

Children are not aware that child care varies in form, function, auspice or regulatory environment. What makes a difference for them are their relationships with teachers and peers. A national system of high quality child care services for Canadian children and their families depends upon the co-operation and support of all segments of the community.

ACTIVITIES

1. Identify barriers to providing high quality child care services.
2. In small groups, identify and discuss indicators of high quality child care from one of the following perspectives: parents, staff, community professionals.
3. Select one dimension of quality and develop the criteria to measure it.
4. Assess the quality of an early childhood setting using one of the following tools:

   - the Early Childhood Environment Rating Scale
   - the Child Care Inventory
   - the Early Childhood Work Environment Survey

5. Choose an aspect of your field placement site where you think quality could be improved. Identify a method, and if possible, implement it.

FURTHER READING

Doherty, G. (1991). *Quality matters in child care.* Huntsville, Ontario: Jesmond Publishing.

National Association for the Education of Young Children (1984). *Accreditation criteria and procedures of the National Academy of Early Childhood Programs.* Washington, DC: NAEYC.

Phillips, Deborah (ed.) (1987). *Quality in child care programs: What does the research tell us?* Washington, DC: NAEYC.

The Role of Government

Each level of government has its own role in child care. The influence of the *federal* government is primarily financial, while the delivery and operation of child care services are the responsibility of the *provincial* and *territorial* governments. The participation of *municipal* governments varies from enforcing local by-laws to directly providing child care. This chapter looks at:

◆ Child care in Canada—the need
◆ The role of the federal government
◆ The role of provincial and territorial governments
◆ The role of local governments
◆ Milestones in legislation, 1960–2001
◆ Legislative offices, acts and provincial advocacy organizations.

Government plays a central role in child care in two very different ways: regulation and funding.

Whether related to child care, banks or broadcasting, regulation is designed to assure minimum levels of quality and accessibility for the entire population. Regulation takes place through legislation shaped by the policy priorities of a particular government.

A government expresses its priorities in an even more concrete way, through its funding priorities. All governments attempt to respond to the needs of society within a constitutionally and legally defined framework, but each government displays its political priorities through how it collects and spends tax revenue. The provision and quality of child care in Canada are heavily affected by government funding priorities, whether these are expressed through federal-provincial transfer payments, direct operating grants, individual subsidies, income tax deductions, or budget restrictions.

Each level of government has its own role in child care. The influence of the federal government is primarily financial, through the transfer payments it makes available to provincial government budgets for child care and related services. Many people argue that the federal government should set national standards and develop a national approach, but so far this has not happened.

The delivery and operation of child care services are the responsibility of the provincial and territorial governments. They are most directly involved in the field of social policy, according to our constitutional division of powers, and so have jurisdiction over legislation and licensing governing child care facilities.

Municipal governments enforce local by-laws such as zoning, building and fire codes, public health regulations, and so on. In some provinces, municipalities have a role in the allocation of subsidized spaces. Some directly operate child care services.

CHILD CARE IN CANADA—THE NEED

Over the last twenty-five years, with the steadily increasing number of families where both parents or the single parent work outside the home, government policy with respect to child care has become a matter of increasing public concern. Children require care while their parents work. For women who are single parents—a social group whose numbers have greatly increased over these same twenty-five years—the availability of child care often makes the difference between independence and welfare. Lack of child care can lead to a perpetual cycle of poverty.

In general, the rapid changes in Canadian families and the growth in the need for child care have moved far ahead of the ability of governments to respond and shift resources. In 1992, the latest year for which full statistics were available at time of publication, there were:

- 32 612 full-time spaces in the formal child care system for children in the newborn to seventeen-month age group. At the same time, there were 188 193 Canadian children whose two parents worked or studied full-time, or whose lone parent worked or studied full-time. This translated into spaces for seventeen per cent of the children, with a lower percentange if we add children with a parent working full-time and another working more than twenty hours a week.

- 34 940 spaces for children in the eighteen-month to three-year-old group were enough for nineteen per cent of Canadian children with a parent or parents working or studying full-time.

- Children in the three- to six-year-old group were the best served. 196 143 spaces provided for almost fifty-four per cent of the children with a parent or parents working or studying full-time.

- With more than one million children between six and thirteen in the comparable category, a little under nine per cent were provided for in the 86 985 available spaces.

FIGURE 2-1
Percentage of children by age, with two parents or lone parent working or studying full-time, who are served by the formal child care system.

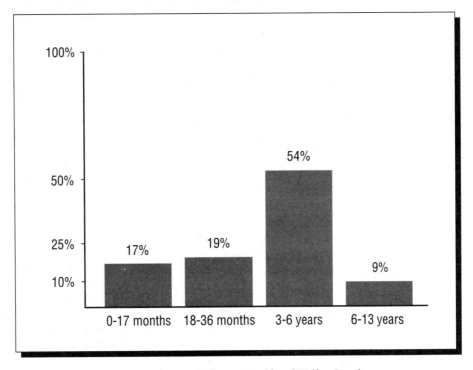

Source: *Status of day care in Canada 1992* (draft copy), Health and Welfare Canada.

These figures indicate the great need for child care, and the even greater unmet need for licensed spaces. Overall, somewhere between fifteen and twenty per cent of the total number of children needing care are in centres. Exact figures for those in informal care are impossible to obtain, but it is assumed to be somewhere over eighty per cent.

School-age children and infants are particularly underserved by the licensed sector. Studies indicate that many more parents would prefer to have their children in licensed care, if space were available and they could afford it.

THE ROLE OF THE FEDERAL GOVERNMENT

Many child care advocates believe a national system needs to be in place in Canada to direct and monitor child care, setting basic standards and levels of accessibility across the country. Federal legislation, combined with federal spending power, has the potential to do this. Debate continues on how far the responsibility of the federal government should go.

There is currently no national legislation or policy developed exclusively for child care. As things stand, the responsibility of the federal government is to:

- set policy direction.
- promote a philosophical point of view that influences provincial or territorial decisions around regulatory systems.
- redress any gaping inequities that exist in access to child care nationally.

Because child care is a political issue, the funding situation may change at any time. The federal government currently funds child care in several ways, as shown on the attached table. This reflects the situation at the time of publication. Each item is explained in detail following the chart.

FIGURE 2-2
The Federal Government's Role in Child Care.

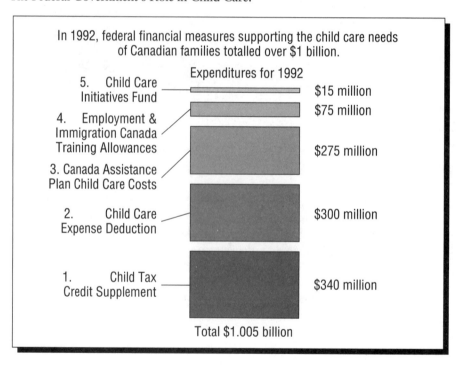

Source: Government of Canada, *Children matter* (May, 1992). Quoted in Zeenat Janmohamed, *Making the connections—Child care in Metropolitan Toronto.* Toronto: Metro Toronto Coalition for Better Child Care (1992).

Child Tax Credit Supplement (Item #1)

Until 1993, the former federal government viewed the Child Tax Credit Supplement as its major source of funding for child care. In 1992 this amounted to $340 million dollars, made available to low-income families with children under seven needing child care. Eligible families received $213 for each child under seven in the 1992 taxation year, an amount irrelevant to the real cost of child care.

In 1993 the federal government implemented the Child Benefit, which combined the existing Family Allowances, non-refundable Dependent Child Credit and refundable Child Tax Credit. Under this arrangement, low-income families get a few more dollars, but middle- and high-income families must have incomes above $100,000 to see even the slightest advantage.

The tax credit system benefits the wealthy, because high-income families have a higher marginal rate of taxation. Middle-class families see no benefits, and low-income families cannot access these credits if their provincial/territorial or local government does not allocate dollars for the matching system.

Child Care Expense Deduction (Item #2)

The Child Care Expense Deduction allows parents to claim direct child care costs related to employment as a deduction on their income tax, but only if they can produce receipts. As much as eighty-five per cent of the total number of children in care in Canada are in informal settings. Many parents pay thousands of dollars annually for unreceipted and unregulated child care, and therefore cannot claim the Child Care Expense Deduction. For those parents able to claim it, the total amount in 1992 was $300 million.

Canada Assistance Plan or CAP (Item #3)

The Canada Assistance Plan (CAP for short) is the main source of direct federal child care funding. In 1992 it provided $275 million for child care subsidies paid on behalf of individual families.

CAP began in 1966 as a major federal-provincial program to address poverty by sharing the cost of providing assistance and a range of social services to persons "in need" or "likely to become in need." The goal was universality: CAP would equalize payments and opportunities across the country.

Child care is one of the social services funded by CAP (it is also a relatively small part of what CAP funds). CAP pays child care costs through funding fee subsidies in child care centres for those families who meet its "needs" criteria. The way it works is this: the province or territory determines if a family qualifies for child care subsidy through "needs testing" that takes into account their budget for housing costs, food, expenses connected with work, debt repayments, etc. This test uses a formula, which varies from province to province and even municipality to municipality, to determine the amount a family is able to pay for child care.

If the family qualifies, and if there is a subsidized space available (there are long waiting lists, because subsidy dollars are scarce), they receive a subsidy to cover the difference between the child care centre's fees and the amount they are deemed able to pay. This subsidy, which is paid directly to the centre on their behalf, comes from three sources: the municipality pays twenty per cent, the province or territory pays thirty per cent, and the federal government pays the remaining fifty per cent through CAP.

The needs test used to determine a family's eligibility for subsidized child care is different from the test that determines eligibility for welfare payments. The needs test for child care subsidy is considerably less stringent than that for welfare, so many families receive subsidized child care without necessarily being on welfare. Some families receive both.

A major intent of the CAP child care subsidy was to reduce welfare costs, by making it possible for single mothers to go out and get jobs. It was determined to cost less to subsidize child care so parents could work, than force them to stay on welfare when they would prefer to be in the paid labour force.

It is important to realize that CAP does not directly fund child care programs. It is a mechanism which allows the federal government to cost-share programs used by children whose parents qualify for a child care subsidy. Under this system, a provincial or territorial government determines how many child care spaces it wants to fund.

In practice, there are limits on the amount of money most provinces can afford to budget for child care. While CAP attempted to create a national standard of social welfare, there was a basic inequity. Poor provinces are unable to match funding as readily as rich provinces, so federal dollars flow disproportionately to richer provinces. The needs criteria set by each province or territory are different from those set by the federal government, and tend to be more stringent. "All of the provinces have set income levels lower, some considerably lower, than those allowable under the federal 'likelihood of need' guidelines. In other words, over the years it is the provinces/territories that have severely limited the cost-shared spending for child care, not the federal government." (Oloman, 1992)

Until 1990, CAP was an open-ended agreement—no limit was placed by the federal government on the amount it would spend in partnership with a province. In theory, if a provincial government had wanted to fund one million spaces and the local governments had put up their twenty per cent, the federal government would have been obligated to pay its fifty per cent. The system of open-ended payment was stopped when the 1990 federal budget placed a limit on CAP funds to the three richest provinces—British Columbia, Alberta and Ontario were limited to a five per cent increase per year. This cap placed on the amount paid each year is commonly referred to as the "cap on CAP."

Unfortunately, "the capping of the Canada Assistance Plan failed to recognize that the poor are not limited to the so-called 'have not' provinces ... it also showed a fundamental shift in federal responsibility for low-income Canadian families." (Janmohamed 1992). The cap on CAP created tremendous shortfalls in funding for child care in Alberta, British Columbia and Ontario, where the already long lists of eligible familes awaiting subsidy increased sharply. Some existing services were cut due to rising costs, and other child care services were delayed indefinitely.

Despite the historic importance of CAP, there have always been limitations in using it to fund child care:

- CAP is basically intended to provide welfare, so only low-income families can qualify for subsidies and there is no thought of a full child care system for all.
- It promotes the notion that child care services are only for the needy, when in reality the need knows no economic boundaries.

- There is no guarantee that a subsidized space will be available even if a low-income family has access to subsidy. Under CAP, parents must find a licensed space. Government funding concentrates on subsidizing parents rather than creating spaces.
- Federal-provincial arrangements make no provision for cost-sharing the capital costs involved in building child care centres or buying equipment for them.

Training Allowances Under Employment and Immigration Canada (Item #4)

Canada Employment and Immigration pays dependent care allowances for trainees in some programs it sponsors. The total paid in 1992 was $75 million (some of it to parents training to become early childhood educators!).

Child Care Initiatives Fund (Item #5)

The Child Care Initiatives Fund (CCIF) was the only part of the projected federal child care policy that remained in place after the 1988 federal election.

The government of the day hoped this fund would improve the quality of child care in Canada by funding demonstration programs, research, innovations in child care, and public awareness. Programs funded under CCIF addressed child care problems related to shift-work, part-time employment, entry or re-entry into the labour force, effective services for Native children, "head-start"-type programs for children with special needs, and the development of non-profit community-based child care services.

The fund began with $100 million, to be expended over seven years ending in 1995 (all had been committed by early 1994).

The Future Role of the Federal Government

The federal government is responsible for ensuring that no unacceptable inequalities exist nationally. In the 1987 report *Sharing the responsibility*, the federal government looked at access to child care and noted that certain provinces had better child care systems than others. As a result, a new National Child Care Policy was proposed before the 1988 federal election, but it was never moved into fact. In spite of many task forces over the years, there is still no national strategy for child care.

THE ROLE OF PROVINCIAL AND TERRITORIAL GOVERNMENTS

Provinces and territories are responsible for:
- the delivery and operation of child care services
- funding arrangements

- regulation of child care programs
- jurisdiction over child care standards, policies and procedures, and guidelines.

These responsibilities can be divided into *financial* and *regulatory*.

Financial Responsibilities

All governments have increased child care services dramatically over the years, and the financial contribution by provincial governments to child care goes beyond spending cost-shared dollars available through CAP. Figure 2-3 provides a look at the total number of *regulated* child care spaces in Canada at the end of 1992 (the latest year for which full figures were available at time of publication), organized by province, dividing the figures according to whether care is provided in a regulated home setting or a centre.

FIGURE 2-3
Interprovincial Comparison of Child Care Spaces.

Provinces/Territories	Centre spaces	Family day care spaces	Centres
Newfoundland	2 764	-	89
P.E.I.	2 482	60	52
Nova Scotia	10 885	1451	181
New Brunswick	6 444	78	179
Quebec	77 269	8 203	2 146
Ontario	118 329	15 078 (estimate)	3 000
Manitoba	11 492	3 328	302
Saskatchewan	4 135	2 283	110
Alberta	45 252	7 893	1 103
British Columbia	22 105	10 590	1 143
Northwest Territories	883	80	25
Yukon	750	152	25
National totals	**302 790**	**47 890**	**8 355**

Source: *Status of day care in Canada 1992* (draft), Health and Welfare Canada.

Figure 2-4 provides another look at how the different traditions and political climate in each province influence child care. Each province and territory makes its own decision as to what kinds of auspice it will fund. In this table, the total number of centre spaces is divided into *non-profit* and *commercial*.

FIGURE 2-4

Interprovincial Comparison of Day Care Centre Spaces by Auspice.

Provinces/Territories	Non-profit	Commercial	Total
Newfoundland	880	1 884	2 764
P.E.I.	1 499	983	2 482
Nova Scotia	6 539	4 346	10 885
New Brunswick	3 122	3 322	6 444
Quebec	65 980	11 289	77 269
Ontario	87 685	30 644	118 329
Manitoba	10 303	1 189	11 492
Saskatchewan	3 930	205	4 135
Alberta	13 853	31 399	45 252
British Columbia	13 331	8 774	22 105
Northwest Territories	808	75	883
Yukon	579	171	750
National totals	**208 509**	**94 281**	**302 790**

Source: *Status of day care in Canada 1992* (draft), Health and Welfare Canada.

How the picture changes from province to province can easily be seen. For example, Newfoundland had no family day care spaces, while the total of these in Saskatchewan approached the total for centre spaces. Less than one per cent of the centre spaces in Saskatchewan were under commercial auspices, compared with sixty-four per cent in Alberta.

There is also wide variation in the cost of child care, as shown in Figure 2-5 comparing centre-based fees by province and territory (the data was collected in 1991).

FIGURE 2-5

Centre Fees for Full-time Children for Each Age Group, by Province/Territory (Figures collected in 1991).

Average monthly fee, in dollars				
Provinces	**Infants**	**Toddlers**	**Preschoolers**	**School-age**
British Columbia	614	435	357	302
Alberta	326	318	307	256
Saskatchewan	457	341	334	287
Manitoba	412	346	330	246
Ontario	668	544	481	359
Quebec	360	359	355	332
New Brunswick	332	299	302	260
Nova Scotia	399	354	357	279
P.E.I.	409	321	310	335
Newfoundland	-	311	319	302
Yukon	461	415	401	373
Northwest Territories	488	495	494	452
National	**458**	**424**	**392**	**309**

Source: *Child care in Canada—Highlights of 1992/1993 background papers.* Lynne Seshagiri, Canadian Child Care Federation.

While the provinces and territories each provide child care subsidies for eligible low-income families, eligibility criteria and the amount of subsidy varies across the country. Each province and territory sets its own limit on the maximum subsidy, and these limits vary widely. Some provinces require parents to pay a minimum user fee for child care regardless of their income level, whereas others expect them to pay a hefty difference between the subsidy rate and the real cost of care. The amount a parent pays is determined by either an income or needs test where a parent must declare amounts paid for rent, food, transportation etc.

As already stated in the discussion under the Canada Assistance Plan, many believe that needs and income tests stigmatize child care and the families on subsidy. A subsidy system does not guarantee low-income Canadian families equality of access or affordability, and has the potential to segregate children based on their parents' economic status.

Provinces provide other kinds of funding for child care besides fee subsidies. These can be divided into grants that continue from year to year to support the annual costs of a centre, and one-time-only grants for special needs. Annual grants available in different jurisdictions cover such things as special amounts to enhance salaries of child care workers, funding to help offset the annual operating costs of a centre, and grants to help with the cost of building maintenance. Special one-time-only grants cover such things as equipment purchases, start-up costs for new centres, and miscellaneous particular special needs.

All provinces and territories now provide operating money in one form or another directly to licensed group facilities. These grants are intended to stabilize essential services which were entirely dependent on user fees and fundraising. Their value ranges widely, from a low of 20 cents per child per day for full time space, to more than $10. Although these grants have helped, fiscal insecurity remains.

Some jurisdictions have recognized that operating funds are not enough to prevent the deterioration or closure of some services, and have developed other forms of support. Examples are special grants for equipment, maintenance and repair, and professional development. A few provinces, for example Ontario and Manitoba, provide salary enhancement grants. In the spring of 1994, the Ontario government concluded a complete review of child care, leading many to hope that a major policy initiative would be forthcoming.

As Chapter 1 makes clear, the most important barrier to high quality child care is staff dissatisfaction, usually expressed through high turnover. The most important cause is the poor salaries, and after that poor working conditions, which are the result of underfunding in other areas. There appears little immediate prospect of improvement, and this is a major reason why every practitioner in the field needs to be aware of the routes to public advocacy (see Chapter 11, "Community, Resources and Advocacy").

Regulatory Responsibilities

The other key area of provincial responsibility is in regulation, the setting of standards. Regulation can do two things: set a minimum below which a centre cannot legally operate, and provide general direction pointing to desired levels of quality. An example of the first is the requirement that each child be allowed so many square metres; an example of the second is that each centre "promote the physical, intellectual, emotional, social, and moral development of children in their care."

Regulations need to be clear, so everyone can understand them. Programs need to know what is expected from them, and government officials need to interpret and enforce standards fairly and uniformly. A functioning system of regulation establishes standards of quality and applies those standards to programs. It specifies penalties and procedures should programs not meet the standards.

As previously mentioned, there is no federal legislation setting standards for child care programs. Provincial and territorial standards usually include criteria for the following:

- group size
- staff-child ratios
- staff training and/or experience
- space requirements per child
- role of parents
- safety standards
- fire regulations
- sanitation
- health approvals
- nutritional requirements.

A centre can be licensed if it meets the basic criteria in these areas. Licensing has traditionally looked after the safety and protection of children, though other important areas such as record-keeping, staff qualifications, personnel policies, etc. must also be determined before a centre can become functional.

The grant of a license to a child care centre means that the province or territory also assumes responsibility for monitoring the centre to check compliance with standards. This can vary from unannounced spot checks to scheduled visits. Doherty (1991), among others, views lack of adequate monitoring as a contributing factor to poor quality child care. The range of enforcement available goes from granting conditional licenses to the removal of licenses, on up to fines and prosecution. In extreme cases, such as child abuse, flagrant lack of safety precautions or outright negligence, a centre may be closed immediately and its administrator or owner face criminal prosecution.

In some centres, overworked or poorly trained staff may be unaware of how to meet particular regulations. Very few programs are actually ordered closed if they do not meet standards, since it is usually felt that parents and children are better served if government officials work in a consultative capacity to improve weak programs. In such a case, the centre is usually given a provisional license, listing improvements that need to be made by such-and-such a date. During this time, officials and/or consultants work closely with the administrator to bring the centre up to minimum standards.

No regulatory system guarantees quality, and many child care facilities meet only the minimum standards required by their province or territory. Others operate at a higher level. The minimum set by regulation should be considered the beginning of high quality care, not the end goal. In any case, it should not be forgotten that less than twenty per cent of the total number of children in care receive it in licensed or regulated settings (including regulated home child care).

There continues to be much change in provincial legislation concerning child care. For current information, consult your provincial or territorial office. Addresses are found below, under the heading "Legislative Offices, Acts and Provincial Advocacy Associations."

THE ROLE OF LOCAL GOVERNMENTS

Like the provinces and territories, local governments have both a *regulatory* and a *financial* role in child care.

Local Regulation

The local or municipal government generally sets requirements in the areas of fire, safety, health and sanitation, building codes, and zoning by-laws. All these must be met by a centre before it can accept children.

The local fire department will require that a child care centre have fire extinguishers, alarms, fire escapes, and a procedure in place for fire drills. Local health and sanitation authorities will inspect food handling, water, toilets, sewage disposal, hand washing and diapering procedures, as well as plans for meeting the needs of children who are ill. Local health departments also set requirements for immunization and the monitoring of health checks for both staff and children. Building codes cover such areas as approval of the type of structure being used for a child care centre, and the local department of building safety will be concerned with plumbing, electrical wiring capacity and other related factors. The local zoning agency will be aware of the building and safety requirements.

Anyone setting up a child care centre needs to be knowledgeable about these regulations, and how to meet them. Often a consultant works with interested parties to assist them with this area (see for example Chapter 5, "Physical Environments").

Administering Subsidies

In many cases, local governments do more than ensure facilities meet local by-laws. They may be responsible for determining the rules making subsidies available to individual families, and administering payment of those subsidies. When this is so, there will be no province-wide uniformity for determining needs assessment. Levels of eligibility will vary from jurisdiction to jurisdiction, and there is no guarantee that a family with subsidy moving from one municipality to another will continue to receive subsidy. Even within the same province, different cities may not be using the same guidelines or income cut-off points in their needs assessment. For example, a family receiving subsidy in Ottawa may no longer qualify if they move to Peterborough, Ontario.

Provincial subsidy funding may be directed to local governments through a transfer of payments for child care. Here, funding limitations have made severe inroads. Provincial and municipal social service budgets pay for welfare as well as child care, and with the steep rise in need since 1990, the provision of subsidies for child care has had to take second place behind welfare. Welfare is a mandated service, whereas providing dollars for child care is voluntary. Thus a number of local governments have reduced the dollars allocated to child care. Expansion of needed child care services becomes impossible as municipalities and provinces are limited in their funding, and it is becoming increasingly difficult to meet needs and costs for existing services.

Municipally Operated Child Care

Some municipalities provide their own child care services, owning and operating their own centres directly. Others enter into purchase-of-service agreements with existing centres, finding it cheaper to buy space than operate a centre. Some local governments do one or the other, some do both, and a few areas still offer no services at all.

When a municipality embarks upon purchase of services, it contracts with a community child care centre to provide so many subsidized spaces. This may mean the local government enters into an individual contract with a centre, either non-profit or for-profit, to enable parents receiving subsidy to use so many spaces in it. Often a local government will purchase services in a geographical areas where parental needs have arisen.

The procedure can be analogous to letting a tender for road repair, where the municipality shops around for the best price. Sometimes local governments use a purchase-of-service agreement to raise the quality of child care. This can be done by imposing requirements additional to those required by the province, such as specifying that a centre must be on a clear license and not a provisional one, or that all staff members must have particular qualifications. A purchase-of-service agreement may also be directed at specific groups of children, such as in the areas of infant/toddler, school-age child care, special needs care, or home child care.

MILESTONES IN LEGISLATION, 1960–2001

Since 1970, numerous commissions and task forces have studied child care services in Canada and made endless recommendations. What is needed now is for some of these recommendations to be turned into action. Put most simply, the proper care and education of young children affects national productivity in two ways: productivity goes down if parents are worried about the care of their children, and future productivity depends on future producers—today's children.

Below are some milestones in the development of child care in Canada since the 1960s. They conclude with the year 2001, when there will be an estimated 2.7 million Canadian children aged twelve years and under. As an early childhood educator, it is crucial that you keep up with current legislation and make contributions for continuous improvements to child care in Canada. Among a few important questions to ask yourself:

- What will be societal and government priorities in supporting new child care services?
- Will new services be funded privately, by government, or through a combination of both?
- Will these new services be accessible, and affordable to all parents and children in need of them?
- Will inaccessibility, high cost or lack of services keep people from having children?
- How can I contribute to, or lobby for support needed for, quality child care services for children and their parents?

Milestones in Legislation, 1960–2001

1960s Insufficient number of licensed child care spaces and the high cost of child care are issues for parents as more women begin to enter the work force. By 1967, women make up twenty per cent of the Canadian work force.

1966 Canada Assistance Plan (CAP) is passed by Parliament. Child care is included among social services for which the federal government agrees to pay half the cost of provincial subsidies for low-income families.

1970s The Royal Commission on the Status of Women calls for government recognition and expansion of high quality child care services, stating that women will not achieve full equality without government involvement in child care.

1971 Introduction of the first tax deduction for child care.

1974 New Canada Assistance Plan policy guidelines make more families eligible for child care subsidies, if provinces agree to extend their own funding entitlements that far. Most provinces do not.

1981 The census reports that, for the first time, mothers in the work force outnumber those staying at home with their children. Fifty-two per cent of mothers participate in the work force, and women make up forty-two per cent of the total work force.

- British Columbia passes its Provincial Child Care Facilities regulations,which succeed the 1970 Community Care Facilities Act.

1983 Canada Assistance Plan sets out specific minimum and maximum income limits for eligibility in its new policy guidelines.

- Nova Scotia passes Facilities for Children in Nova Scotia, succeeding the 1978 Daycare Act and Regulations and Guidelines for Operating Daycare.
- Quebec passes Regulations Respecting Day Care Centres, succeeding the 1979 Act Respecting Child Day Care.

1984 The soon-to-be-defeated Liberal federal government commissions the Task Force on Child Care, chaired by Katie Cooke. Its mandate is to examine the need for child care services and parental leave in Canada, and make recommendations on the federal government's role in the development of a national child care system.

- Federal election year. For the first time, all three major parties make child care a campaign issue. The newly elected Conservative government promises a national child care program.

1985 New Brunswick passes Day Care Facilities Standards, which succeed the 1980 Child and Family Services and Family Regulations Act.

1986 The Task Force on Child Care chaired by Katie Cooke releases its report. Its principal recommendations are: a publicly funded, universally accessible national system of licensed group and family child care should be developed over fifteen years; public funding should support only government-run and non-profit services; and parental leave provisions should be improved.

- Newfoundland passes Daycare and Preschool Licensing Requirements, Newfoundland and Labrador Department of Social Services, succeeding the 1975 Act Respecting Daycare and Homemaker Services and 1982 Daycare and Homemaker Regulations.
- Yukon passes its Day Care Act.

1987   Statistics Canada reports that the participation rate in the work force of mothers with children under the age of 16 has increased to sixty-five per cent.

- The federal government releases its report of the Special Committee on Child Care, chaired by Shirley Martin, entitled *Sharing the responsibility.*
- *Caring for Canada's children—A special report on the crisis in child care* is published. This report, commissioned by the federal NDP opposition, reaches different conclusions from the Martin report.
- The Ontario government publishes *New directions for child care,* stating that it "recognizes child care as a basic public service, not a welfare service." This approach represents a fundamental shift in the way government views child care. Planning and spending for child care is to be based on three-year cycles, and initiatives are designed to expand the child care system while concentrating on issues of affordability, quality and integration.
- The federal government proposes its National Strategy on Child Care. Included are a $5.4 billion child care program to take effect over seven years, child care tax deductions for receipted child care expenses, a research and development fund (the Child Care Initiatives Fund), and a commitment to a national child care act. The Child Care Initiatives Fund is to operate for seven years and support projects totaling $100 million.
- Alberta passes the Social Care Facilities Licensing Act and the Day Care Regulation, which succeeds the 1980 Social Care Facilities Licensing Act and the 1981 Day Care Regulations.
- Manitoba passes new regulations under the Community Child Day Care Standards Act.
- Ontario passes revisions to the Day Nurseries Act. School-age programs, human resources and training, as well as development of innovative and flexible models for ill children, extended hours and rural communities come under consideration.
- Prince Edward Island passes the Child Care Facilities Act and regulations, succeeding the 1980 act.

1988   Statistics Canada identifies the country's ten worst-paid jobs. Day care workers are at the bottom of the list, behind housekeepers, waitresses, bartenders, and farm labourers. It is noted in the media that zookeepers earn more.

- The Ontario government provides direct operating grants to be used by centres to either lower parent fees or enhance salaries. The amount per staff member is $3,500. Average salaries before this raise in Toronto are about $16,000. The national average is about $8,000.

- The Northwest Territories passes the Child Day Care Facilities Act and regultions, succeeding the 1980 Policy Respecting Subsidized Day Care.
- Saskatchewan passes the Child Care Act, succeeding the 1981 Day Care Regulations.
- The federal government announces its Canada Child Care Act. It is a federal eletion year, and there is not enough time to pass the act. The Conservative government wins the election and begins a second term.

> "I believe a decade hence, the Canada Child Care Act will be regarded as perhaps the most important social innovation of the 1980s, and child care regarded as a fundamental right."
>
> —Prime Minister Brian Mulroney: August 11, 1988.

1989 The re-elected federal Conservative government announces it will reconsider the Canada Child Care Act, as too many interest groups are critical. The act does not reappear.

1990 The federal government limits annual increases to five per cent on Canada Assistance Plan payments to Alberta, British Columbia and Ontario (the "cap on CAP"). This is a radical departure from the original open-ended agreement, and signals a change to the notion of universality.

1991 Federal revisions to Unemployment Insurance grant parents an additional ten weeks of maternity benefits, which may be taken by either parent.

- The 1989 United Nations Convention on the Rights of the Child is ratified by Canada.

1992 The Ontario government fully funds up to 20,000 subsidized child care spaces in the non-profit sector, over a three-year period, to support parents who gain employment through its Jobs Ontario Training Fund.

- The federal government releases its report *Brighter futures: Canada's action plan for children*. There is no mention of a national child care system or policy.

> "Child care is now considered a last priority ... I had the privilege to be (its) killer."
>
> —Benoît Bouchard, federal minister of health: February 29, 1992.

- The Canadian National Child Care Study releases its report as *Parental work patterns and child care needs*. This study, funded by the Child Care Initiatives Fund, provides a comprehensive review of the child care arrangements and needs of Canadian families, based on a nationally representative sample collected in the fall of 1988, of Canadian families with children from newborn to twelve years of age. It confirms that most Canadian families have two working parents.

1993   A federal election replaces the Conservative government with the Liberals under Jean Chrétien. Although child care is not a major election issue, the incoming government does make a commitment to increasing the national total of high quality spaces available, when the economy improves.

2001   It is estimated that there will be 2.7 million Canadian children aged 12 years and under. Will Canada have a national child care policy or strategy?

LEGISLATIVE OFFICES AND ACTS
PROVINCIAL ADVOCACY ORGANIZATIONS

Alberta

Who Governs Early Childhood Programs
Ministry of Family and Social Services

Addresses of Legislative Offices
Day Care Programs
Family and Social Services
11th Floor—7th Street Plaza
10030—107th Street
Edmonton, Alberta
T5J 3E4

Provincial Act Governing Child Care or Most Recent Amendment
- Social Care Facilities Licensing Act, 1980
- Day care regulation—Alberta regulation 333/90

Provincial Organizations and Addresses
Alberta Association for Young Children
Avonmore School, Room 31
7340—78th Street
Edmonton, Alberta
T6C 2N1

British Columbia

Who Governs Early Childhood Programs
Ministry of Advanced Education, Training and Technology (training)
Ministry of Social Services and housing (funding, i.e., CAP and special needs)
Ministry of Health (licensing, certification of teachers and approval of training programs)
Ministry of Women's Equality (child care grants and support programs)

Addresses of Legislative Offices
Program Manager, Child Care
Community Care Facilities Branch
Day Care and Infant Development Program
Ministry of Health
7th Floor, 1515 Blanchard Street
Victoria, British Columbia
V8W 3C8

Child Care Branch
Ministry of Women' s Equality
Government of British Columbia
3rd Floor, 756 Fort Street
Victoria, British Columbia
V8V 1X4

Support Services Division
Ministry of Social Services
3rd Floor, 614 Humboldt Street
Victoria, British Columbia
V8V 1X4

Provincial Act Governing Child Care or Most Recent Amendment
- Community Care Facility Act, Chapter 57. 1979
- Community Care Facility Act: Child care regulation 319/89; Order-in-Council 147/89.
- Guaranteed Available Income for Need Act, Revised Statutes Chapter 158, 1979
- Guaranteed Available Income for Need Act Regulations, 1989
- British Columbia Child Care Regulations, amended 1990

Provincial Organizations and Addresses
Early Childhood Educators, British Columbia (ECEBC)
3998 Main Street
Vancouver, British Columbia
V5V 3P2

Manitoba

Who Governs Early Childhood Programs
Ministry of Family Services

Addresses of Legislative Offices
Department of Family Services
Child Day Care
114 Garry Street, 2nd Floor
Winnipeg, Manitoba
R3C 1G1

Provincial Act Governing Child Care or Most Recent Amendment
- The Community Child Day Care Standards Act (Chapter C158 of L. R. M., 1987)
- Manitoba regulation 62/86

Provincial Organizations and Addresses
Manitoba Child Care Association, Inc.
364 McGregor Street
Winnipeg, Manitoba
R2W 4X3

New Brunswick

Who Governs Early Childhood Programs
Department of Education (school-based ECE programs)
Department of Health and Community Services

Addresses of Legislative Offices
Provincial Coordinator, Early Childhood Services
Office for Childhood Services
Department of Health and Community Services
P. O. Box 5100
Fredericton, New Brunswick
E3B 5G8

Provincial Act Governing Child Care or Most Recent Amendment
- Family Services Act, Chap. C-2.1, Part II. Community Placement Resources, 1983
- Family Services Act Regulation 83-85, under Family Services Act order-in-council 83-457 (consolidated to June 30, 1985)
- Day Care Facilities Standards, Department of Health and Community Services, June 1, 1985

Provincial Organizations and Addresses
Early Childhood Coalition Petite Enfance
123 York Street, Suite 202
Fredericton, New Brunswick
EOG 2WO

Newfoundland

Who Governs Early Childhood Programs
Department of Social Services

Addresses of Legislative Offices
Day Care and Homemaker Services
Department of Social Services
3rd Floor, Confederation Building, West Block
P. O. BOX 8700
St. John's, Newfoundland
A1B 4J6

Provincial Act Governing Child Care or Most Recent Amendment
- The Day Care and Homemaker Services Act, 1990
- The Day Care and Homemaker Services Regulations, Newfoundland Regulations 219/82 (under The Day Care and Homemaker Services Act, 1975)

Provincial Organizations and Addresses
Association of Early Childhood Educators of Newfoundland and Labrador (AECENL)
P. O. Box 9783
St. John's, Newfoundland
A1A 4J7

Northwest Territories

Who Governs Early Childhood Programs
Department of Social Services Child Day Care Section

Addresses of Legislative Offices
Day Care Coordinator
Child Day Care Section
Family and Child Services Division
Department of Social Services
500—4920 52nd Street
P. O. Box 1320
Yellowknife, Northwest Territories
X1A 3T1

Territorial Act Governing Child Care or Most Recent Amendment
- Northwest Territories Child Day Care Act, 1987 (1), c. 13. (as amended by SI 101-87[1], c. 13)
- Child Day Care Standards Regulations, 1987 (pursuant to Subsection 39 [1] of the Child Day Care Act)

Territorial Organizations and Addresses
N. W. T. Child Care Association
5004—54th Street
Yellowknife, Northwest Territories
X1A 2R4

Nova Scotia

Who Governs Early Childhood Programs
Department of Community Services

Addresses of Legislative Offices
Day Care Services
Family and Children's Services Division
Department of Community Services
Family and Children's Services Division
P. O. Box 696
Halifax, Nova Scotia
B3J 2T7

Provincial Act Governing Child Care or Most Recent Amendment
- Day Care Act and Regulations, 1990. (Chapter 120 of the revised statutes)

Provincial Organizations and Addresses
Association of Early Childhood Educators
60 Thornehill Drive
Dartmouth, Nova Scotia
B3B 1S1

Ontario

Who Governs Early Childhood Programs
Ministry of Community and Social Services (licensing and funding)
Ministry of Education and Training (school based ECE programs and Training)

Addresses of Legislative Offices
Child Care Branch
Children's Services Division
Ministry of Community and Social Services
2 Bloor Street West, 30th Floor
Toronto, Ontario
M7A 1E9

Provincial Act Governing Child Care or Most Recent Amendment
- The Day Nurseries Act, 1990 (under revision)
- Ontario Regulation 760/83, under the Day Nurseries Act (under revision)

Provincial Organizations and Addresses
Association of Early Childhood Educators, Ontario (AECE, O)
40 Orchard View Boulevard, Suite #217
Toronto, Ontario
M4R 1B9

Prince Edward Island

Who Governs Early Childhood Programs
Department of Heath and Social Services
Department of Education (school based ECE programs)
Child Care Facilities Board (enforcement and licensing for Child care facilities act)

Addresses of Legislative Offices
Early Childhood Services Co-ordinator
Early Childhood Services
Corporate Services Division Department of Health and Social Services
P. O. Box 2000
Charlottetown, Prince Edward Island
C1A 7N8

Provincial Act Governing Child Care or Most Recent Amendment
- Child Care Facilities Act, R. S. P. E. I. 1988, Chap. C-5
- Child Care Facilities Act Regulations (including any amendments to December 31, 1990)
- Guiding Principles for the Development of Child Care Services, 1987

Provincial Organizations and Addresses
Early Childhood Development Association of P.E.I.
C/O The Park Day Care
West Royalty Industrial Park
Charlottetown, Prince Edward island
C1E 1B0

Quebec

Who Governs Early Childhood Programs
L' Office des services de garde à l'enfance, under the Minister for Women's Issues
Ministère de la Main-d'oeuvre et de la Securité du revenu (subsidy programs)
Ministère de l'Education (start up and operating grants for school boards and training)

Addresses of Legislative Offices
Présidente
Office des services de garde a l'enfance
100, rue Sherbrooke est
Montréal, Québec
H2X 1C3

Provincial Act Governing Child Care or Most Recent Amendment
- Loi sur les services de garde à l'enfance L. R. Q., chapitre S-4.1 1979 (incluant les modifications apportées jusqu'au 1er octobre 1992) (An act respecting child care, 1992)
- Reglement sur les services de garde en garderie, dernière modification: 17 octobre 1991, à jour au 16 février 1993 (Regulations respecting child care centres, 1993)

Provincial Organizations and Addresses
Association de l'education préscolaire du Québec
600 rue Fullum, 6ième étage
Montréal, Québec
H2K 4L1

Saskatchewan

Who Governs Early Childhood Programs
Ministry of Social Services

Addresses of Legislative Offices
Child Care Branch
Department of Social Services
11th Floor, 1920 Broad Street
Chateau Towers
Regina, Saskatchewan
S4P 3V6

Provincial Act Governing Child Care or Most Recent Amendment
- The Child Care Act, Chapter C-7.3, 1989
- The Child Care Regulations 948/90, Chapter C-7.3, Reg. 1 Section 27 1990

Provincial Organizations and Addresses
Saskatchewan Child Care Association, Inc.
#1—3002 Louise Street
Saskatoon, Saskatchewan
S7J 3L8

Yukon Territory

Who Governs Early Childhood Programs
Department of Health and Human Services

Addresses of Legislative Offices
Child Care Services Unit
Department of Health and Social Services
Yukon Territorial Government
P. O. Box 2703
Whitehorse, Yukon
Y1A 2C6

Territorial Act Governing Child Care or Most Recent Amendment
- Child Care Act, Statutes of the Yukon, 1990 (Bill 77)
- Child Care Centre Program Regulations, Order-in-Council 1990/115, pursuant to section 40 of the Child Care Act
- Child Care Subsidy Regulations, Order-in-Council 1990/116, pursuant to section 4 of the Child Care Act
- Family Day Home Program Regulations, Order-in-Council 1990/117, pursuant to section 40 of the Child Care Act

Territorial Organizations and Addresses
Yukon Child Care Association
Box 5439
Whitehorse, Yukon
Y1A 5H4

ACTIVITIES

1. Would you make any changes to your province or territory's legislation for child care? If so, what would you like to see changed and explain why.
2. Construct your own "milestones chart" for legislation and other relevant facts, for the last twenty-four months. Discuss what has been happening nationally, provincially/territorially and locally. What changes would you like to see in child care during the next twenty-four months?
3. Write to your local provincial member for the latest publications from his or her party concerning child care.
4. Outline who parents should contact and see for child care subsidies or financial assistance in your local government. Where are these officials' offices located? Are they easily accessible?
5. Make a list of the steps you would take to license a child care centre in your province or territory.

FURTHER READING

Janmohamed, Zeenat (1992). *Making the connections—Child care in Metropolitan Toronto*. Toronto: Metro Toronto Coalition for Better Child Care.

Oloman, Mab (1992). *A child care agenda for the 90s: Putting the pieces together—child care funding*. Toronto: Ontario Coalition for Better Child Care/Canadian Day Care Advocacy Association.

Seshagiri, Lynne (1993). *Child care in Canada—Highlights of the 1992/1993 background papers*. Ottawa: Canadian Child Care Federation.

3

The Philosophy Statement— A Framework for Success

The philosophy of an early childhood education centre is its general statement of beliefs and goals. The philosophy statement should underpin all aspects of a centre's operation; it is so crucial it is even required by law in some provinces. This chapter will outline:

◆ The importance of the philosophy statement
◆ How to develop a philosophy statement
◆ Implementing and assessing a philosophy.

THE IMPORTANCE OF THE PHILOSOPHY STATEMENT

In an early childhood setting, the philosophy statement is used to hire staff, focus the direction and evaluation of the curriculum, draft informational brochures, and recruit parents. An explicit statement of philosophy is needed to guide and support a centre's curriculum and policies, and establish a basis of common understanding between staff and parents. It isn't enough to say, "Our basic objective is to do a good job and run a good child care centre." These are good intentions, but not sufficient basis for the daily operation of a quality child care centre.

The philosophy statement governs the teaching and the general approach to children. It has a direct bearing on the development of the curriculum in all areas, and should affect budget allocations, staff hiring, scheduling of routines, degree of parent involvement, and use of community resources.

The philosophy statement may be a few paragraphs or a few pages, but it is important that it be written, and available to all who are in contact with the centre. These include the supervisor, board of directors, staff, parents and potential parents, training institutions, students, visitors, community agencies, and even the children themselves. If the centre functions in a multicultural setting, the philosophy should reflect this, and will need to be translated into the necessary languages.

Parents who are approaching a centre for the first time should be able to use the philosophy statement to make informed choices about the care of their children. The philosophy statement provides the basis for initial decisions in choosing a child care centre. If a particular family finds a program philosophy does not match their needs and values, they should be referred to a program whose philosophy does.

A philosophy draws together many strands—an understanding of child development, current research, personal beliefs and values, trends in parenting styles, and general societal expectations. All these areas are continually evolving. As a centre's philosophy becomes part of the daily life at that centre, it should be continually re-evaluated and adapted, so that it becomes a living statement fitting the desired practice of the centre and the needs of those who use it.

A philosophy of early childhood education also has a personal dimension. In the same way as each centre needs a spelled-out philosophy, each practitioner needs to think through their own personal philosophy of early childhood education.

Examples of How a Statement Functions

The following example shows how one line in a centre's philosophy statement evolved over time in response to the needs of its clientele. Name changes reflect changing trends in early childhood education, and time changes reflect the needs of people living and working in the community.

Year	
1965	"The Child Care Centre will be open from 8:30 a.m. to 5 p.m. to meet the needs of student parents and working parents and their children."
1980	"The Early Childhood Centre will be open from 7:30 a.m. to 6 p.m. to meet the needs of student parents and other working parents and their children."
1990	"The Early Childhood Development Centre will be open from 6:45 a.m. to 6:30 p.m. to meet the needs of parents and their children."
2001	"The Child Care Centre will maintain 24-hour flexible care for infants, toddlers, preschoolers and school age children of working parents, from 6 a.m. Monday until 2 a.m. Saturday weekly."

The philosophy statement serves to direct the action and behaviour of the staff, and allows caregivers to ensure they are comfortable with the rationale for the curriculum. In the previous example, only caregivers comfortable with flexible 24-hour care would apply for jobs with the Child Care Centre in the year 2001. When a philosophy is in place and the staff works towards its goals, then programming and related activities and experiences will be directed to helping children develop and learn in a particular manner. Individual staff members must be committed to the philosophy, if this focusing of effect is to happen.

The next examples show how different approaches to learning can derive from the same statement of philosophy. Each approach is positive, but each illustrates a different emphasis.

Philosophy statement:
"Staff in the centre are committed to providing curriculum to assist in building children's confidence and self-esteem."

Centre 1:	Centre 2:
Most of the children are from families that appear confident of their literacy skills. The staff is committed to providing a wide arrangement of dramatic play opportunities for children to widen and strengthen their social interactions and knowledge. They also believe in *child initiated* play, under the protective eye of the teachers. Each day staff members make special efforts to chat with the parents as they drop off and pick up their children, to keep them up to date on progress toward the common goals in the statement of philosophy.	Most of the children are from families with limited educational backgrounds. It is realized that the children would benefit from a year or two of head-start type programming, to help prepare them for the school system. The staff is committed to providing carefully selected activities for the children to widen and strengthen their social interactions and knowledge. This staff believes in more *teacher directed* play and activities. For example, special play activities will be set up to build skills and knowledge in the use of telephones. Parent meetings are held regularly to explain the goals in the statement of philosophy, how they are being met in the centre, and how parents can reinforce them at home.

HOW TO DEVELOP A PHILOSOPHY STATEMENT

A philosophy statement is developed when a new child care setting is opening, or any time that changes are wanted in the operation of an existing one. It provides a collective understanding of goals, so that board, supervisor, staff, parents, and student teachers all work toward them as partners. The board is responsible for monitoring the implementation of this collective understanding, as it is ultimately responsible for the content of the philosophy.

The statement must express a series of goals. For example, one goal in a high quality early childhood program is likely to be the fostering of a positive self-concept. To meet this goal, staff and parents need to work together to help children develop confidence in their abilities. For example, staff might present many opportunities for children to chant or sing together, giving them a sense of accomplishment without singling out individual strengths or weaknesses. They might also fill the room with children's artwork or projects. They can also value the child's culture by providing opportunities for parents, grandparents and others to participate with the children in reading stories from their childhoods, or in preparing food for the centre.

Another goal may be that children learn to play and work together co-operatively and harmoniously. In such a setting, an early childhood educator would not get a group of children ready for outdoor play by saying, "O.K. Let's see who can get out the door the fastest and grab a tricycle." Instead she could say, "When you are ready, you may go out. Remember to share the tricycles." As the basis for a centre's policies, program and procedures, a philosophy needs to be concrete, operational and measurable.

The statement can be developed from the top down, the bottom up, or as a collaborative effort. Parents should have an opportunity to contribute, and the philosophy should express the relationship between setting and community. Most often, a collaborative model is used, because this gives everyone ownership and thus a solid reason to uphold it. The collaborative model about to be described was actually built by school-age children.

PAL (for "Programs After Learning") is a school-age child care program in Kingston, Ontario. A few years ago the children put a lot of energy into building a model city they called "Palville." They realized their city would function better if it had some rules or structure, so they decided to have a leader, and since it was a city they called the leader the mayor. The actual mayor of Kingston was invited to visit Palville and did. As the children continued to build, they added city officials and departments as needed. They invited each city official to visit and each one came.

As they learned more about organizing themselves and their city, the children realized cities have structures to live by. They began to develop guidelines as they thought of or needed them, dealing with how their city should be used and how everyone should behave while playing in it. Palville was so much fun that the children developed similar guidelines for their whole school-age program, and these guidelines became their philosophy. These guidelines have continued to evolve and still remain in place today in the "Pal Promise," repeated every day by the children as their philosophy.

The PAL Promise
• PAL belongs to me.
• Today I will do my best to make PAL a safe and happy place to be.
• Today I will be careful not to hurt anyone at PAL.
• Today I will think before I speak. If what I am about to say is unkind, or may offend someone, I will not say it.
• Today I will think before I act. If what I am about to do may hurt someone I will take time out to become calm and in control.
• Today I will remember that when I am angry or upset, words are the best way to express my feelings.
• Today I will try to help someone when I can.
• Today I will try my best to be pleasant and co-operate with others.
• Today I will remember that I am special and you are special.
• We are PALS!!!

Many early childhood educators have found it useful to develop their own personal philosophy statements to guide their individual practice. The process of developing a personal philosophy is in many ways similar to that of articulating a centre's philosophy. In both cases, the development of a statement would involve the following steps:

1. Research.

Anyone preparing a statement must have a clear understanding of different theories of child development and learning. For example, you could research the contributions made by such theorists as Johann Pestalozzi, Frederick Froebel, Jean Piaget, John Dewey, Arnold Gesell, Susan Isaacs, Maria Montessori, and Benjamin Spock. Such research gives the statement credibility. Following a review of existing theories of learning and development, you can integrate your conclusions with your own values and beliefs.

Example: After reviewing several educational philosophies, you choose a combination from the learning theories, add your own ideas, and begin to build your own philosophy. You should feel free to modify it often as you gain more experience and work in a wider variety of environments.

2. Consult with peers and colleagues.

It is important to get feedback from others. Share and discuss ideas with colleagues, college faculty, supervisors, parents, licensing officials, and other practitioners in the field. These consultations widen the base of knowledge and experience supporting a statement of philosophy.

Example: Your early childhood centre has just hired a new staff member whose background is Mexican. He shares his knowledge and ideas with the centre, including the fact he thinks the centre's lunch menus are limited and bland. Based upon staff discussion, the centre reviews its existing philosophy and decides to make a change. The old philosophy states: "Health is a primary concern for all. Good nutrition is essential to maintaining good health." This is changed to: "Health is a primary concern for all. Good nutrition, and providing a wide range of food opportunities reflecting many cultures, is essential to maintaining good health and a sense of pride and well-being."

3. Integrate your research.

Always make sure that what you know is brought into contact with your daily practice.

Example: Your province has just issued new multicultural guidelines showing how different learning theories can be used to reinforce multicultural awareness, but no one seems to find time to read them. One day a new child and his mother come to your centre. They are black. A staff member shows them around the centre, and you overhear her ask, "What country do you come from?" The mother pleasantly replies, "We're fifth-generation Canadians."

That same day, you give each staff member a copy of the new multicultural guidelines, and announce a special staff meeting to begin discussions about how to implement them.

4. Reflect philosophy in program development.

After discussing with your colleagues and weighing your common understanding of child development and learning theories, you begin to formulate program procedures to meet your basic objectives.

Example: It is understood in child development that basic needs must be met. Children arriving very early in the morning may not have had time to eat an adequate breakfast and may feel hungry. The centre philosophy states, "Basic needs are a first priority," so the centre decides to provide breakfast as part of the program.

5. Evaluate.

The expectations used in evaluation should emerge from the centre's statement of philosophy and the job descriptions used to hire staff members. These job descriptions will themselves be based on the philosophy. When evaluations are implemented and effectively used, they can facilitate self-growth and build confidence. Used improperly they can cause both morale and performance to plummet.

Example: As the new director of a centre, you ask each staff member to list their perceived strengths and weaknesses. You then use a list of questions to interview them. At the end of these two exercises, you have solid evidence that the staff as a whole has a major area of weakness around professional development, even though the centre philosophy states that the professional development of staff should be supported. No staff member had been to a professional conference in five years, and three staff members had never been to a conference at all—not even as students in training! The staff has been feeling professionally isolated. You present these results to the board, who recommend funds for professional development, and work with you to strengthen the commitment to professional development in the philosophy. Staff are given a list of conferences, and invited to choose. Morale, productivity and enthusiasm skyrocket!

6. Be open to new information.

As a program operates from year to year, the philosophy should be re-assessed to make sure it continues to reflect current thinking on the development of children, the emerging needs of the parents and community it serves, and the understanding of staff.

This is equally true in the development of a personal philosophy. As an educator in the field, you should continue to consider and assess your own views, alongside new information you gather from practice in the field. You can acquire new information from courses offered through continuing education programs, educational journals, and membership in professional organizations.

Example: Several early childhood education students feel children should sleep in their own beds at night, and find it difficult to accept that their field placement will embark upon flexible child care in the fall. On the weekend these same students go to a party. At 2 a.m., when they call a taxi to take them home, they find the driver has an infant in a carseat in the front. She apologizes because her child care arrangements have broken down. How is a single parent in her position to keep her job?

The students hadn't considered a dilemma like this. As they think this experience over, they see a real need in their community for flexible child care—not only for taxi drivers, but workers in the hospitality industry, hospital staff, and many others.

IMPLEMENTING AND ASSESSING A PHILOSOPHY

Specific goals and objectives in the statement of philosophy set the direction of the program and determine how the activities are carried out. The supervisor and board are responsible for how these goals are achieved.

Staff members must feel comfortable with the philosophy and how specific goals are to be achieved. In order to give it their full support, staff members need a philosophy compatible with their own, and involving them in the development of the philosophy statement gives them a stake in it. Here are examples of a successful and an unsuccessful fit between staff member and program philosophy.

Statement:
The program philosophy stresses positive support, non-punitive guidance and the value of play for children, along with professional development for staff.

Teacher 1:	Teacher 2:
The substitute teacher is thrilled to be called so often by the school-age centre. This is her fifth year working part-time there. It's an enjoyable place to work, and she feels she is being paid to do the thing she likes best—interact with children in an enthusiastic environment.	When she was hired, the new staff member said she agreed with the centre's philosophy. However, her own upbringing had been abusive, and she had not enjoyed her training because of her difficulty in not being punitive with children. During her three-month probation in her new job, she realized she disliked working with children and their parents. Her colleagues helped her obtain career counselling to find another career.

When you talk with prospective parents, take time to discuss the centre's philosophy. Make sure they understand it, and that it is consistent with their values and traditions. For example, is the setting sensitive to cultural distinctiveness? Are all staff members—including cook, secretary, janitor, etc.—sensitive to the presence of children from different faiths? Are vegetarian meals available without a fuss? Such discussion will ensure a better fit between parents and staff, who must work together in the interest of the children in their care.

The philosophy statement also provides a basis for understanding between the centre and training institutions. Training programs, and the students they place in the early childhood setting, should be aware of the centre's philosophy and prepared to follow it. In order for this to happen, field placement agencies should provide an orientation process, or the centre must be prepared to provide one during each placement.

Methods for Monitoring and Assessing a Philosophy

Regular review of a centre's philosophy will help guide future strategic planning. Such review or evaluation should be built into the program, usually on an annual basis. The review should include research, observations and suggestions from staff, parents and the board of directors (and sometimes from the children as well), to see whether the work of the centre still reflects the statement of philosophy, and whether program goals and objectives are being met. While input from outside consultants can be beneficial, the responsibility remains primarily in the hands of the supervisor, the board of directors and the staff. If a philosophy is to be responsive to parent needs, parent feedback must be a part of the process.

Children need the security of consistency in routines and activities planned by staff so they have a sense of completion in their lives. Staff need direction from a clear statement of philosophy in order to maintain continuity and consistency in their work. Parents need to know what they can expect from the centre, how they can contribute to it, and what is expected of them. The centre needs to explain to the community what it stands for and how it operates.

The evaluation of a philosophy statement should take into account:

- the structure of the program
- the environment in which the program operates
- the changing needs of the community
- the way in which the program is funded.

Evaluation can range from developmental checklists of children to complex research processes. After discussing a number of child development theories and methods of evaluation, Evans (1975) concludes that empirically-based evaluation methods are probably most appropriate. This is because philosophy statements, and their resulting policies and programs, often assume a life of their own as centre staff continually re-evaluate their role and mission.

While recognizing the value of evaluation, early childhood educators often feel they lack the knowledge, time or funds required to do it adequately. Consultants can be useful here. Assessment tools have also been developed that can be useful as well as time saving—for example, Jorde Bloom's *A great place to work: Improving conditions for staff in young children's programs*, Harms and Clifford's *Early childhood environment rating scale* (also available: *Infant/toddler* and *Family home day care*), and the *Guide to accreditation by the National Academy of Early Childhood Programs: Self-study, validation, accreditation* (NAEYC 1985). Validated instruments can often be used successfully after a minimum of staff training. The areas measured must be consistent with your centre's philosophy—any tool is valid only if it measures what the program views as quality.

Evaluation time should be made a priority. It is necessary to budget adequately for evaluation, because costs exist both directly, as in the purchase of materials, and indirectly, as in staff time. The program should also budget for and commit itself to program development, training and staff development.

ACTIVITIES

1. Begin building a living philosophy as an early childhood educator by writing a personal statement of philosophy. Discuss it with peers and at least two other professionals (director, staff or board member) working in your community. Include: beliefs/goals/mission; theories underlying these beliefs; and how to reach the goals.

2. In the appendix to this chapter you will find three "sample" philosophies, each designed with imperfections for discussion purposes. You will also find a sample program statement of philosophy from the current Ontario Day Nurseries Manual. Discuss these critically.
3. Collect two statements of philosophy from early childhood centres in your area. Visit these centres. Look for examples of how goals, values and beliefs are implemented in the programs. What do these philosophies have in common? How are they different?
4. Read newspaper articles, listen to the radio and watch television for items involving children. Discuss how the media shapes a societal philosophy toward children and their parents and how this assists or hinders progress in child care services in Canada.
5. Identify and use (or develop) a tool to measure an aspect of philosophy, such as "self-esteem" or "cultural appropriateness."

FURTHER READING

Ayles, T., and S. Becker-Griffin (1990). *Daily operations manual with supplement on finance management.* Toronto: Umbrella Central Day Care Services/Child Care Initiatives Fund, Health and Welfare Canada.

Ayles, T., and S. Becker-Griffin (1990). *An A-Z handbook for boards of directors of non-profit community-based child care programs.* Toronto: Umbrella Central Day Care Services/Child Care Initiatives Fund, Health and Welfare Canada.

Harms, T., and R.M. Clifford (1980). *Early childhood environment rating scale.* New York: Teachers College Press.

Sciarra, D. J., and A.G. Dorsey (1990). *Developing and administering a child care center.* Albany, NY: Delmar Publishers Inc.

Taylor, B.J. (1993). *Early childhood program management—people and procedures.* New York: Merrill.

APPENDIX A: THREE SAMPLE PHILOSOPHY STATEMENTS

As you explore the sample philosophy statements that follow, keep in mind
that imperfections have been built into them for discussion purposes.

Sample Philosophy #1

The Child Development Centre's educational philosophy is based on meeting
the developmental needs of individual children as well as children in group settings.

The theoretical frameworks for programming to meet each child's emotional, social,
cognitive and physical needs are derived from the works of Pestalozzi, Froebel and Dewey.
The educational program is based on growth taking place in predictable sequences or stages.
Each successive stage depends on the outcome of the previous stage. Therefore, children
will be given time to complete each stage through a wide variety of opportunities that
are considered to be developmentally appropriate for each stage.

Adults are responsible for assisting each child in growing and flourishing according
to his or her natural rhythms and maturational forces, in order to develop to the fullest
potential. As each stage of development is recognized, curriculum is designed to nurture
and facilitate growth at that stage. This is reflected in the Centre's continuous
re-evaluation of program activities.

Sample Philosophy #2

The philosophy of the Child Care Centre is to provide the child with a stimulating
and supportive environment. This environment is designed to motivate the child
to develop and widen his or her individual mental and physical capabilities.
The program offered is designed to achieve these objectives by:
- providing each child with a variety of physical environments, toys, materials
  and situations which will assist in the development of gross and fine motor skills;
- encouraging the growth and development of self-esteem in each child as an individual,
  a member of the family, and a member of the peer group through exposure to
  the warm and trusting environment of the Centre;
- maintaining for each child opportunities for self-expression through the development
  of language skills and reasoning abilities;
- providing each child with the opportunity to share in group activities and thus learn
  group mores and the benefits of co-operating with peers and teachers; and
- establishing, maintaining and encouraging open and honest discussions
  between staff and parents to ensure the needs of each child and the family
  are fully met in the most practical manner possible.

Sample Philosophy #3

The Centre's philosophy is based on a cognitive-interactionist approach which emphasizes:
  • an environment that is child-centred,
  • a program designed for self-teaching, and
  • a style that is discovery-oriented, through the incorporation of play
    opportunities.
Play is a prime vehicle for learning and enjoyment in the Centre as the Centre's Board, director and staff believe all children:
  • are active learners,
  • need freedom to explore,
  • need to discover nature, and
  • explore the environment openly.
   Therefore, the daily program allows for large blocks of time to allow children to explore and investigate their surroundings. Children are seen as active explorers in their environment and are encouraged to select from it, with the help of staff as facilitators of the learning environment, the materials and situations that stimulate their interest.
   The staff structures the environment by organizing learning centres that stimulate children's interests and foster their curiosity and desire to learn.
   This learning environment is continuously re-evaluated through staff observations of the children's development and questions. The staff continually gathers information from these observations and questions to guide the selection of additional learning materials and activities that will widen the children's interests and skills.
   Continuous open communication between parents and staff is encouraged so that the needs of the child and family are met within the framework of this philosophy.

APPENDIX B: SAMPLE PROGRAM STATEMENT FROM THE ONTARIO DAY NURSERIES MANUAL

Philosophy

Day Nursery X attempts to provide a positive learning environment for your child that enhances his or her level of development. Through play experiences and the guidance of specially trained staff, your child will be exposed to situations that will stimulate:
   1. curiosity, initiative, and independence;
   2. self-esteem and decision-making capabilities;
   3. interaction with, and respect for others;
   4. physical activity that develops gross motor skills;
   5. communication skills; and
   6. fine motor development.

Program development

Programs are re-evaluated regularly to reflect changes within the Day Nurseries Act and ideologies on early childhood education. Workshops are also offered for both staff and parents to review program content. At regular intervals throughout the year, a newsletter will be sent informing you of these workshops, as well as topics of interest, events and nursery news. You are invited to contribute to these newsletters.

Ages of children

Day Nursery X has facilities to accommodate the following children:
1. Ten infants, 16 weeks to 18 months
2. Fifteen toddlers, 18 months to 2 1/2 years
3. Twenty-four preschoolers, 2 1/2 years to 5 years

Days and hours of operation

Both full- and part-time care are provided 52 weeks each year.
1. Full-time care is offered between 7:00 a.m. and 6:00 p.m., five days a week.
2. Part-time care is offered:
    a) Four days a week, or less
    b) 7:00 a.m.–11:30 a.m., five days a week
    c) 1:00 p.m.–6:00 p.m., five days a week

Admission and discharge policy

An interview will be arranged to familiarize you and your child with the philosophy and surroundings, and to answer questions and complete admission forms prior to enrollment. A non-refundable registration fee is also required, and can be paid at this time. For the first week you are encouraged to stay with your child at the beginning of the day in order to reassure him/her and minimize fears until you and your child become more comfortable.

Written notice of permanent withdrawal must be given two weeks in advance. If notice is not received, full program fees will be charged. A permanent space cannot be guaranteed if you wish to temporarily withdraw your child. Therefore, your child will be placed on a waiting list. Day Nursery X may terminate services if policies are not followed or fees are not paid.

Arrival and pickup

Young children depend on regular routines for their own sense of security. We recommend that you establish fixed hours to pick up and drop off your child. When your child arrives, notify a member of the staff as to your child's presence. Similarly, when picking up your child, enter the building and make sure the staff knows you are leaving. Unless otherwise arranged, children will not be released to any person other than those specified on the admissions form.

Parking

A drop-off area is provided for cars. However, if you anticipate staying at the day nursery for any length of time, kindly park at the facilities located within easy walking distance of the nursery.

Specialized services

Day Nursery X is an approved integrated centre for handicapped children. In addition to participating in the daily routine, individual programs for developmentally or physically handicapped children are conducted by a qualified resource teacher.

A program has been arranged with the neighbourhood swimming pool for supervised lessons twice a week. Parents who are interested in enrolling their children in this activity should notify the supervisor.

Nutrition

A nutritious midday meal and morning and afternoon snacks will be provided. Children's special dietary needs and allergies will be posted in the cooking and service areas. Weekly menu plans will be posted for the current and following week to assist you in menu planning at home.

Health and administration of drugs

The Day Nurseries Act stipulates that prior to admission, each child must be immunized as recommended by the local medical officer of health. Day Nursery X also requires that a medical certificate confirming a complete medical assessment be submitted at this time. Regulations require daily outdoor play for each child. Therefore, it is our policy that children too ill to play outside remain at home. If a child becomes ill during the day, temporary care will be provided until you can be contacted and your child taken home. Day Nursery X will administer both prescription and non-prescription drugs to children, in accordance with provincial legislation. This requires that parents provide:

1. written authorization, including the dosage and times any drug is to be given; and
2. medication in the original container, clearly labeled with the child's name, name of the drug, the dosage, the date of purchase, and instructions for storage and administration of the drug.

Medication is not to be left in the cloakroom area. Kindly give it directly to a program staff member.

Clothing and possessions

Your child should be dressed in clothing that is appropriate for physical activity, the weather and the season. A second set of clothing should be kept at the nursery in case of accidents. Also, all clothing and toys should be labeled with your child's name.

Discipline

Children are disciplined in a positive manner at a level that is appropriate to their actions and their ages in order to promote self-discipline, ensure health and safety, respect the rights of others, and maintain equipment.

Spanking or other forms of corporal punishment are not permitted.

Methods of discipline are discussed at staff meetings, and consistent disciplinary measures are agreed upon. A workshop on discipline is planned, so that parents and staff may exchange ideas.

Parental involvement

Daily contact with parents and staff will be supplemented by individual interviews, group meetings and workshops. You are encouraged to participate in the daily program and visit your child in your free time.

Field trips

Throughout the year, trips are made to special places of interest. A notice will be sent home in advance of the excursion informing you of the destination, time and date. It will also include a permission slip to be signed and returned. You are always welcome to accompany us.

Holidays/sick leave

Day Nursery X observes the following statutory holidays: New Year's Day, Good Friday, Easter Monday, Victoria Day, Canada Day, Civic Holiday, Labour Day, Thanksgiving, Remembrance Day, Christmas Day, Boxing Day.

In addition, each child may be absent for two weeks vacation/sick leave a year, where payment of fees is not required. There are no refunds for any additional days missed. Written notice of an intended vacation is required at least one month in advance.

Fees

Monthly fees are required on the first day of each month. Fees can be paid by cheque or money order. A late fee may be charged if payments are not made on time. Monthly receipts will be given for income tax purposes. Subsidized services may be available to eligible families. Further information may be obtained from the supervisor.

Fee schedule

Full day   _____ $

Half-day   _____ $

Infants   _____ $

Toddlers   _____ $

Preschoolers   _____ $

Fees for children in part-time care may be negotiated.

Source: *Revised day nurseries manual.* Ontario Ministry of Community and Social Services. Toronto: March 1988, pp. DN-02-02-02. Used by permission.

4

Developing Curriculum—
the Supervisor's Role

Curriculum is a key dimension of the "high quality" child care discussed in Chapter 1. As the person who monitors the implementation of the program philosophy, the supervisor is responsible for the development, implementation and evaluation of curriculum. This chapter will discuss:

◆ What is curriculum?
◆ Three major positions on child development
◆ Developing curriculum—where to begin
◆ Developing curriculum—the supervisor's responsibilities.

WHAT IS CURRICULUM?

Curriculum can be defined in several ways. Different definitions illustrate different points of view on what an early childhood program should be. Those designing curriculum, whether boards of directors, supervisors, community members, staff, consultants, or some combination of these, should choose the definition which best reflects the philosophy of the setting and the needs of the children and families who use it.

Some define curriculum as "what happens" in an early childhood setting (Schwartz and Robison 1982). In this definition, the child decides: the teacher provides an environment rich with possibilities and supports the choices the child makes. Such a program is *child-centred*. Rather than setting out the day's activities ahead of time, teachers plan a variety of activities to fit a range of developmental levels and interests.

In another approach, Seaver and Cartwright (1986) use the term curriculum to refer to "activities deliberately selected and systematically implemented by staff." This definition implies a more *teacher-directed* program, which sets out goals and objectives, and views the activities as a way to reach them. The goals may be short- or long-term, general or specific. While they provide an overall structure for the program, they are general enough to allow staff some flexibility in adapting plans to children's needs and interests.

A more formalized curriculum for children may consist of a detailed set of written plans, or a syllabus which identifies what is to be taught and the sequence in which it is to be presented. Such a plan will generally specify learning outcomes and how to evaluate them.

If staff lack consensus about what curriculum is, the program will exhibit lack of consistency. The definitions discussed above would result in programs that differ sharply from each other, in how far the activities are preplanned, the role of teachers, and the specific expectations for children. The process of defining curriculum can serve as an excellent starting point for the development or revision of a program philosophy. The discussion can help staff clarify their beliefs about the role of early childhood programs in the lives of young children and their families, enabling them to work more effectively.

What is Good Curriculum?

Curriculum development involves a number of decisions, each with different implications for how the program is constructed. Ask ten individuals to describe a good program for young children and you will probably get ten different answers, although there will be common elements. Consensus is often difficult to reach, but a shared understanding is essential to the provision of high quality child care.

Several professional organizations have developed position statements with guidelines for early childhood curriculum. The Association for Early Childhood Education (Ontario), the Canadian Child Care Federation, and the U.S. National Association for the Education of Young Children (NAEYC) have each produced statements which provide a blueprint for good early childhood programs. The NAEYC has also produced a position statement on developmentally appropriate practice which provides comprehensive guidelines for quality programs for young children.

These documents share common elements, and the following list represents a synthesis of these shared ideas. A good early childhood curriculum:

- provides opportunities for the child's active participation.
- provides experiences which contribute to all areas of a child's development: emotional, social, physical, and cognitive.
- is developed based on the program's philosophy or program rationale.
- reflects both individual and group developmental needs and interests.
- provides a balance of quiet and active experiences.
- challenges children to think, explore, problem-solve, and discover.

- provides choices and encourages independence and the development of autonomy.
- reflects the values of parents and the community.
- is based on observations and records of each child's interests, strengths and needs.

As discussed in Chapter 3, a philosophy should reflect a collective understanding of how children grow and change, forming the basis for commitment to common goals. The philosophy provides the basis for curriculum development, so there needs to be consensus regarding the philosophy for the centre before the curriculum is developed.

THREE MAJOR POSITIONS ON CHILD DEVELOPMENT

You will already be familiar with the three major theoretical positions on how children develop and learn. We will briefly review them here, since each theory has different implications for the teaching/learning process and thus forms the basis for a particular kind of curriculum design.

Staff in a centre that is developing its curriculum may have different understandings and beliefs about how children develop and learn. They can work to achieve consensus in one of two ways. The first is to "start from scratch" and brainstorm, sharing their beliefs about child development. Common elements can then be identified, and compared with the three major theories in an attempt to find a match. Identifying the theory that best fits the staff's beliefs will provide a foundation for curriculum development and evaluation.

The other approach would be for staff to examine the major theoretical positions, to find the one that best reflects their views of early childhood. Either way, staff must articulate their beliefs and reach agreement, or the result will be patchwork curriculum design and an inconsistent program.

The Maturationist View

Maturationists view the development of the young child as the result of biological and genetic factors. Development is determined by heredity, and change is the result of the natural unfolding and maturing of physiological structures. Children enter each new stage of development as they mature.

If this theory is used as a framework for curriculum design, the responsibility of the early childhood educator is to provide an environment rich in possibilities and allow the child to choose her or his own experiences. The child needs to be "ready" for experiences, and the teacher's role is to match children with activities that are developmentally appropriate. Maturationists believe it is unlikely that a teacher's planned activities will shape a child's development, although they may help it unfold as it should.

The Behaviourist View

While maturationists believe that change is determined by biological factors within the child, behaviourists ascribe change to environmental forces outside the child. They view the child as a "blank slate" (you sometimes hear *tabula rasa*, which is Latin for "blank slate") whose development can be moulded. Learning is a continuous hierarchical process. As learning accumulates, it forms the basis for the acquisition of more complex ideas. Reinforcement strategies play a key role in development, as they can be applied systematically to shape desired behaviours.

Behaviourist programs for young children are teacher-focused. The teacher makes key decisions related to the teaching/learning process, deciding what is to be learned and how. She uses reinforcement systematically to shape learning, and thus children acquire skills through deliberate stimulation and reinforcement.

The Cognitive-Developmental View

Cognitivists see the child's development as the result of interaction between internal and environmental factors. Children are viewed as intrinsically active, constructing knowledge of the world through interactions with their peers and environment. According to cognitivists, children progress through a series of developmental stages, each qualitatively different from the other. These stages are sequential, and are characterized by different ways of thinking and reasoning. The child sees the world quite differently from one stage to another.

In this view, children are active participants in their learning who "construct" knowledge. Educational experiences should provide opportunities for children to explore and experiment, and the educator's understanding and knowledge of the world has little impact on the child. The teacher doesn't explain, the child discovers. It is the teacher's responsibility to provide challenges and experiences that foster discovery. This requires both an environment rich in possibilities, and a teacher who is trained to assess cognitive development and interact appropriately.

Common Principles of Child Development

Despite their differences, the three theories agree on several basic developmental principles that affect curriculum design across the board:

- Development follows a predictable sequence.
- There are individual differences. While the sequence of development is predictable, timing is flexible.
- Behaviour becomes increasingly differentiated and complex.
- There is a genetic component to development.
- There are critical periods in development.

DEVELOPING CURRICULUM: WHERE TO BEGIN

There are a number of possible starting points for designing curriculum, from creating a design specifically tailored to the needs and interests of the children in your care, to selecting something prepackaged. Written plans are useful in providing direction to the program, a framework for organization and a guide for interactions with children. Planning formats include long-range, weekly and individual activity plans.

Long-range plans should be flexible, to accommodate later fine-tuning and adaptation to children's learning needs and interests. They provide information about upcoming activities for parents and may form the basis for ordering supplies.

Weekly plans identify the major activities of each day and provide a framework for planning specific activities. Planning may be based on specific developmental goals and objectives, a thematic approach, or regularly scheduled activities such as story time, music, outdoor play, etc.

Individual activity plans can be particularly useful for beginning teachers, as they provide guidelines for interactions and the evaluation of planned experiences. They may include items like objectives for the activity, materials required, directions on how to proceed, and an evaluation to be completed afterwards. See Appendix for an example.

Regardless of format, it is important that planning responsibility be clearly articulated in job descriptions, and that time be allotted for it.

Licensing Requirements and Regulations

Each province or territory sets licensing requirements for day care, specifying minimum standards, health and safety requirements, space minimums, and staff qualifications. These may be specified in the legislation, or outlined in accompanying regulations. They must be considered in planning curriculum.

These regulations do not provide guidelines for optimal programming—rather, they state the minimum of what is acceptable. Some advocates of high quality care argue for the establishment of national standards, while others prefer that individual provinces develop improved standards.

British Columbia

The program must include a comprehensive and co-ordinated set of activities for the development, care and protection of children, based on individual developmental needs. Activities which provide for physical, intellectual, language, emotional, and social development are defined by a set of program standards, the "Program Standards for Early Childhood Settings."

Alberta

The program should meet the developmental needs of children and provide a variety of indoor and outdoor activities. In addition, the program should be flexible and provide for rest, toileting, nourishment, and rigorous and quiet activities for groups and individuals.

Saskatchewan

The environment must be supportive of the normal development of the individual child. Periods of rest and sleep, according to the age and needs of children, are required. Young children with special needs should be integrated into the "regular" program.

Manitoba

Every person is required by the regulations to promote the "physical, social, emotional, and intellectual" development of children. The program should include daily individual and small-group activity, physical, cognitive, language, and social activity, and both child-initiated and adult-directed activities. Outdoor play must be provided on a daily basis. Sleeping and toileting should be provided according to the development and capability of each child.

Ontario

A written statement outlining the philosophy, program and method of operation is to be discussed with the parent prior to admission, and reviewed annually. The program should be varied and flexible, as well as appropriate to developmental levels. It should include group and individual activities, active and quiet play, and activities that provide for the development of fine motor, language, cognitive, emotional, and social skills. Children in each age group should be separated for indoor and outdoor play. The program should provide a rest period for children. Outdoor play should be provided for two hours a day, weather permitting.

Quebec

The applicant for a child care permit must undertake to provide children with child care and a program of activities to promote their physical, intellectual, emotional, social, and moral development.

New Brunswick

The setting must provide a positive, stimulating atmosphere and structure conducive to the total development of children. In addition, the program is required to provide a support service to family. A written daily program is required. Children unable to walk are to be separated during play period. Children under six are to be separated during play period. Children attending the centre for more than seven hours are to have up to two hours outdoor activity.

Nova Scotia

The daily program should facilitate and stimulate intellectual, physical, emotional, and social development appropriate to the developmental level of children. Activities designed to encourage language development should be included. Facilities may be licensed to provide a child care program for young children with special needs.

Newfoundland and Labrador

A flexible program suited to the age and developmental needs of children is required. The program should provide experiences designed to facilitate intellectual, perceptual and language development. Activities should encourage creative expression and allow for freedom of choice. Outdoor play and a rest period must be provided each day. Efforts should be made to provide child with male identification figures. Television is to be used only for viewing educational programs.

Prince Edward Island

The program should foster a sense of self-worth, respect family values and involvement, and further the comprehensive development of the child. The program is required to plan for the integration of special needs children. Outdoor activity should be provided according to the child's developmental needs, with a minimum of one hour in winter and two hours or more in summer.

Yukon Territory

Programs must provide a planned, but flexible, daily schedule for rest, toileting and nourishment. Activities should be age-appropriate and designed to facilitate cognitive, perceptual and language development. Opportunities for creative expression and decision-making should be provided. Young children with special needs should be integrated into the program, "as much as possible."

Northwest Territories

The daily program should facilitate children's intellectual, physical, emotional, and social development. Activities should be developmentally appropriate and reflect the cultural and ethnic background of the children. Children with special needs should be integrated into the daily program as much as possible. Community services may be used to enhance the quality of the program.

Cultural Diversity

Early childhood programs should include developmentally appropriate materials and activities which reflect cultural diversity. These activities should be integrated into the fabric of the program, not set apart.

For many early childhood educators this approach will be new, requiring the development of new skills. The supervisor can be a catalyst for this growth by identifying professional development needs and providing the necessary resources.

Parents may be challenged by this new approach and should be involved in the early stages. Questionnaires designed to identify the cultural heritage of families will help to sensitize parents to the need for a program which reflects cultural diversity. When the feedback is summarized and shared with parents, the results may be surprising. Some parents may want to contribute to the new focus by providing resources; for others, sharing information about their cultural heritage will contribute to a new sense of partnership with their child's setting. A resource that is useful in this context is Kenise Kilbride's *Multicultural early childhood education: A resource kit* (1990).

Developmental Diversity

As more children with special needs are integrated into early childhood settings, supervisors and staff face the imperative to adapt curriculum and centre environments to meet the resulting wide range of developmental needs. Both the nature of the special needs and the number of children with them need to be considered in designing curriculum.

Age Groupings

Finally, the ages of the children in the early childhood setting will of course determine the types of activities provided. A space designed for infants and toddlers is dramatically different from one designed for preschoolers. From the size of the space to the type of play materials, the differences reflect the developmental needs of each age grouping.

DEVELOPING CURRICULUM—THE SUPERVISOR'S RESPONSIBILITIES

Working with Staff

A key part of the supervisor's role is to provide leadership to staff. For example, she may plan a meeting to consider the merits of implementing a new approach to program planning, and encourage staff to problem-solve the benefits from a number of perspectives. She creates the structure within which staff members discuss their values and beliefs about how children develop.

The supervisor must be a curriculum specialist with the skills necessary to design and implement a high quality program. These skills enable her to provide staff with concrete goals.

Chapter 6 discusses the developmental stages of early childhood educators as defined by Lillian Katz (1972). The staff in a centre will be at different stages in their understanding of curriculum—some may be recent graduates and thus relatively inexperienced, while more experienced staff may be in a creative rut, relying too heavily on old lesson plans. The supervisor must work with staff as individuals, and support their skill development by providing support and access to resources where they are needed. To support professional development needs, the supervisor may:

- support staff members in their own professional development plan.
- provide in-service workshops.
- enable staff to attend conferences or workshops providing opportunities for specific skill development related to curriculum design.
- provide time for staff to visit other settings noted for their programs.

Since these activities will require financial support, the supervisor must ensure funds are budgetted for professional development, to ensure staff growth and renewal. She may need to convince her board of the importance of providing the necessary funds.

Developing curriculum takes time. If staff are to develop a high quality program, the supervisor must provide planning time for these activities. She must implement strategies to relieve staff from classroom responsibilities for two hours or more per week, to give them the opportunity to work as a team in developing curriculum. Substitute staff may need to be hired.

On a more basic level, the supervisor must ensure staff have input into the ordering of supplies and resources to support a high quality program. While early childhood educators are experts in locating free materials such as leftover wood and "beautiful junk," they still need an adequate supply of paint, scissors, construction paper, etc.

In consultation with staff, the supervisor must structure a process for evaluating the curriculum, both formally and informally. Criteria for a high quality program such as those outlined by the Association for Early Childhood Education, Ontario, the Canadian Child Care Federation or the U.S. National Association for the Education of Young Children should be part of a framework for program evaluation.

Working with Children

The supervisor may sometimes substitute for a staff member, or depending on her other responsibilities, she may choose to work with the children on a regular basis. For instance, she might assume responsibility for a particular curriculum component, such as planning science activities. In this way, she can get to know the children and assess the program from the staff's perspective, while acting as a role-model for them.

In some larger centres, the supervisor may only have time to do this a little, while in others she may alternate half-days teaching and administering. This may also vary depending on the province or territory—for example, in B.C. most supervisors do double duty as regular teaching staff.

The supervisor is also responsible for structuring a process to assess the children's progress, and ensuring this is an ongoing part of the centre's activities. In consultation with staff, she should structure an assessment process, create timelines for assessment, and monitor implementation.

Working with Parents

Parents need information to understand the rationale for the activities their child is involved in, the more so since their own early childhood experiences were likely quite different. For example, a parent may not understand a particular centre's approach to toilet training. The supervisor must help them understand the centre's activities, providing informal opportunities for sharing information, formal interviews, orientations, and newsletters.

A part of this is providing staff with the time to talk with parents, and the opportunity to develop the skills to communicate effectively.

Program Evaluation

Evaluation should be a collaborative process leading to a shared commitment to continuous program improvement, and validating the successful aspects of the program. For it to be successful, all staff need to support the process, and share responsibility for ongoing program improvement.

The supervisor plays a key role in leading the evaluation process, ensuring that a collaborative approach for gathering and analyzing information is in place. She needs to ensure that the process is trusted by staff, and that information is shared openly and honestly. In addition, resources such as time, assessment tools and inservice training are required to support the process.

The standards for evaluating the program need to be identified. *The early childhood environment rating scale* (Harms and Clifford 1980) or the *Child care inventory* (Abbott-Shim and Sibley 1986) each provide a useful framework for evaluation. Alternatively, staff can develop their own standards, using the philosophy and goals of the centre for reference. Regardless of the mechanism, standards must be measurable.

Procedures for gathering information may include observations, interviews, surveys, standardized tests, and a review of program records. To ensure its validity, information must be gathered from different sources. These include children, parents, staff, administrators, students, and other resource persons.

As the evaluation team analyzes their information, they should refer back to the program philosophy in order to establish priorities for change. They need to establish an action plan, with possible solutions to the identified problems as objectives. This plan should be monitored to see if it is reaching its objectives, and modified as necessary.

Evaluation should be an ongoing process. It may be useful to "start small" and choose a specific focus for evaluation in order to ensure success.

Developing high quality curriculum for young children is not easy. It requires time, energy and teamwork from a knowledgeable staff who are committed to the process, and a supervisor who can provide the necessary leadership.

ACTIVITIES

1. Select two program evaluation tools. Implement an assessment of an early childhood environment using each tool, and compare the results.
   a) Which tool provides the most useful results? Explain.
   b) Which tool is easiest to use?
   c) Are the results similar?
2. In an interview, a parent is concerned that his child plays all day and asks, "When are you going to start teaching?" How would you respond?

3. You are hired as a supervisor in an established early childhood program. There has been little staff turnover; the newest staff member has been working in the centre for five years. You soon realize that there are some problems with the program—the staff seem to be in a rut, and appear to put little energy into curriculum development. What would you do?

FURTHER READING

Association for Early Childhood Education, Ontario (1988). *High quality child care statement*. Toronto, Ontario.

Bredekamp, S. (ed.) (1987). *Developmentally appropriate practice in early childhood programs servicing from birth through age 8*. Washington, D.C.: National Association for the Education of Young Children.

Brown, J. (ed.) (1982). *Curriculum planning for young children*. Washington, DC: National Association for the Education of Young Children.

Canadian Child Day Care Federation (1991). *National statement on quality child care*. Derman-Sparks, Louise and the A.B.C. Task Force (1989). *Anti-bias curriculum: Tools for empowering young children*. Washington, D.C.: National Association for the Education of Young Children.

Jorde Bloom, P., M. Sheerer, and J. Britz (1991). *Blueprint for action: Achieving centre-based change through staff development*. Mt. Rainier, MD.: Gryphon House Inc.

Schwartz, S., and H. Robison (1982). *Designing curriculum for early childhood*. Boston, MA: Allyn and Bacon.

Seaver, J., and C. Cartwright (1986). *Child care administration*. Belmont, CA: Wadsworth.

Spodek, B. (1970, October). "What are the sources of early childhood curriculum?" *Young Children*.

APPENDIX: PLANNING SHEET

Activity: _____

Date of Activity: _____

Number of Children: _____

Ages of Children: _____

Goals for Children	Objectives for Children
Write broad general aims for the children. Use words such as develop, enhance, increase, and expand.	The objectives should be related to the goals. Each objective should refer to specific, short-term tasks and skills in which the children will be engaging.

Procedure
List the procedure in a step-by-step format. Be specific in describing the introduction, implementation and conclusion of the activity. Also include a plan for transitional activities. Identify open-ended questions to be asked.

Evaluation
1. Describe the children's response to the activity. 2. If you were to implement this activity again, describe the changes you would make to improve the experience.

a

b

Physical Environments

This chapter provides a systematic look at how to organize physical space both indoors and out, keeping in mind both designing new areas and re-arranging old ones. The headings are:

◆ Developmental considerations when designing space: Infants, toddlers, preschoolers, school-age children
◆ A systematic approach to the use of existing space
◆ Designing new environments
◆ Planning outdoor environments.

The physical environment of an early childhood program is an important factor in its success. Space must be developmentally appropriate for children, secure, aesthetically pleasing, and convenient for staff.

Early childhood educators, parent volunteers and others working in the child care field have needed to call on many talents to create physical environments that are inviting and stimulating for young children. Many spaces built for quite a different purpose, such as church basements or old coach houses, have been reinvented to create space for early childhood programs.

The supervisor monitors and evaluates the ongoing use and care of the physical environment. Her challenge is to provide alternative approaches, while overseeing the safe, effective and appealing use of the available space. Above all, her role is to draw on the creative ideas of staff.

DEVELOPMENTAL CONSIDERATIONS WHEN DESIGNING SPACE

It is critically important to consider the developmental needs of children when designing space for quality child care programs. Many centres now have programs for children ranging in age from four months to twelve years. This presents a considerable design challenge, as well as requiring careful thought for the future should the ages of children needing care in the centre change.

Designing Space for Infants

We know from research and experience that infants need an environment that makes them feel secure and stimulates them through varying levels of challenge. Infants in group care usually range in age from four to eighteen months, a developmental range that requires careful planning by staff.

One of the many benefits for infants grouped together in this age span is the opportunity for the younger ones to experience varied social interactions. Younger children imitate and respond to their older peers, who enjoy helping and comforting the younger ones.

Young infants need secure and comfortable places to view and interact with their environment. Very young infants need to be protected from beginning walkers, and it is equally important for the older infants to have space to practice their developing skills. Infants also have different individual needs and temperaments. Some require orderly, quiet environments, while others seem to do best in environments that are busy and highly stimulating. A range of options needs to be available.

As demand steadily grows, more and more centres are incorporating care for infants. Studies by Wachs (1989) underscored the importance of environmental factors such as noise, overcrowding and spacial arrangements in supporting positive and negative responses in children. As space becomes more and more expensive to build and renovate, we must increase our ability to use what we have effectively and flexibly. Space for infants must offer:

- an environment where supervision is easy
- quiet areas and spaces to be alone
- areas that encourage and support small group social interactions
- room to allow for a wide range of movement
- areas to stimulate the senses
- opportunities to offer change, challenge, novelty, and enjoyment.

A centre should reserve one particular area for infants of varying ages. An infant area can be defined by large, stable dividers, or by full or half-walls of tempered glass. Keep in mind that there are many times when safety requires keeping all the infants together. Large foam-covered areas with low foam walls provide a space where older infants can interact with younger ones, ensuring the physical separation necessary to keep them safe, while allowing crawlers to get about and stumbling new walkers to try out independence (see photo "A" on p. 72). Flexibility in design is needed, to meet all the needs of this age group.

There are many specific requirements in a physical space for infants that should be kept in mind:

- an array of sensory areas that are aesthetically pleasing

- space where staff can carry nonmobile infants about to explore their environment
- ample floor space for mobile infants to experiment with the use of their bodies through toys and materials
- play areas that allow for hiding, imitation, grasping, banging, dumping, and filling up
- spaces that encourage young children to move in and out of social interactions with their peers
- serving areas that are easily sanitized, with convenient appliances
- feeding areas with tiled floors to allow finger foods and quick cleanup
- places where infants can pull themselves up safely and be sufficiently cushioned when they tumble or fall
- a division between the nonmobile and mobile areas, that promotes exploration while also ensuring safety
- permanent sleep rooms with individualized beds that promote security and permit individualized schedules
- adult-height change areas with large sinks where staff can wash children comfortably
- individual storage areas for each child's clothing and personal belongings
- accessible and handy storage for bulky diapers, extra toys and materials
- counter space for parents to change outerwear, fill out daily forms and share information about the child with the teachers
- easy access to the infant playground with storage for triple strollers and other outdoor equipment.

The physical care of infants is demanding. An effective arrangement of space allows staff to focus more of their caregiving time on pleasant teacher-child interactions. If space is poorly laid out, staff become frustrated and time spent with the children is less productive.

Parents are often anxious about leaving a very young child in group care. Their confidence in the centre will be increased if they perceive the physical environment is thoughtfully laid out, safe and aesthetically pleasing.

Designing Space for Toddlers

What a fascinating group of active young learners—move equipment aside and give them space! They want to use their bodies to do just about everything. They push things, fill and empty wagons and buggies, pails and purses, as they practice and refine their skills. Toddlers are doers who need the security of some defined space and the flexibility of large areas. This sensory-motor stage leads them into testing every skill over and over again. They test their bodies by climbing stairs, hills and slides. They prefer large toys, moving them around with a stuffed animal parked under one arm. In their mind there is nothing they can't do!

How do we design space to incorporate what we know about toddlers? Much of what we said about infants also applies to toddlers—for example, they need change areas, easily cleaned surfaces and convenient storage areas. Unlike infants, toddlers are mostly all mobile, moving, adjusting, re-arranging, piling, organizing, knocking down, and rebuilding. A centre needs space where they can accomplish such energetic tasks.

Washrooms in, or adjacent to, the playrooms foster self-help skills and peer toilet training. Low sinks they can use to wash their own hands and get a drink further foster these skills.

Toddlers need space to experiment with their bodies, space without sharp corners or cluttered areas. Toddlers like to sprawl and spread out their toys, with little interest in putting them away. Low cupboard areas encourage little ones to put away their toys and make more space to clutter all over again. They like to pick up large objects and carry them around, unconcerned that the objects may be as large as they are.

It may be possible to build different levels, ramps and slides into the playroom for the sensory-motor toddlers. Stairs that take toddlers to safe platforms where they can look down at the adults give them a feeling of power (see photo "B" on p. 72). A space under the platform allows others to read books quietly and be by themselves, or with one or two others. Open areas for walking about, pushing buggies and pulling wagons is as important to consider indoors as it is outdoors. Such different levels can become a permanent part of the room, to be used in a variety of ways. At the same time, leave enough open space to allow you to adapt the environment quickly to meet changing developmental needs.

Safety is a fundamental consideration for all ages in child care centres, but toddlers are most vulnerable. Infants are dependent on adults to get around, and preschoolers have learned some basic safety rules, but for toddlers the understanding of what is safe is often secondary to curiosity and the drive for independence. Space for toddlers must be secure, padded whenever possible, and free from obstacles that impede their play and interaction with their world.

Designing Space for Preschoolers

The developmental needs of preschoolers also cover a very broad range. In most provinces this group includes children from two-and-a-half to five, or until they are eligible to attend either junior or senior kindergarten. Initial decisions about how to arrange physical space needed to facilitate children's optimum growth depend on the philosophy of the centre. Will preschoolers be family-grouped or age-grouped? part-day or full-day? and so on. Once these decisions are reached, environments can be planned.

Preschoolers need ample opportunity to become independent problem-solvers involved in their environment. A positive self-concept is reinforced when children are given opportunities to make choices, time to carry them out, and a planned environment to feel safe and comfortable in. Staff must also consider the changing and developing needs of each individual in the group, as well as the needs of the overall group, so activities and experiences must be provided at varying degrees of ease and difficulty.

Opportunities for problem-solving or divergent thinking are important during the preschool years, so the environment should provide a wide range of choices. A developmental curriculum for preschoolers usually results in a variety of learning centres, each with its own characteristics and properties. Placing learning centres in close proximity to each other allows children varied opportunities to test and transfer their learning.

Educators set the stage for learning by providing activities with a range of ease and difficulty in each of the learning areas. For example, the science area can have many simple materials for the beginning manipulator to explore, as well as more complex materials to challenge others. Such blending of resources throughout the playroom encourages social interaction, peer assistance and more in-depth and varied questions from the children.

The layout of the room should generally reflect program goals and expectations, giving behavioural cues to the children. When space is totally open and provides no clear guidelines for the children to follow, play spills over from one area to another. This may encourage children to develop some level of skill in conflict resolution, but it tends to inhibit the concentration of play involvement and increase the number of negative interactions.

Children need clear definitions between play areas, so allow a clear space for each small group of children, with open areas where they can use their bodies to enhance their involvement. This results in more productive play. Social skills develop slowly in young children, and their development is supported by placing small groups in large, defined areas. This is an important consideration for children in all care settings—as adults we also do best when our interactions are limited to reasonable numbers of other people at one time.

The arrangement of space dictates the level of teacher involvement needed to help children remember the expectations for inside play. Clear pathways, or traffic patterns that lead from one area to another, must be visible from the child's eye level so they can move freely and independently. This physical layout and space definition helps children understand that some want a quiet space to reflect, while others are always ready for new playmates. All developmental areas should be clearly accessible, so children have opportunities to choose many different experiences. For example, if something like the block area is hidden from easy view, some children may miss its fabulous play potential.

Dramatic play is critical during this developmental stage, and requires large amounts of space. Dramatic play can take many forms, from creative movement to representations of daily living that children try out over and over to help them make sense of their world. Settings that can be duplicated in play with the help of a few teacher-supplied props include parent workplaces, outdoor camping, shopping malls, pet stores, libraries, and many others.

Defining play space effectively is a difficult task, especially for the beginning teacher. Each group of children brings a separate culture which takes time to understand and incorporate into the environment, and what works with one group may not work with another. As children become more competent in their play, educators may want to involve them in the setup of the room. A very confident teacher is often more willing to provide this experience for the children. Planning with the children, defining goals and expectations, and physically involving the children in the room arrangements, can be a valuable and rewarding experience for both children and staff.

The development of independence and self-help skills continues to be important during the preschool years. Washrooms should be conveniently located, so children can go on their own with minimal guidance. That way, visual supervision by staff tends to replace physical assistance, fostering independence in the child while giving staff more time for creative work. Similarly, children's personal items and clothing should be located close to the playrooms in order to enhance their self-help skills. Windows in the playroom walls looking out to the coat area allow for supervision while increasing the sense of independence.

Designing Space for School-age Children

Within the last ten years, the ages of children housed in child care centres has expanded to run the whole gamut from infants and toddlers at one end to school-age children at the other. This great developmental range means supervisors face many challenges in assigning staff, and using space, equipment and financial resources wisely.

Canadian children enter formal schooling between the ages of 3.8 and six years, depending on the province or territory, and children between 3.8 and twelve are considered school-age children under some board of education definitions. However, school-age children are generally defined as five- to twelve-year-olds. Depending on individual needs, child care centres may enrol these children before school, at lunchtime, after school, after or before kindergarten.

Staff-to-child ratios may be lower than those required for younger children, but space requirements are higher. School-age children need many and varied opportunities for gross motor activities, sturdy equipment that is developmentally appropriate, space for large-scale projects, opportunities to change equipment, and greater emphasis on recreational activities.

Developmentally, older children require increased opportunities to plan their own activities, structure their own schedules, and participate in group decision-making and project development. They are developing their own hobbies, interests and life skill activities, and require both space and time to work in groups, as well as quiet, reflective areas to do homework or just be private.

Since school-age children spend all or part of their day in school, they need different kinds of experiences in the child care centre. Ideally, recreational programming should be a primary consideration. While it may be possible to install basketball hoops or provide co-operative games, most centres rapidly come up against their own limitations. Older school-age children love hockey, baseball and other team sports, although incorporating these into the program may be difficult. Any alternative sports require dedicated space as well. Many school-age programs are housed in schools, and may be allowed to use the gym or playground. In other cases, recreational space can sometimes be found in a nearby community centre or church.

Quiet areas for relaxation, reading and doing homework should be set away from the noise of more rambunctious play. Often, the space used by school-age children is used by other ages during the day, so locked portable cupboards are required to keep school-age materials secure.

A SYSTEMATIC APPROACH TO THE USE OF EXISTING SPACE

It is often difficult to analyze the present use of existing space, especially if your program has been running for some time and the staff are used to doing things a certain way. A systematic approach to analyzing your centre's physical environment will speed up the process, give you a rationale for your plans when you present them to staff, and ensure that you take all aspects of the program into account. If you change one room or area at a time without having an overall plan, you will not get the most efficient and effective use of the space in the long run. In this section, we will proceed with systematic analysis step by step.

1. Review your statement of philosophy and your centre's overall goals.

- What are you trying to accomplish with the children, parents, staff, and the local and professional community you belong to?
- What have the staff agreed about how children best learn and grow?
- What do the staff agree upon as developmentally appropriate practice for young children?
- Do your staff have a good understanding of the developmental needs of each of the age groups in your centre?
- How do the staff want to involve parents?
- What are the staff's long- and short-term goals?

Once you have re-examined your philosophy and overall goals for the centre, you can begin to assess how the physical environment can best meet these needs.

2. Look at your present or anticipated enrolment.

What are the ages and number of children in each group? We have seen how the set-up of the physical environment supports developmentally appropriate practices. A review of the developmental needs of the children served by a centre is essential in your analysis of the best use of an existing environment.

3. Evaluate the existing physical space.

Go through your centre with measuring tape and graph paper in hand, and actually measure each area that is presently part of your centre. Don't be satisfied with rough estimates for each area. If you are lucky there may be a set of plans you can work from, but this is often not the case. Completing this exercise has several advantages:

- It helps you develop a clear idea of spacial relationships. You may think you know what an 8×12 metre room looks like, but you may be surprised when you actually measure out the space.
- It helps you develop a clear visual image of your overall centre, and the size of each area in relation to other areas.
- You begin to get the "big picture" and become more methodical in your thinking about how best to use your space.

4. Draw a plan of your centre.

This doesn't have to be a masterpiece in design and layout. Decide on a scale, make it an easy one, and lay out your centre according to the measurements you have taken in each area. Scale your space large enough so that you can sketch in shelving units and equipment, using a constant scale so that eventually you can move your equipment around in your rooms as you try out different arrangements.

5. Establish priorities.

Develop several lists to be considered in your planning. The first list would include the things that are impossible or extremely difficult to change in your present setting—kitchen and bathrooms, windows, and structural considerations such as bearing walls.

The next list would contain the areas where you need additional information before you can make a decision. Costs might well be a determining factor; or if you share space with another organization, you need to examine how your changes would affect them.

Develop a list of the areas you can change. You may find that a consideration on one list should be moved to another. For example, you may have wanted to move a wall and make a large room out of two small rooms, and then had to give it up when you found out the wall was a bearing one and could not be moved. Upon further examination, you discover you can open the two rooms up with a large archway, which solves your supervision problem and still leaves the bearing wall with sufficient strength. Don't eliminate possibilities before looking at a range of ways for solving the same problem.

6. Move to the "what if" stage.

"What if we moved the staff room into the storage room, found some storage in another area of the centre, and used the staff room as the extra space we need off the playroom? This location for the staff room would provide more convenient access to the playroom, and the storage area tends to be a 'throw it in and close the door' kind of room."

"What if we moved the coat cubbies to the other end of the hall, and left this end open in order to divide the children into smaller groups for circle time?"

"What if, what if ..." You have now opened your mind up to new possibilities you may not have been aware of before. Staff can have input into how the centre might be laid out as they experiment with the various arrangements on the scaled drawings. The more you stimulate ideas, the greater the possibilities. The old response,

"Yes, but we tried it that way once and it didn't work," may be heard for the last time. Often that response was born from the fact that staff didn't relish the idea of lugging equipment from one end of the room to the other and back again while a final decision on its resting place was decided. There's no way to avoid physically moving the equipment, but after the staff have become involved and excited about the new physical arrangement, only one move will be required to put it into place.

By scaling your equipment to size in your drawing, you can try out many possible arrangements of space. Make scale cardboard templates of the equipment, furniture, storage areas, shelves, and so on. Now you can begin to get an idea of the possible ways to use your centre without actually lifting the equipment around. Careful attention here saves much time and difficult work, and avoids the trap of "Just leave it there—I'm not moving another thing."

7. Consider health and safety issues.

Careful review of all health and safety conditions is critical. This should take place both before you lay out the room arrangement and after you complete it.

As you consider changes in your existing setup, examine your local licensing regulations to make sure you are not overlooking some fire regulation. You may need to arrange a visit from the fire department to ensure that you are not interfering with the fire exits. Sometimes rules change so that you gain more flexibility in the use of some areas. Sometimes the opposite is the case, and you find you are inadvertently breaking some new regulation.

You need to consider such things as play areas near drafty doors and windows, and washrooms that cannot easily be supervised. The floor surface in each area is a health and safety issue. Carpets that can't be cleaned easily may collect dirt and dust, causing health problems, particularly in children with allergies. Surfaces that become slippery when wet can be a hazard. Saving a carpeted area by putting plastic under messy areas such as painting activities may create a safety hazard. A safe traffic pattern must be established in each area to prevent accidents and protect children who are using the floors for play.

While it is the responsibility of every staff member to be alert to health and safety issues, one person should be assigned the task of completing a checklist of such issues on a regular schedule. Otherwise some areas of the centre may get overlooked. A checklist is the best method to use to feel confident that each area of the centre has been examined for health hazards or safety concerns.

Any areas identified as potential hazards should be noted, and an action plan put in place. The list should also indicate when the correction will take place, and the date of the next inspection. Educators have too many details to keep in mind to trust the health and safety aspects of the centre to memory. A systematic way of monitoring potentially dangerous health and safety issues leaves staff more able to supervise with ease and freedom. A sample checklist is given in the appendix to this chapter.

8. Determine accessibility and proximity.

When existing space limits access from one area to another, staff have to come up with creative solutions. For example, what if there are no sinks near the creative area?

Portable sinks could be used, as long as they are kept sanitary. It reduces tension to have water nearby, rather than watch a three-year-old trail a thick path of goop and finger paint across clean floors and rugs.

The developmental needs of the children will dictate the kinds of activities you make available. A few suggestions might help you decide the proximity and accessibility of one area to another.

The planning and provision of learning areas seems to be the most commonly used approach in implementing a developmental curriculum. There must be space for:

- science and nature activities
- cognitive experience, fine motor development and quiet games
- creative endeavours
- the development of gross motor skills
- listening centres for music, enjoying stories and other language experiences
- privacy and quiet reflection
- sensory experiences and exploration
- imaginative and dramatic play
- experimentation
- blocks with many properties.

9. Don't forget empty space.

While consideration must be given to the curriculum areas listed above, it is also important to evaluate the amount of empty space available to the children in each room. Each province has guidelines setting the minimum space to be provided for each child. In your space planning you need to include open or empty space for children to use.

Kritchevsky et al.'s book *Planning environments for young children* (1983) discusses the need to include areas of empty space in proportion to the group size. It would appear that the larger the number of children, the higher the proportion of empty space needed by each child. It is recommended that one-half of the room space available should be uncovered surface.

Kritchevsky et al. also refer to dead space, usually occuring in the middle of the playroom without visual or tangible boundaries. Often such space invites running, and less constructive play requiring more teacher intervention.

10. Consider the proximity of one activity to another.

Once you have laid out your room on paper, cluster the activities by considering the kind and amount of space they need. Then think about their proximity to other activities. For example, large blocks and dramatic play take far more space than cognitive games. Activities of the first kind need space for construction, rearrangement, and finally tearing down, while the latter require less movement. Activities that are alike should be clustered together, providing opportunity for children to transfer their learning and practise their skills on a number of different materials and media.

Traffic flow or pathways must be organized so that children see and use them effectively. Learning centres must be protected by some kind of partition so that activity does not get disrupted when other children pass by. At the same time, painters can get inspired by the activities they can see in another section of the room.

Other Considerations in Redesigning Space

The surface of the floor in each area is also a consideration. A corner area may seem appropriate for a quiet book place, but it may be the only area where the creative activities can take place, because of limited options in floor surfaces.

Areas with natural light may also influence decisions about where certain activities need to be placed. After you have listed the learning centres and curriculum areas you wish to include, you may find that natural lighting is required for some of them. Ventilation in the room becomes even more important if you house pets. The nature and science area may require sunlight for some part of the day. Fish tanks should not get direct sun, while some experiments require it.

Aesthetics must also be addressed. Pictures, mobiles, plants, and art work can help create a warm, soothing environment. Attractive surroundings including a variety of textures and so on allow children opportunities for sensory experiences. When the centre is arranged to allow children opportunities to touch and explore, they can be encouraged and expected to help care for their own environments.

A chart could be developed to organize the many variables related to the use of space. This chart would be helpful in other ways as well. It should include:

- the various activities included in the curriculum
- aesthetic considerations
- equipment and materials needed, and their relative size
- pathways and desired traffic patterns
- the desired amount of open space
- noise considerations
- areas with natural and artificial lighting
- doors and windows in the room
- location of washroom and coat cubbies.

Each centre has its own strength and drawbacks. Systematic analysis will help you make the best use of any environment.

Environmental Health Considerations

Recent research has begun to look at health hazards that may exist in indoor environments. These are particularly an issue if you have a sealed space with a central air supply, without opening windows. Rapidly growing young children may be particularly sensitive to indoor environmental hazards.

Noxious vapours can be given off by new carpets, paint and cleaning agents. Common areas need disinfecting, but do not use cleaning agents that are harsh or leave a lingering odour. Carpets and curtains can hold dust and moulds that are circulated through air conditioning and heating systems, feeding sickness and allergies. Humidification is necessary in winter, but avoid bacteria buildup by making sure the humidifier is cleaned out regularly.

An area which is still controversial concerns children's sensitivity to the electro-magnetic fields (EMFs) given off by electric cables and appliances. Recently a kindergarten was closed in Toronto because of unacceptable EMFs originating in power cables running under the floor. Again, rapidly developing young children are seen as being most sensitive, and jurisdictions as far apart as Sweden and New York City have recently passed rigorous standards limiting the strength of EMFs to which children and pregnant women can be exposed. That old computer you leave running in the corner for the children to play on may be emitting fields far above the New York school board limit.

Exercise common sense, keep children well back from electrical appliances and away from transmission lines. If you are concerned, your local hydro authority may come in to measure fields in your centre. These measurements should reflect the actual situation at your centre, so make sure they are not done at times when electrical use is unusually low.

DESIGNING NEW ENVIRONMENTS

While early childhood educators often become expert at the adaptation of existing space, the best way to make sure a child care centre meets all the requirements is to design a new one. Helping design a new centre can make people anxious, but it is certainly exciting to put a vision of what young children need into the reality of new physical space.

Although architects and other professionals are becoming more and more knowledgeable about the needs of young children's environments, you are the expert on what children, staff and parents need. Just as a doctor must describe to an architect what kinds of activities go on in her office, an early childhood educator needs to describe, in full detail, what goes on in a quality child care program, and what the environment requires to be successful. A great deal of preliminary work is required from the staff to clearly lay out and fully explain the activities, routines, daily schedules, and space requirements. The architect needs a clear picture to design a space to meet well-defined needs.

Sometimes altering or adding to an existing space appears to be a quick and simple solution to a long-standing problem. "If only we could add to the storage area it would solve all our problems." Sometimes the solution may be just that simple. But the systematic approach is just as necessary when considering an expensive addition. No change, or expansion, is without cost. Look at what you want to achieve in the overall scheme of things before you make a final decision on building or altering space. You may find that there is need for extra space, but you may also discover versatile uses for it which were not part of your original thinking.

Translate the Centre's Philosophy and Goals into the Physical Requirements

Once you are clear about what you want to accomplish in your centre, you will have to translate these needs into terms an architect can understand. For example, if increased independence in self-help and personal hygiene is one of your long-term objectives for the children, the physical environment could encourage this goal by providing child-size personal cubbies and washrooms easily accessible from the playroom.

If your goals stress parental involvement in the centre, this must must be reflected in a design providing places for parents to engage with the centre. The final design must reflect your written philosophy about how you feel children best learn and grow, and the role parents should have in that process.

Describe the Needs of Staff and Parents

Comfortable staff areas must be included when centres are being designed or redesigned, to allow staff to return to the children refreshed and enthusiastic. Staff need work areas to prepare curriculum materials that are separate from the lounge section, so they can have a real break and don't feel pressured during their time off. A workroom with proper storage to house large rolls of paper, gallons of paint, wonderful junk, and all the other supplies will enable staff to prepare their materials efficiently. Individual work areas could be included so staff can keep their records up-to-date and store their personal resources. A small kitchenette will reduce the volume of traffic in the kitchen, particularly during the hectic noonhour schedule. Adult washrooms should be included adjacent to the lounge area, along with closets for bulky winter outerwear.

This kind of staff space will keep the centre organized and free of clutter. Centres can't provide office space for each individual staff member, but a common room to be scheduled for parent interviews or to discuss the progress of student teachers will meet this need. Depending on the size of your centre you may have a reception area, a supervisor's office, or both. Whatever the case, they should be located near the entrance, accessible to entering parents. A space to keep an ill child who is waiting to be picked up is also required by some licensing bodies, and a location near the supervisor's office is advisable.

Parents' areas are also important. As outlined in Chapter 10, we are gaining more and more information about the benefits of parent involvement. The more parents feel confident and comfortable with the staff and the children's environment, the easier it seems to be for children to settle in and learn from their new experiences. If there is space designed to increase parental involvement, then parents will spend more time in the centre and become familiar with the staff and the program. Bulletin boards providing current information, a coffee area with books and articles, and private space to meet with the staff, all add to their involvement.

Interpret the Regulations of the Local Licensing Body

This could be a simple or more difficult task depending on the complexity of regulations governing your province or territory. Most mention the following areas:

- requirements of the local health, fire and zoning authorities
- teacher-child ratios
- age groupings
- group sizes and room capacities; square metres per child, both indoor and outdoor
- curriculum planning and daily records
- staff qualifications and training
- use of indoor space
- playground requirements
- health and safety regulations
- amount and types of toys and equipment
- administrative procedures
- regulations regarding the physical plant.

Reading the regulations is one thing; clearly understanding their implications is another. Your role is to make sure all parties involved in the design agree about what they mean. A regulation may require one toilet and sink for every fifteen preschoolers, but not specify the location. It is up to the child care professionals to think about where the toilets should be placed. Regulations typically refer to minimal requirements that are just that—minimal. It is cheaper and less disruptive to determine the centre's growth needs at the time of construction than it is to rip up areas later.

The regulations take time to incorporate into your overall planning and should not be taken lightly. When you are designing a new centre, the preliminary plans are usually sufficient to get approval in principle from your licensing body. Your local licensing body should be able to provide you with other helpful information to assist in the development of your centre. Understanding the procedure to follow is the most important aspect for us to consider here, since regulations vary so greatly across the country.

Incorporate Health and Safety Features

A hazard-free environment offers more opportunities for children's free use of the space without anxious staff overseeing their every move. Children must be protected from such hazards as poisonous substances, hot tap water, slippery floor surfaces, uneven rugs, electrical outlets, sharp edges, and unsafe windows and stairs. For example, area rugs over tile do not work with young children. The ends become frayed, children like to lift them and slide under, and sometimes they become a safety problem. In areas where children are going to play on the floor, wall-to-wall rugs are safer.

A single-storey centre is safest, if the land site makes it feasible. Stairs require the enforcement of safety rules often forgotten by young children. The relationship of the playground to the building is another safety feature. Direct access from indoors to the playground will ensure that children do not stray when one of the eyes in the back of the teacher's head is blinking. Parents should be able to go directly to the playground to pick up their child.

The location of swings and creative climbers must also be clearly considered from a safety point of view. Space to walk easily and safely around each piece of equipment is essential. Hills for tobogganing must be placed so that they point away from the building, and away from fences and other pieces of equipment. When visiting a centre one day, the author was taken to see a newly constructed playground. It looked very attractive, contained the variety and scope of equipment that encourages gross motor development, and included some nice areas which might stimulate social interaction. The playground contained a hill with good ascent for slipping and tobogganing. In fact, it appeared to be an exemplary setup. By midwinter the supervisor was at her wit's end: what looked like a well-considered playground turned out to be a disaster when ice formed. The gently sloping hill changed into a slippery nightmare only bobsledders could use. The speed the children came down at took them directly into the fence. No amount of salt and sand seemed to make a difference, and the staff spent the rest of the winter slipping and sliding on the hill to retrieve children eager to give it another run.

The location of parking for the parents is another safety consideration. Little feet too tired to move from the snack table suddenly spring into action as parents struggle to get them and their precious belongings into the car. Safety bumps and clearly marked traffic patterns all assist in making dropping off and picking up safer.

Look at everything with a critical eye. Think of how the building, the equipment or any other aspect of the program might become a hazard for young hands, bodies and minds.

Ensure the Design Allows for Flexible Enrolment and Programming

When you are designing a new centre you usually have a given number of children in mind. The number in each group is often determined by the staffing ratios established by the licensing regulations governing your area. For example, if the staff-child ratio is 5:1 for toddlers, and your maximum group size is fifteen, then you may plan for a group of fifteen toddlers. You may decide that ten toddlers in a group is a better overall size, but after further consideration three staff is an overall safer situation. Economics and safety may together determine your final decision to have fifteen in the group.

If your staff-child ratio is 8:1 for preschoolers and your maximum room size is twenty-four, you have another decision to make. Do you have two groups of sixteen children with two staff in a room, to make a more appropriate group size for young children, or one group of twenty-four?

Developmentally appropriate practices and the philosophy of your centre should be the most important considerations in your decision, although the financial viability of your centre will also play a role. Further growth may also be a factor for the board to consider. Long-term plans may involve a phase-in schedule.

Once you have determined the beginning capacity and age groups you are starting with, consideration should be given to the flexibility of the space in terms of its use by various ages. Let's say that your beginning capacity is ten infants, fifteen toddlers, thirty-two preschoolers and fifteen school-age children. Registrations are coming in, and you find that your predictions are being matched for the infants, toddlers and preschoolers, but there are only one or two requests for school age. Now what?

Back to the "what if" theory. What if we gave the parents of the two school-age children the option of incorporating their after-kindergarten children into the oldest preschool program for the half day, and use the school-age room for the extra toddlers requesting care. Good idea! If we have included the necessary requirements for flexible use in our design, we are ready to accept the second group of toddlers. Keep in mind that many of the physical characteristics necessary for one program can have another purpose with a different age. For example, change areas with large sinks in the toddler room would make very useful creative areas with another age. When a checklist of needs for each area has been prepared, another column could be added for alternative use with other ages. This procedure can be followed throughout the centre.

Enrolment may suddenly change, after remaining consistent for several years. Another centre may open or close in your area, the board of education may do a pilot project, or new adult education programs may increase the demand for a particular age group. Whatever the case, flexible programming is important to meet the needs of the families in the community, and it makes good sense from the point of view of economics.

Explain the Need for Accessibility, Proximity and Clustering of Activities

This is a big undertaking and encompasses almost every other consideration discussed to this point. What activities do you want to cluster together? How do you ensure safety for the children? Where should the support services be located? What about staff, parents and entrance areas?

One way to begin to get a handle on this task is to decide which activities go together and why. Activities and activity areas related to the children themselves make the first cluster. You can visualize the clusters as circles including related activity areas.

- playrooms, storage of toys, supplies, beds, etc.
- washrooms
- gross motor area, indoor/outdoor storage
- coat cubbies, personal storage
- dining area
- playground, indoor/outdoor storage.

Activities related to the provision of services require another cluster:

- kitchen
- pantry
- sleep room (if separate from playrooms)
- laundry room
- janitorial room
- storage for extra toys, equipment, supplies
- seasonal storage.

Draw another circle and include these areas. Don't worry at this point if you are not entirely sure what should be included in a particular cluster. Fine tuning comes later, but for the moment you want all areas included.

Make a third cluster for staff areas:

- lounge
- supervisor's office
- reception area
- work area and supply area
- interview room
- personal space and resource storage
- kitchenette
- adult washroom
- area for a sick child.

Make a fourth circle for the inclusion of parent needs.

- lounge
- information area
- meeting room.

Keep in mind that the point of this exercise is to look at what you want to include in your centre, and how each area relates to others. Each centre will have a different set of priorities and needs that will guide the layout.

You may want to take one area out of a certain cluster and put it into another. For example, you may decide the staff washroom should be clustered with the children's area so that staff can use it easily. Or you may want the washroom required for school-age children to double as a second staff washroom near the children's area.

After the activity areas are grouped in circles, bring the circles together, overlapping the ones you think should relate to one another most closely. For example, you will want to locate the playground, gross motor room and indoor/outdoor storage close to one another. A washroom easily accessible from the playground is essential for supervision and the avoidance of unnecessary untidiness from messy and snowy boots. Playrooms should be close to one another to allow flexibility of use, easier supervision in times of emergencies, and versatility of programming. Access from one room to another allows multiple use, so that different groups of children can share space, age groupings can reflect changes in enrolment, and curriculum can be adjusted as needs of the children change throughout the year.

The philosophy of the centre will dictate some further decisions about how you cluster areas together. The reception area, supervisor's office or both should be near the entrance for easy parental access. The parent area or areas should be easy to reach from the entrance, and should invite parent involvement. The staff room may have to be placed away from the supervisor's office, since there is only so much space in one area.

Other Considerations

Planning to reduce noise

Young children are easily stimulated and react to the activities around them. Some activities require concentration which is easily broken by the sudden screech of excitement when a block is finally balanced on the top of the pile. You do not want to discourage this productive sound, but you also want an atmosphere where children can "get into" an activity requiring quiet concentration. Consequently, the dilemma!

More and more professionals are becoming involved in the design of child care centres, studying ways to reduce the impact of noise. These include special acoustic strategies not considered in the past, with a combination of more familiar architectural concepts. Children react to noise around them in varied ways. Some are able to ignore it, some become louder in their play as the noise level accelerates around them, and some react very negatively to various levels of sound. It is important to include an acoustical expert in the planning of a centre in order to implement solutions specific to each site.

Storage areas

Although it may seem obvious, the provision of adequate storage needs to be emphasized when preparing final plans for building or alterations. Storage space is critical—for beds, indoor/outdoor gross motor equipment, seasonal material like bicycles, wagons and holiday decorations, and much else. Clutter is inevitable in a centre for children, but a lack of proper closed storage makes child care impossible, both aesthetically and practically. Stress the need, make a case, and stick to it!

Maintenance

Children play hard and are not as much in control of their bodies as adults may sometimes like them to be. Surfaces must be durable and washable. Tiled floors should be of good quality for the heavy washing they will need. Rugs should have good underpads and be of sturdy fabric that can be sanitized. Wall surfaces must be durable. One of the best solutions is to have attractive arborite glued on the walls, with wood trim. This may be more expensive initially, but in the long run it is economical. Cautions and concern for maintenance are essential, and the time and effort spent in carefully planning this area will be rewarded financially and aesthetically.

Further features to keep in mind

Other specific features that require attention include:

- washrooms in, or directly adjoining, each playroom and playground
- adult-size sinks in each playroom
- closed storage for curriculum toys, games, supplies, beds, and equipment in each playroom
- access from one playroom to another
- consideration for multi-purpose areas
- a minimal number of doors and corridors
- glassed areas to create an impression of spaciousness
- in the group areas, separation for learning centres and space for privacy or solitary play
- entrances that are aesthetically pleasing and comforting to the child (open and airy), with the avoidance of long halls and corridor-like cubbies
- storage that is accessible from both indoor and outdoor for gross motor equipment
- exits for parents from the centre or the playground
- service entrance to pantry from outside
- direct access to the playground from as many playrooms as possible, for indoor/outdoor programming in good weather
- parking for staff
- parking for parents that is convenient and safe for children.

PLANNING OUTDOOR ENVIRONMENTS

Outdoor space needs to be organized as much as indoor space. Many of the principles discussed for indoor environments can be applied to playgrounds or outdoor space. Developmental needs for each age group should be reflected in the playground layout to enhance children's social, emotional, cognitive, and physical growth.

Canada's four seasons bring new challenges, learning potential and excitement of discovery for children. While some children prefer to be inside, many blossom and thrive in the space, freedom and vitality presented to them in the outdoors. Children have a greater sense of discovery outside even when they are burdened with a bulky winter snowsuit—running, experiencing different sounds and using language in new ways, enjoying less structured opportunities for self-expression.

Safety

Playgrounds must be safe for use by any age group. Smaller, more vulnerable children need to have adults that check and re-check the safety of the playground. People passing by may inadvertently throw something over the fence that could harm infants and toddlers. Gates and fences must be checked constantly to ensure that children cannot hurt themselves or escape to an unsafe area. Outdoor areas require extra vigilance.

Proximity

The cubbie area, a washroom, and playrooms need to be close to the playground. This is crucial for infants and toddlers, and highly desirable for the preschoolers. The school-age children have developed sufficient self-help skills that priority should be given to the younger children to access these areas more readily. When playrooms and outdoor areas are close to one another, staff can extend inside play to the outside as weather allows, while maximizing staff supervision.

Playground Equipment

As Esbensen (1987) states, the quality of playground equipment and its location, together with the surface type and the condition of the playground, can present safety hazards for young children. All equipment must include such safety features as adequate handrails, child-size steps, soft and absorbent landing areas, clear boundaries for safe traffic flow, recessed bolts that protect small hands and fingers, and locations that make supervision possible from many angles. The playground layout should allow staff to be in assigned areas so that each adult on the playground can assist children readily and quickly. Because of the complexity and size of the gross motor equipment, it is usually best to open areas as staff are available to supervise them, rather than trying to supervise too large or complex areas. Safety is the critical factor that determines whether or not children should use the equipment.

Staff are often able to relax a little outdoors. The playground time may allow opportunities for staff to "get off their feet" for a few minutes. Incorporating equipment that children and teachers can enjoy together may help reach this goal. Safe, comfortable swinging or stationary benches, picnic tables, low dividing walls, and other environmentally attractive seating areas can be incorporated into the playground design.

Private companies involved in the design and layout of safe and effective playgrounds are now often available to consult with child care centres. Once staff have an overall idea of what they want to achieve in their outdoor area, these professionals can assist with the location, quality, design, and maintenance of equipment and surface areas including asphalt paths, type of fencing for the given area, recommended landscaping, natural mounds, levels, building overhangs or covered areas for wet days, storage space, and so on. The final design is critical, given the expense, the relative permanence of the playground, and its importance in meeting the centre's developmental goals.

Some staff naturally enjoy the playground activities while others prefer to be indoors. However it is important (and required by law) that children spend parts of the day outdoors. Attractive, comfortable space that is safe and convenient to supervise will entice "indoor" staff to want to be outdoors more and to increase the amount of time they stay outside.

Playground Space—Designated Areas

The size and shape of the playground will probably be determined by how much space is available. Provinces and territories have minimum requirements—for example, Ontario requires 5.6 square metres per child. Other factors to be considered include ages and number of children in the centre, the location of the playground in relation to the centre, what play areas are to be incorporated, use of surrounding land, nearby traffic and noise from outside, and the ratio of open to closed space.

Experts support the notion that dividing a playground into areas or zones helps children define space in a way that encourages particular types of play, and supports positive social interactions. The specific layout of designated spaces will be determined by the goals of the centre. Clearly defined areas, with boundaries easily understood by the children, would contain space for quiet reflection, social/dramatic areas, large gross motor or physical play areas, and creative/cognitive space. Walsh (1988) simplifies the description by calling them open areas, active areas and quiet areas.

It is important to highlight the importance of open space outdoors. While gross motor equipment such as swings, slides and a complex climbing apparatus is important, open space allows children to engage in self-directed activities. These experiences can change from day to day as children use props with increasing creativity and imagination. Where staff believe that children should have many opportunities to problem-solve, be spontaneous and make decisions, the outside environment will provide open space for these goals. It's always easier to provide movable equipment and materials that allow children to use open space constructively, than it is to change permanent structures.

In conclusion

We have done no more than provide an introduction to the complexity of child care centre design. Try to capture a sense of a child's perception of the world, and incorporate this point of view into the environment. Designing a child care centre is a procedure where new challenges are raised by every task solved. The information in this chapter will hopefully encourage you to continue to search for new and innovative ways to meet the needs of children, parents and staff.

ACTIVITIES

1. Visit a centre and observe one program for half an hour. Draw the floor plan of the room you observed and answer the following questions:
   a) What was the traffic pattern in the room, and how did it affect the children's involvement and behaviour?
   b) What was the noise level in the room, and what effect did it have on the children?
   c) What was aesthetically pleasing in the room, and what would you have changed?
   d) Did the room include sufficient open space for the number of children in the group?
2. Talk to one or two early childhood educators who have been working with children for several years. Find out what areas of the physical design in their centre have facilitated their ability to present curriculum and have enhanced teacher-child interactions, and what areas have been a hindrance.
3. What would you list as the three most important areas to include in the centre's physical design for each of the following age groups: infants, toddlers, preschoolers, school age?
4. Spend an hour in a playground. Make a list of the important developmental needs of the children using that playground. List the areas in the playground that help foster those needs.

FURTHER READING

Esbensen, S.B. (1987) *The early childhood education playground: An outdoor classroom.* Ypsilanti, MI: High Scope Press.

Frost, J.L. (1992). *Play and playscapes.* New York: Delmar.

Kritchevsky, S., E. Prescott, and L. Walling (1983). *Planning environments for young children: Physical space.* Washington, D.C.: National Association for the Education of Young Children.

Lovell, P., and T. Harms (1985). "How can playgrounds be improved? A rating scale." *Young Children* 40 (3): 3-8

Ministry of Culture and Recreation, Ontario (1982). *A guide to creative playground equipment.* Toronto: Government of Ontario.

Sciarra, D., and A. Dorsey (1990). *Developing and administering a child care centre.* Albany, NY: Delmar Publishers.

APPENDIX: HEALTH AND SAFETY CHECKLIST

HEALTH AND SAFETY CHECKLIST
Inspection completed by _____   Date _____
Summary of concerns from last inspection _____
_____
_____   Date of last inspection _____

INSPECTION AREA	YES	NO	COMMENTS
INDOORS			
Surfaces that are easy and quick to disinfect			
Floors that provide warmth and comfort			
Rugs secure to prevent tripping			
Non-slip floor surfaces			
Rounded or padded corners			
Climate control and draft-free environment			
Good ventilation with all systems working			
All areas are well-lighted			
Acoustic and noise levels are appropriate			
Safe, locked storage for hazardous materials			
Controlled systems for food storage and refrigeration			
Sanitary diapering procedures posted			
Sanitary food handling procedures posted			
Hand washing procedures posted			
Electrical outlets at children's level have dummy plugs when not in use			
No electrical or phone wires at child's level			
Furniture is stable, washable, not peeling or chipped, without toxic paint			
Safety glass in doors and windows, securely fastened			
Child size furniture and equipment to avoid accidents			

INSPECTION AREA	YES	NO	COMMENTS
Equipment and toys have no protruding edges and are in safe working order			
Science and nature materials are non-toxic and safe			
Toys and equipment are stored safely when not in use			
Toy shelves and cupboards are stable			
Water play is changed after use			
Sand is disinfected regularly			
Woodworking equipment is organized and safely stored			
Pathways in rooms are uncluttered, at child's eye level and easy to follow			
Toilets and sinks are at child's level			
Step stools used are wide, strong and stable			
Faucets used by children are temperature controlled			
Paper towels are readily available for children to use			
Children can access paper cups and a drink of water easily			
Kitchen is out of reach for children			
Dangerous equipment in kitchen is well out of reach of children			
Storage areas are uncluttered and have safe passages			
All areas of centre are cleaned daily (floors, washroom, kitchen, counters)			
Intensive cleaning is completed on a regular schedule (walls, doors, windows washed)			
Staff areas are organized and uncluttered			
OUTDOORS			
Playground can be accessed safely from building			
The entire playground is visible			
Playgrounds have clear and safe pathways			
Grounds are clean, garbage free and well-maintained			
Fencing in all areas is at least four feet high			
Fences are in good shape, latches working and secure			
Bushes and tree limbs are strong and sturdy			
Surfaces are free from holes and protrusions			
Sandboxes are covered or inspected for debris			

INSPECTION AREA	YES	NO	COMMENTS
Equipment is confined to designated areas			
Drainage is working well			
Washrooms and drinks are readily accessible			
Gross motor equipment is well anchored			
Equipment is free of holes, gaps, rough edges			
Equipment has no protrusion that clothes can catch on			
Equipment has space between each area			
Equipment is easy for staff to supervise			
Equipment is developmentally appropriate			
Children are protected from sun, wind and cold			
Surfaces under equipment have good cushioning			
Water play areas are changed at least daily			
Plants, shrubs etc. are non-poisonous			
Swings are checked to ensure safety			
Slides have no pinch points or protrusions			
Riding paths are in good shape			
Wood on equipment is smooth and splinter-free			
Bolts and screws are recessed			
Riding toys are checked for safety			
Equipment is developmentally appropriate			
Children are protected from sun, wind and cold			
Surfaces under equipment have good cushioning			
Water play areas are changed at least daily			
Plants, shrubs etc. are non-poisonous			
Swings are checked to ensure safety			
Slides have no pinch points or protrusions			
Riding paths are in good shape			
Wood on equipment is smooth and splinter-free			
Bolts and screws are recessed			
Riding toys are checked for safety			

ALL CONCERNS OR PROBLEMS WERE REPORTED TO THE SUPERVISOR ON _____

BY _____

6

Staffing—The Key to Quality

This chapter examines the supervisor's roles and responsibilities in relation to staffing, and then discusses professionalism in early childhood education and how it can be enhanced. The headings are:

◆ Defining a competent early childhood educator
◆ Developing effective recruitment and hiring procedures
◆ Stages of professional growth
◆ Supporting staff development
◆ Is early childhood education a profession?
◆ Methods of enhancing professionalism.

If you ask an experienced early childhood educator what is the single most important thing determining quality, you'll probably get an answer like "Teachers are the key to quality—the teacher can make it or break it." The importance of staff in early childhood programs can't be overemphasized. Doherty, in *Quality matters in child care* (1994), reviews research studies conducted over the past ten years in a number of countries that confirm the critical role good staff play.

The supervisor plays a key role in staffing, by selecting staff and ensuring they work at their optimal level. Along with the board or owner, the supervisor has these responsibilities:

- defining a competent early childhood educator
- developing effective recruitment and hiring procedures
- conducting staff performance reviews
- providing opportunities to staff for ongoing professional growth
- ensuring the environment meets staff needs.

DEFINING A COMPETENT EARLY CHILDHOOD EDUCATOR

What personality traits, values, beliefs, knowledge, and skills are most important in working with children? What makes a competent early childhood educator?

Current research demonstrates that program quality is strongly related to staff education and training. In a high quality child care program, qualified staff use specialized skills to meet the needs of the group as a whole, while remaining focused on the needs of each individual child. The kind of specialized knowledge gained through teacher preparation includes a foundation in the theory and research on child development, and the development of appropriate programs for young children that are individualized, concrete and experiential.

Whitebrook (1990) found that working with young children requires skills and knowledge that are provided through formal education and training programs. Formal training alone does not guarantee high quality child care, but several studies indicate that the standard of care is raised if staff are educated in child development and early childhood education. This is shown through the children's increased social interaction with adults, development of prosocial behaviours, and improved language and cognitive development.

As the field of early childhood education expands and diversifies, the specific training needs for early childhood educators are being re-examined. Some hold the view that early childhood education extends to age eight or even twelve, whereas others concentrate from birth to five. Since staff should have specialized training for the age group they work with, the span of the ages of children served in early childhood programs may affect the length, content and structure of teacher education programs.

One proposal for teacher education suggests a three-year diploma, with all students participating in a common core program for the first two years. In the separately streamed third year, students would choose an area of specialization such as working with children with special needs, administering child care programs, or specializing in an age group such as toddlers or school-age. A different model offers the year of specialization as a post-diploma program.

Apart from formal education, good teachers must have the right personal characteristics for working with young children. Almy (1975) identified the qualities of a good early childhood educator as a high energy level, patience, warmth, nurturance, openness to new ideas, a tolerance for ambiguity, flexible thinking, and maturity. Others (Peters 1988) would also add a positive self-concept, along with positive attitudes and expectations about children's achievements.

We know intuitively that these are important qualities. It is more difficult to concretely demonstrate their impact on the quality of children's experience, but attempts have been made to clearly and systematically determine what qualities make an effective teacher. Individual staff members can be evaluated through observing their interactions with children, parents and staff, and monitoring their implementation of curriculum.

The early childhood educator must receive broad-based professional training in such areas as human growth and development, program planning, working with adults, interpersonal communication, and behavioural management. A field placement experience is a critical factor. More specialized knowledge and skills may be added around this core, as required. For example, many educators are increasingly aware of the need to address the area of employee rights on the job. In order to keep pace with rapid changes in the field, educators must be prepared to participate in ongoing professional development throughout their careers.

DEVELOPING EFFECTIVE RECRUITMENT AND HIRING PROCEDURES

Given the importance of good staff, an administrator needs to make all efforts to attract and keep them. A recruitment strategy that is well planned and implemented is essential.

Job Description

The first step is to ensure there is a complete and concise job description. This should be in tune with the centre philosophy, and should include:

- the *title* of the position
- *accountability*—to whom the person reports
- *minimum qualifications*—education, experience, personal qualities
- *responsibilities*—for example, to establish and maintain a safe, healthy environment; to advance physical and intellectual competence; to support social and emotional development; to provide positive guidance; to establish positive and productive relationships with families; to ensure a well-run, purposeful program responsive to children's needs; to maintain a commitment to professionalism.

Once the job description is completed, the supervisor should sit down with existing staff and evaluate their skills and strengths as a team. This gives everyone an opportunity to have input into the recruitment process and assess what skills might complement the team, thus defining new job requirements that will help enhance the overall program.

A supervisor wants to develop a team that works together with a shared philosophy, where each members supports and complements the others. This not only provides a richer program for the children, it provides opportunities for in-service training where staff can share their expertise and skills with one another.

A job description gives the broad outlines of a position's responsibility and relationship to other positions. Although it should not be restrictive, a job description should be specific enough to measure performance and give staff a clear outline of their responsibilities. In fact, it is usually a fairly general document that leaves room for more specific requirements that can be included in the advertisement. A job description might state that the candidate should be able to plan, prepare and implement an overall development curriculum for toddlers. The advertisement might further specify that the successful candidate should possess particular skills in music and movement to supplement the skills of the existing staff.

Advertising and Interviewing

The next task is to find a candidate who meets your requirements. A good match is critical, when you consider the time it will take for a new staff member to get to know the children, parents, co-workers, and overall operation. If you hire someone and they don't work out, you will have spent a good deal of time and energy only to begin the process over again. Repeated change in staffing is also very unsettling to children.

Post the job internally. Make sure present staff know about it and have a chance to apply. They shouldn't hear about it from outside, and they may know of a good candidate to recommend.

Determine the interviewing team before the applications are reviewed. Involve the board of directors, by getting one or two members to be part of the team. You should also involve the staff member who will be working most closely with the new person. This contributes to building a compatible team.

Many supervisors use a four-step process for hiring. The initial screening of résumés and first interviews narrow the field by determining how well the candidates' qualifications parallel the program's needs. In the second stage, several candidates are invited to participate individually in the playroom for a minimum of two hours, to allow the director and staff to observe their skills in interacting with children and other staff. The third stage begins when staff, parents and director discuss what they observed, and finally a follow-up session is held with the candidate to discuss and clarify the observation.

Then the supervisor, along with the board or owner, makes the decision to hire. In a case where there are two equally qualified applicants, an additional question and answer period may be necessary. In a unionized setting, there will be specific rules to observe with regard to internal candidates and seniority.

You will want to cover these areas when you are interviewing a candidate:

- education and experience related to the position
- attitude
- interpersonal skills
- knowledge and understanding of child development
- ability to plan a developmentally appropriate curriculum
- methods used for guiding and supporting children's behaviour
- evidence of problem-solving strategies and conflict resolution style
- methods suggested for involving parents in the centre
- commitment to professional development.

It is important that all applicants be asked the same questions. In addition, the interviewing team must be aware of human rights legislation, and know which questions are not allowable.

Time spent in planning a thoughtful and thorough interview process will ensure that both your interviewing team and the candidate have ample opportunity to exchange information in order to make a well-informed decision about job placement. Remember, while you are interviewing a candidate, they are also interviewing your program. Effective hiring procedures result in greater compatibility between employee and program, a higher level of job satisfaction, and ultimately a higher quality program. Ensure that a candidate provide references, and that you follow them up. British Columbia legislation requires a criminal record check.

Once you decide on a candidate, you present an offer that includes salary, the details of the benefit package, and terms of employment. At the same time, you should outline the probationary period and the system for evaluating performance.

Staff Orientation

The recruiting and hiring process introduces new staff members to general aspects of the program like philosophy, objectives, curriculum, program design, and level of parent involvement. A detailed orientation process is necessary when they start the job.

A staff handbook helps new employees become familiar with the administrative policies and procedures in the centre. It should include information like:

- centre philosophy and goals
- policies and procedures—health, safety, sanitation, nutrition
- organizational structure—board of directors, staff reporting
- performance review process and probationary period
- personnel policies—holidays, sick days, benefits, etc.
- arrival and departure procedures
- record-keeping requirements
- behaviour management policy
- child abuse policy and procedures
- confidentiality.

This list can be added to by a centre's specific needs.

Make sure you allow for on-the-job orientation, where the new staff member can spend time with you discussing the staff manual and learning the specific responsibilities of the position. In the long run, time spent in carefully introducing new staff to the children, parents and overall centre operation is time well spent. Remember, you are building a long-term relationship with your staff members. They will feel respected and valued by being part of this process.

Performance Appraisals and Staff Reviews

Many supervisors view performance appraisals as one of the most difficult, time-consuming, and emotionally challenging tasks they face. But when they are carefully and consistently implemented, staff reviews can become the springboard for professional growth, program improvement and staff motivation. Many programs use the job description as the basis for the performance appraisal (see sample performance tool in appendices). The annual review provides an opportunity to reflect on staff performance, as well as to ensure the job description is updated to represent increased responsibilities. Supervisors can use the review process to identify strengths and needs, provide opportunities for addressing and reinforcing those areas, and develop the unique potential of each staff member.

In a supportive climate, the review process builds motivation, competence, and commitment to the organization. An effective staff development program can go a long way toward influencing and increasing professional development skills and self esteem among early childhood educators.

Everyone needs to know they are valued and respected for their work. It is a major challenge for a supervisor to create an atmosphere that encourages all staff to enhance their skills and participate in self assessment, and helps them plan experiences that result in better teaching. A supervisor plays a vital role by providing ongoing support for staff and by giving them open, honest and regular feedback. While it is up to the individual to make the decision to change behaviour, this feedback on performance provides direction for change. It makes individuals aware of what they do well, and may help them improve their performance in areas that need attention. Such feedback need not be directive when it is based on an evaluation model where director and teacher work together to generate solutions and explore alternatives.

This appraisal model concentrates on a staff member's behaviour, rather than on her or his character traits—on how a person acts, rather than on some judgement of who they are. It is specific rather than global, and focuses on the future rather than dwelling on the past. Regular open communication like this may have a more enduring impact on an individual's self esteem and overall performance than any specific resources that are provided to them. Caruso (1986) provides a comprehensive look at supervision practices, within a perspective that acknowledges stages of employee development.

The relationship between the supervisor and the teacher is the most critical element in producing improved performance. The quality of the supervisor's skills, combined with the degree of trust between supervisor and staff, determines the success of the evaluation process. Effective supervisors use the appraisal process as an opportunity to promote trust and motivation in the program's most valued resource—its staff.

Evaluation can acknowledge superior performance, give feedback on the selection process, and provide a basis for career planning and professional development. By clarifying the expectations of the program, feedback is especially helpful to beginning teachers. The appraisal system used must fit the professional skills, maturity, and experience of the staff. A comprehensive approach to assessing staff performance will use a variety of formats to meet the needs of individual teachers in each stage of their development.

STAGES OF PROFESSIONAL GROWTH

Glickman, Katz, VanderVen and others have defined predictable developmental stages that early childhood educators go through. Individuals vary greatly in the length of time they spend in each stage.

- Stage I—Survival
- Stage II—Consolidation
- Stage III—Renewal
- Stage IV—Maturity

Katz describes a teacher's typical behaviour at each of these stages, and identifies specialized training and professional development appropriate to each level (see Figure 6-1).

FIGURE 6-1
Stages of Development and Training Needs of Preschool Teachers

Developmental Stages	Training Needs
STAGE I **SURVIVAL**	On-site support and technical assistance
STAGE II **CONSOLIDATION**	On-site assistance, access to specialists, colleague advice, consultants
STAGE III **RENEWAL**	Conferences, professional associations, journals, magazines, films, visits to demonstration projects
STAGE IV **MATURITY**	Seminars, institutes, courses, degree programs, books, journals, conferences

Stage I—Survival

In this stage, which usually lasts through the first year of teaching, the beginning teacher feels the impact of full responsibility for a playroom of young children. This experience is often jarring and anxiety-filled, and the individual typically experiences self-doubt and feelings of insecurity.

Teachers in this stage need encouragement, insight into the reasons for children's behaviour, and instruction in specific skills. On-site support and training from other teachers and/or the supervisor is most appropriate.

Stage II—Consolidation

As they pass the survival stage, teachers stabilize and begin to exhibit some degree of confidence in their skill level. They begin to interpret what is happening in their classroom and are eager to seek alternate approaches. They learn by observing, modelling and doing, and thrive in a supportive environment that encourages problem solving and sharing.

At this stage, educators benefit from more focused observations and feedback that identify challenges, problems, and new classroom approaches. An administrator can provide encouragement to develop resources and form a support network.

As they develop further and master classroom fundamentals, teachers are ready to develop more challenging skills. They require exposure to new ideas to stay motivated and avoid burnout. In the later stages of the consolidation phase, individuals are ready for evaluation systems that facilitate introspection and personal goal setting. Possible methods include self-administered checklists, video analysis, or a mentor approach. Such a mentor relationship can be formal or informal, but most often it involves the supervisor or a lead teacher, along with regular opportunities to formally review issues that have arisen in the course of daily practice.

Stage III—Renewal

These teachers have reached a professional plateau. After several years of teaching the same curriculum to children at the same age level, they may no longer feel challenged. They may search for stimulation, asking: "What's new in the field? ... Are there new areas of curriculum I haven't considered before?"

When this occurs, the teacher has reached the renewal stage. Professional development opportunities that are particularly beneficial at this stage include attendance at conferences and workshops, taking a course, and active involvement in a self-assessment process.

Stage IV—Maturity

Mature teachers view themselves as committed professionals. They have developed a philosophy of education and care, and recognize the critical nature of early learning. Mature teachers acknowledge the need for continual professional growth and self-renewal. They are committed to the improvement of the teaching profession, and see the role of sharing information as an essential part of it. They are often searching for the meaning of social, economic, historical, and political influences on society.

SUPPORTING STAFF DEVELOPMENT

A major challenge for supervisors of early childhood programs is to create an atmosphere that enables staff as well as children to develop. Such an enabling environment contributes to the development of relationships within the program, and should flow from the program philosophy. To grow professionally, teachers need to share ideas and problems with other teachers, and to receive appropriate in-service training.

Supervisors can explore different ways of expanding opportunities for staff to enhance their knowledge base and develop new skills and competencies. It is important to provide release time for teachers to visit other early childhood programs. Professional conferences and workshops provide opportunities for staff to receive new information and discuss practice-based issues with colleagues. Such activities not only rejuvenate individual teachers, they often provide a rippling benefit when new ideas and resources are shared with other staff members.

Supervisors need to ensure that money and resources are available for staff development. Staff opportunities for continuous growth not only bolster morale, they also enhance the program's ability to foster children's healthy growth and development. Some programs provide money for teachers to take relevant courses through colleges or universities, and allow staff members time to complete their field placements and daytime courses.

There should be a bookcase in the staff room stocked with professional magazines, journals, and books for staff to read. Relevant articles should be circulated among staff, students and parents. Investing in these resources is a cheap way of enhancing program quality.

Ensuring the Work Environment Meets Staff Needs

Early childhood education is both physically and emotionally demanding. The supervisor is responsible for making sure policies, practices, the physical environment, and organizational values are responsive to staff needs.

Children need environments where they feel secure and free from anxiety. Minimal staff turnover and stable staff-child groupings build security for the children and allow for consistent application of the program philosophy. High staff turnover adversely affects both the children and the morale of the remaining staff, in turn further affecting the children and their program.

A number of surveys (Whitebrook 1990; *Caring for a living* 1992), as well as current studies, show that caregivers stay in the field longest when they have appropriate training, wages commensurate with their training, and good working conditions.

FIGURE 6-2

Wages in Early Childhood Education—Provincial Averages

		National	British Columbia	Alberta	Saskatchewan	Manitoba	Ontario	Quebec	New Brunswick	Nova Scotia	Prince Edward Is.	Newfoundland	Yukon	Northwest Terr.
Hourly wage across all positions		9.60	9.06	6.95	7.94	9.85	11.38	9.30	6.50	7.95	7.73	6.20	9.75	11.80
Average wages by position														
Assistant teacher	Hourly	8.29	7.85	6.23	6.59	8.60	8.84	9.06a	6.03	6.22	7.29	5.57	8.44	8.68
	Annual	15,337	15,307	12,440	13,125	16,815	17,652	16,960	12,448	12,420	15,504	11,586	17,072	18,978
Teacher	Hourly	9.71	8.94	6.76	7.52	9.29	11.51	9.06a	6.20	7.64	7.25	6.03	9.58	11.34
	Annual	18,498	17,433	13,498	14,977	18,164	22,983	16,960	12,799	15,256	15,419	12,542	19,378	22,231
Teacher Director	Hourly	10.76	10.14	8.14	9.42	12.25	12.49	b	7.50	9.31	9.40	6.54	11.13	12.54
	Annual	20,498	19,773	16,254	18,761	23,951	24,940	b	15,483	18,590	19,992	13,603	22,514	24,583
Administrative Director	Hourly	13.51	12.73	10.45	12.52	15.36	14.78	b	9.53	12.53	-	13.57	14.59	17.81
	Annual	25,804	24,824	20,867	24,935	30,031	29,512	b	19,674	25,020	-	28,226	29,513	34,915
Percentage higher wage when staff is represented by a union		33%	39%	88%	0%	15%	18%	25%	c	39%	c	c	c	c
Percentage higher wage for staff in non-profit centres over staff in commercial centres		25%	17%	30%e	d	25%	10%ef	36%	12%	44%	-14%	25%	d	d
Staff with post-secondary credentials		68%	71%	38%	50%	63%	85%	65%	50%	79%	69%	63%	42%	60%
One year certificate		10%	34%	15%	19%	11%	4%	6%	27%	13%	13%	17%	7%	29%
Two or three year certificate/diploma		46%	29%	18%	19%	31%	66%	46%	10%	39%	40%	26%	14%	27%
Degree		13%	8%	6%	11%	21%	15%	12%	13%	26%	16%	20%	21%	4%
Turnover rate		26%	28%	42%	26%	22%	19%	23%	28%	24%	16%	27%	84%	65%

a Assistant teacher and teacher positions combined   b Returns too low to be reliable   c No unionized staff responded to survey   d Commercial staff returns too low to be reliable
e Does not include municipal centres; staff in municipal centres in Alberta received 26% more than staff in non-profit centres and 63% more than in commercial centres;
  in Ontario, staff in municipal centres received 22% more than staff in non-profit centres and 33% more than in commercial centres
f This calculation has been adjusted to reflect estimated additional unreported Direct Operating Grant income received by staff in non-profit centres

Source: *Caring for a living—A joint project of the Canadian Day Care Advocacy Association and the Canadian Child Day Care Federation*
Data collected in June 1991

In *Improving the quality of work life* (1986), Jorde Bloom identifies a number of factors affecting the quality of the work environment and ultimately the quality of care. These include the amount of support received from the supervisor, opportunities for professional development, clarity of job expectations, an equitable reward system, and the physical work environment.

Over the past decade, considerable energy has been devoted to the improvement of wages and working conditions in child care settings. Most early childhood educators are underpaid and feel they are undervalued by society. But even recognizing this underlying dissatisfaction, they can still feel that their own program's policies are equitable and just. It is essential for administrators to have systems in place to ensure that pay, job security and promotion policies are fairly administered and communicated to all staff.

Employees of child care programs are entitled to the same legal rights as other workers. Both federal and provincial laws protect workers with respect to minimum wage, overtime pay, and a variety of working conditions. Supervisors, owners and boards of directors must be aware of these laws and ensure their personnel policies reflect them.

A good deal of attention in the field has focused on how the physical environment of early childhood settings can be made responsive to children, but little attention has been paid to adult needs. The general layout and design of space can help or hinder staff in carrying out their jobs, and powerfully influence moods and attitudes. Staff must have the proper equipment, materials and resources to do their work effectively. This aspect of child care is discussed in detail in the previous chapter, "Physical Environments."

The supervisor must be concerned with potential health hazards in the work place. *Well beings* (1992) cites the following health hazards in early childhood education: increased risk of illness, toxic substances in art supplies and cleaning agents, back problems from heavy lifting and frequent bending, physical strain from using furniture and an environment designed for children, poor lighting, high noise levels, and stress. Another major health hazard comes from the common tendency early childhood educators have to ignore their own health needs, because they lack health benefits and time off, and because they feel responsible for meeting children's needs first.

With the support of the board of directors, the program supervisor is responsible for creating a program environment sensitive to the needs of adults as well as children. These issues can be addressed by:

- ensuring there are personnel policies responsive to staff needs, such as a staff health plan.
- creating a positive healthful environment.
- assisting staff in looking after their own health needs.

Some of these are issues with no easy short-term solution. Chapter 11 addresses the need for child care practitioners to advocate on their own behalf, to increase public awareness and help gain access to necessary resources.

The Role of Unions

As early childhood educators experience the frustration of fighting individually for improved wages and working conditions, questions often emerge about unions, federations or professional associations—a group who will represent the field and gain the right to bargain with employers on the conditions of their employment. Who should perform this function for child care is emerging as a key question for the 90s.

While wages, benefits and hours are the items most frequently associated with collective agreements, they usually cover many other important issues: personnel policies, grievance and hiring procedures, performance review and promotion systems, provision for in-service training, breaks, and input into program decision-making.

These non-salary benefits are frequently as important to job satisfaction as the salary benefits are. They can be critical in helping staff provide better services. For example, input into centre decision-making can be an important guarantee in a contract. Members of Services Employees International Union (SEIU) Local 299 in Moose Jaw negotiated a provision guaranteeing their employer would meet with them once a month to evaluate concerns affecting the quality of care in the centre. Examples of other innovative contract provisions include a staff room "for the use and enjoyment of employees," and reimbursement for the cost of cleaning and shampoo occasioned by an outbreak of lice at the centre.

Many workers recognize the union or professional association as a long-term political ally that can assist child care workers in advocating for better funding and expanded services. The strength and unity of representation can be used to influence government funding for child care.

For workers who are employed by corporate child care chains, unions have been quick to point out organizations operating with huge profit margins and thus well able to increase staff wages without raising parent fees.

Only a small percentage of the child care workforce is unionized. The diverse and isolated nature of the child care delivery system, coupled with an unusually high turnover rate, has worked against the development of successful organizing campaigns. For more information on unions, refer to *Taking matters into our own hands* by the Child Care Employee Project (1990).

IS EARLY CHILDHOOD EDUCATION A PROFESSION?

Many believe the quality of child care is influenced by the level of professionalism in the field of early childhood education. Early childhood educators need recognition of their professional role. *Professionalism* refers to a combination of competence in a particular field of knowledge and identification with a group of colleagues who can collectively define and support quality practices.

Better salaries, improved working conditions and increased recognition of educational qualifications usually accompany professional status, and these are clearly warranted and appropriate goals for which to strive. Recognition of educational responsibility is crucial—many people are unaware that early childhood education has a distinctive professional knowledge base that informs practice. It is crucial to meet these conditions, in order to attract and keep good and experienced caregivers. Early childhood educators are familiar with the impact of low wages, high staff turnover, and inadequately trained staff. Unionization and advocacy have evolved as significant avenues to improve these areas.

The differing perspectives of unionization, advocacy and professionalism need not be mutually exclusive. Regardless of the approach taken, professionals require and deserve working conditions that enhance competence. Professional growth requires opportunities for learning new skills and time for planning and acquiring appropriate resource materials.

Katz (1985) identifies six criteria for looking at the professional nature of early childhood education:

- specialized knowledge
- standards of practice
- prolonged training
- a code of ethics
- autonomy—internal control over quality and self-regulation
- altruism.

An examination of early childhood education in terms of these characteristics will lead to mixed conclusions as to whether it is yet a profession.

Specialized knowledge in early childhood education is derived from developmental psychology and many other fields. A great deal of knowledge exists about how to care for and educate young children from birth through age twelve, and research demonstrates that those with access to this knowledge provide better care and education for young children. Professional judgement involves assessing events, weighing alternatives, and estimating the potential long-term consequences of decisions and actions based on that knowledge. Our choice of courses of action is based not only on common sense, but also on specific expertise acquired through professional training and ongoing professional development. We must continually challenge and evaluate our professional judgements and practices, to ensure they are based on the best available information. The knowledge base of the field has expanded greatly over the last decade, and it continues to grow as the needs of children and families increase in complexity. Practitioners need to upgrade their knowledge through readings, courses, conferences, and discussions with colleagues.

Prolonged formal training ensures that early childhood educators learn the knowledge base and techniques necessary for informed and effective work in their field, both before they begin work and throughout their career. A variety of instructional formats can be used for training, such as internships, field work, in-service workshops, professional literature, and conferences.

One of the major tasks ahead for Canadian early childhood educators is to develop and articulate professional standards of practice. The U.S. National Association for the Education of Young Children (NAEYC) has published *Developmentally appropriate practice in early childhood programs serving children from birth through age 8* (1987), which serves as an important guide to high quality standards of practice. Organizations in several provinces have recently begun to develop Canadian equivalents.

Professional standards based on the best available knowledge and practice are set for typical situations all members of the profession can be expected to encounter. Practicing professionals are committed to performing at the same high standards consistently, without allowing personal matters or moods to affect their work or their relations with those with whom and for whom they work. Regardless of the setting, young children deserve to be cared for and educated by adults who possess the appropriate knowledge and skills. The process of professionalizing creates greater consensus among practitioners regarding the meaning of critical terms and concepts. Greater consensus supports working toward shared goals.

The hallmark of professionalism is a shared code of ethical conduct. The protection of vulnerable children demands that all individuals working with children conform to the highest standards of ethical conduct. Professionals not only agree to operate according to a high standard of behaviour, they also agree to monitor the conduct of others in the field.

The process of developing a code of professional ethics may begin with the describing of standard predicaments that caregivers confront in the course of their day-to-day work. Stephanie Feeney has examined a number of these situations in a series of articles in *Young Children* (1985, 1987). For example, teachers may occasionally be forced to choose between a parent's and a child's needs. A code of professional ethics can facilitate decision-making in such instances, since it provides a basis for discussion or action. Such a code is created through shared collegial reflection on dilemmas that occur regularly within the profession.

To claim to be a professional is to declare publicly that one adheres to goals and values which go beyond immediate interests. In order to attain true professional status, all practitioners must adopt a common code of ethics within a national community. Penalties (financial, suspension or termination of one's right to practice) should be levied against members of the profession who are incompetent or who fail to act in accordance with standards of ethical practice.

Lastly, a profession is said to be altruistic in its motives—ideally, members are expected to perform their services with unselfish dedication. On this criterion, early childhood education is doing very well!—since it is well known that teachers of young children are poorly paid for performing demanding work. Since we are dealing with human lives, we have to be accountable—we have to care about what we do and how we do it.

The application of all these criteria to the field of early childhood education suggest it is on its way to developing into a profession.

METHODS OF ENHANCING PROFESSIONALISM

Although early childhood education is not yet a profession in the formal sense, competent practitioners will seek out opportunities to improve their skills.

Self-assessment is an indispensable route to professionalism. It helps us to be accountable to others, and even more importantly it makes us accountable to ourselves. This process of validating our accomplishments and identifying what we need to work on can lead us to feel more confident about our role. Supervisors and peers can assist us, by providing feedback on our strengths and supporting us in the areas we want to improve.

Certification and accreditation were mentioned in Chapter 1 as means of assuring quality in child care programs. Both methods incorporate self-assessment as part of the process. These programs can improve standards of practice and promote the professional image of early childhood education.

Certification is a way of identifying those persons who possess the competencies needed for successful teaching. In its certification program, the province of Manitoba defines a competent child care worker as one who:

- conducts himself in an ethical manner
- meets the specific needs of children
- works with parents and other adults
- nurtures children's physical, social, emotional and intellectual growth in a child development framework.

The qualifications required for certification guarantee that certified practitioners possess specified levels of professional competence. Eligible individuals voluntarily participate in the certification process to develop their skills and knowledge in the field.

At the present time, the status of certification in Canada seems to be in a state of flux. There are no certification standards for early childhood educators across the country equivalent to those for kindergarten and primary school teachers. This lack is probably rooted in economic interests as much as academic ones. Early childhood educators are the lowest paid, and raising educational requirements would further increase the pressure for higher pay, thus increasing the cost of child care services.

Accreditation is a way that the public and other professionals can recognize high quality child care programs. This is a process whereby standards are established by a representative body recognized by the community. Accredited programs meet or surpass these standards of quality. There is currently no accreditation system available for child care in Canada.

Accreditation of early childhood programs benefits parents, children, staff, and community in the following ways:

- It assists parents in their search for high quality programs for their children.
- As documented standards of good care are met, the quality of programs for young children and families is improved.
- The accreditation process provides staff with a professional development experience.
- Accreditation assures funders that they are purchasing a high quality program.
- Accreditation provides professional, public and government recognition of high quality early childhood programs.

As the profession evolves, we are becoming more knowledgeable about theories of development and learning, and more skillful in applying these in our daily work with children. We are working on professional issues including ethics and standards of practice. We must continually strive to do our best for young children and families through informed, ethical practice. Further, we must be willing to share this perspective with others. Chapter 11, "Community, Resources and Advocacy," provides a variety of strategies for public education.

As early childhood education comes of age, we are more aware of our specialized expertise and training. But we still have a way to go in developing our professional image, so the present is a critical time for practitioners to serve as advocates. As educators work together on common goals they invest part of themselves in the process, and this investment contributes to our shared professionalism. This enhanced sense of collective purpose is what makes us willing to become involved in voluntary efforts surrounding the improvement of child care.

In the words of one professional: "It is in this subtle area of private endeavour that a profession, in its totality, achieves greatness. Sometimes it is called professional spirit. It is the result of the association of men and women of a superior type, with a common ideal of service above gain, excellence above quality, self-expression beyond motive, and loyalty to a professional code beyond human advantage."

This is the commitment needed to realize high quality child care for every Canadian child.

ACTIVITIES

1. As a teacher of young children, which developmental level would you place yourself in. Why?
2. Develop a plan for the next six months for your professional development. Identify resources and supports you will need to carry out your plan.
3. Write a job description to be placed in a newspaper for one of the following positions:
   - toddler teacher for centre-based care
   - staff for school-age program
   - infant room teacher

   Review to assess whether the aspects as listed in the sample job description have been adequately covered.
4. Obtain a copy of the Directory of Canadian Child Care Organizations published by the Canadian Child Care Federation. Review the list of groups in your area, and identify which ones you want to learn more about. Contact them and arrange to attend a meeting and/or subscribe to their newsletter.
5. Talk to some early childhood educators about the aspects of their job that are the most satisfying. What is the least satisfying, and what can they do about it? Compare their responses to your own goals and expectations.
6. Develop three questions that could be used when interviewing an applicant.
7. Using the section on recruitment and hiring, develop a short staff handbook of procedures for this area.

FURTHER READING

Bloom, Paula Jorde (1986). *Improving the quality of work life: A guide for enhancing the organizational climate in the early childhood setting*. Evanston, IL: National College of Education.

Caruso, J,. and M. Fawcett (1986). *Supervision in early childhood education: A developmental perspective*. New York: Teacher's College Press.

Spodek, B., O. Saracho, and D. Peters (eds.) (1988). *Professionalism and the early childhood practitioner*. Columbia University: Teacher's College Press.

APPENDIX A: SAMPLE CHILD CARE STAFF JOB DESCRIPTION

Title: Early Childhood Educator
Reports to: Supervisor of Centre
Responsible for: a group of sixteen three-year-olds in co-operation with one other early childhood educator

Major responsibilities

The early childhood educator is expected to co-operate and take an active role in planning and carrying out an education program for children from three to four years of age. Communication with other members of the centre and the parents of the children is a major area of responsibility as well.

Representative responsibilities

1. Provides a warm, nurturing environment where children are valued and respected with emphasis on self-esteem, security, choice-making, acceptance of the individual, independence, and trust.
2. Plans, prepares and implements a curriculum based on developmentally appropriate and anti-bias practices that includes fine and gross motor activities, cognitive, receptive and expressive language, social-emotional and self-help skills both indoors and outdoors.
3. Supervises and educates children in nourishment routines.
4. Observes and assesses the development of individual children.
5. Supervises children in rest periods.
6. Arranges and supervises all transition periods.
7. Reports unusual situations, such as allergies, accidents, parental requests and concerns, or behavioural irregularities to the supervisor.
8. Provides or arranges for first aid in case of emergencies.
9. Attends, shares information and participates in staff meetings in order to discuss the implementation of the overall program, and works with individual children and their families.
10. Completes intake interviews, initiates the sharing of information with parents on a regular basis, plans and attends parent interviews and parent evenings, and acts as a resource to parents in problem-solving situations.
11. Actively takes responsibility for personal and professional growth and development.

APPENDIX B: SAMPLE CHILD CARE STAFF PERFORMANCE APPRAISAL

Employee: _____   Date: _____

Classification: _____

Department: _____   Location: _____

Supervisor: _____

_____

Type of Review: Three month   Six month   Annual

The purpose of the appraisal is to provide employees with some measure of how well they are performing in their current job, and to identify any training/development requirements. Comments should include whether they meet or exceed expectations, or need improvement. Please give specific behavioural examples to support your ratings.

Review position description form and revise if necessary. Identify status.

Key Job Areas	Performance Indicators	Comments
Demonstrates positive human qualities with children	• provides warm, nurturing environment • values and respects children • fosters child's self-esteem, sense of security and trust • encourages choice-making and independence	
Plans, prepares and implements a developmentally appropriate curriculum	• plans and posts curriculum for specific ages of the children • has resources readily available • carries out planned curriculum for fine and gross motor, receptive and expressive languages, social, emotional, cognitive and self-help skills both indoors and outdoors • supervises and educates children in nourishment routines, rest periods and all transitions	

Key Job Areas	Performance Indicators	Comments
Reports unusual situations to team leader	• reports unusual situations, such as allergies, accidents, parent requests or concerns, and behavioural irregularities to team leader • provides or arranges for first aid in case of emergencies	
Directs student teacher in field practicum	• be a positive role model • provides support and ongoing feedback • complete mid-term and final evaluation	
Liaises with ECE faculty	• shares information on student teachers • contacts faculty regarding areas of concern • clarifies mid and final evaluations • follows through on faculty's suggestions and ideas	
Functions as team member	• respects colleagues • resolves conflicts with children, parents, co-workers and centre operation • shares own resources, skills and materials	
Supports parental involvement	• initiates the sharing of information with parents on a regular basis • acts as a resource to parents in problem-solving situations • supports and maintains rights of parents as able • completes intake interview and attends parent evening	
Performs professionally	• punctual • ensures confidentiality • fulfils responsibility • wears clothing that suits workplace • seeks and obtains directions and assistance when needed • acts on previously established objectives • responds to child care issues • maintains requirements of legislation	

Leadership Styles and Challenges

Even though leadership skills are fundamental to the supervisor's success and the quality of the environment for both children and staff, they are not usually addressed in the study of the administration of early childhood settings. This chapter addresses this lack, by examining:

◆ What is leadership?
◆ Leadership styles
◆ Decision-making in a collaborative environment.

Earlier chapters have sketched the responsibilities of the supervisor and pointed to some of the roles she fills. Among these roles, leadership is central. The supervisor:

- functions as the point of contact between the board of directors and the staff, interpreting the board's directions to the staff and the staff's concerns to the board.
- provides advice to the board, helps to focus its decisions when necessary, and makes sure it is kept informed of anything of note that occurs at the setting.
- works with board and staff to develop a philosophy statement that reflects the collective wisdom and values of those involved in its development.
- works with board and staff to ensure that policies and procedures are developed for the centre and adhered to.
- guides the relationship between the centre and the external community.
- is responsible for ensuring the development and implementation of a high quality program, with a developmentally appropriate curriculum reflecting the

cultural diversity of children and their families.
- provides a vision to guide the work of the staff, and gives ongoing support, evaluation and encouragement.

In a privately-run for-profit centre, the supervisor would work with the owner in similar capacities.

Each of these responsibilities represents a different aspect of a supervisor's position. Her success in each area depends on her ability to bring individuals together and motivate them to work toward common goals in the effective operation of the centre.

WHAT IS LEADERSHIP?

According to Johnson and Johnson (1991), leadership is "the art of ensuring that group members work together with the least friction and most co-operation." This definition implies that leadership is a skill that people can learn, through experience and practice. It is a skill that involves interacting effectively with other people, influencing how they interact with each other and work together toward a common goal. Leadership is the art of influencing the common work of a group so that it performs most productively. It depends on sharing ideas and information in an atmosphere of mutual respect.

Leadership means moving forward—it involves working with others to move forward to the realization of common goals. Viewed in this way, leaders are catalysts for change.

Such a discussion of leadership in the abstract becomes useful when it is placed into the context of our own personal experience. Think of people you have encountered who were in positions of leadership—how were they the same, and how did they differ? How did they come to be in positions of leadership? Do you think some of them were "born leaders," or is leadership a skill people can learn?

Several theories provide useful frameworks for thinking about leadership. We shall look briefly at three general theories of leadership, deciding that situational theories offer the most potential for understanding. Then we'll look at different leadership styles.

Trait Theories

Is leadership an inherited skill? Are leaders people who are born with a natural ability to lead others? Throughout history, this has been a common belief—kings and queens, for example, were seen as people divinely endowed with an ability to lead.

In the last few years, a number of people have undertaken studies designed to identify personal attributes and abilities that make people stand out as natural leaders. The belief that there are such identifiable qualities or character traits is known as *trait theory*. Trait theory tends to be static—if some people are born leaders and some are not, you either have it, or you don't. According to this theory, if you weren't born a leader, there's not much you can do about it.

The findings of these studies have not supported the belief that leadership is based on inherent traits. There seems to be no definitive set of personality characteristics or unique behaviours that makes someone a leader. Some leaders are charismatic, outgoing individuals who inspire others to follow them; others are relatively quiet types, who set goals and methodically set out to accomplish them. Leadership seems to depend on situation more than it does on personality.

Influence Theory

Another set of theories defines leadership as the balance of "influence" in a group. The leader is the one who holds this balance of influence, the one to whom others look for comment or direction.

Unlike trait theory, this is a dynamic theory—it talks about how you can work to develop leadership abilities. It also has the advantage of considering leaders in the context of the group they lead. It understands leadership as a reciprocal relationship—the leader influences the group because the group is prepared to be influenced by him or her. However, this theory is limited in how far it can be used to analyse a given situation, or in the guidance it gives someone in a leadership position who wants to know how best to act.

Situational Theories

The most useful way of looking at the question is through theories that relate leadership skills to the particular situation they are used in. Not only is it generally agreed that there is no such thing as inherent leadership skill, it appears that no one set of leadership skills will work in every situation. Different situations require different leadership skills.

One of the best-known leadership studies, by Hersey and Blanchard (1977), focused on the dynamics of situational leadership—i.e., what it takes to be a leader in different situations. Two dimensions of leadership were studied: the extent to which the leader initiated *task behaviour* and gave the group direction; and *relationship behaviour*, the ways the leader provided support and guidance to individual members of the group.

The study found that different leaders tended to stress one of these over the other. Some focused on accomplishing tasks, while others paid more attention to providing emotional support to their staff. The study went on to find that the maturity of the group was the determining factor in deciding which particular combination of leadership skills was most effective. Generally speaking, groups who demonstrate a high level of individual maturity are more able to assume responsibility for their work, and respond well enough to a leadership style with a low emphasis on task accomplishment and a low level of emphasis on relationship.

Groups with less maturity are less able to set their own goals or assume responsibility for their own behaviours, and in this case a combination of high task emphasis combined with low relationship emphasis results in the most effective leadership. The primary lesson to be drawn from this is that leadership style should be varied to fit the group.

LEADERSHIP STYLES

The distinction between styles that emphasize results and styles that emphasize relationship is a useful one in work situations. Which style is right for a situation depends on the group. In their 1991 book, Jorde Bloom et al. keep these distinctions, and add a third possibility halfway between, to give us three major leadership styles to consider:

- task-oriented
- people-oriented
- transactional

It is unlikely that any supervisor would fit entirely into one of these categories, but they do provide useful ways of looking at how different leadership styles would work in an early childhood setting.

Task-oriented Style

A task-oriented supervisor focuses on achieving the stated goals and objectives of the program. Carrying out the centre's philosophy statement is central to her interactions with both staff and parents. This supervisor would stress the need to follow procedures regardless of the situation, and would provide detailed expectations to her staff through their job descriptions, the policy and procedures manual and the philosophy statement.

A supervisor who was at the extreme of being task-oriented would typically make decisions with little input from others. As the "control centre" for the program, she would provide considerable direction in the development of the program, and in its day-to-day operation.

Naturally, any supervisor would display most of these behaviours some of the time. Few would go to the extreme, which has a variety of drawbacks. An extreme task-oriented supervisor would have little opportunity for involvement with the children at the centre, and would want to deal personally with all inquiries from parents and staff. When there is little or no collaboration with staff, the supervisor is likely to be seen as the "boss" rather than a member of the team. This can alienate staff members, particularly those who are mature and experienced.

When staff are not part of the decision-making process, they cannot share responsibility for the success or failure of the program—these rest on the shoulders of the supervisor. The tighter the supervisor's control and the more her individual responsibility, the greater her stress and the greater the danger of eventual burnout.

People-oriented Style

A people-oriented supervisor focuses on the needs of staff, children and parents, and pays less attention to giving specific direction for accomplishing specific tasks. While policies and procedures are always important, this supervisor is more likely to consider individual needs in her decisions, which may at times skirt around the centre's written policies. The majority of this supervisor's time involves attending to the relationships of people within the setting; enhancing the quality of these relationships is her primary goal.

Whereas an extreme task-oriented supervisor would make most of the decisions, an extreme people-oriented supervisor would encourage staff to work autonomously. This supervisor is more likely to be viewed as a colleague, another member of the team. She is likely to be involved in the program working directly with the children, who view her as another teacher. This supervisor would have close involvement with parents, and would be viewed by her staff as a source of emotional support.

The potential negative consequence is that as the supervisor attends more to people and less to tasks, the program will tend to reflect the style and preferences of the individual teachers. This can result in a program that varies in the extent to which it reflects the centre's philosophy. An extreme people-oriented style would provide too little direction, and the program would stagnate. Another danger is that a strong-minded staff member will set the program direction, with many potential negative consequences.

Transactional Style

Both task- and people-oriented styles have strengths, and both show weaknesses when taken to extremes, or applied in the wrong situation. In many ways, the transactional style represents a point midway between the two.

A transactional supervisor tends to balance the needs of the centre with the needs of staff and others. This is the most situational style, one where the supervisor can shift the balance according to the particular needs of the situation. In the words of Jorde Bloom et al. (1991), "Achieving both centre goals and maintaining high morale is important in this leadership style. This director is flexible and fair, recognizing that different situations may require a different emphasis on centre-wide needs or individual needs."

A transactional supervisor will adapt her style to fit each staff member's level of professional development, as outlined in the schema by Lillian Katz described in Chapter 6. She will provide different levels of support to teachers, according to their maturity and experience. For example, a staff member in Katz's stage 1, "survival," will require concrete strategies and ongoing support. The supervisor may ask a more experienced staff member to work with her as a mentor, focusing on specific skill areas. On the other hand, a staff member at stage 3, "renewal," may require new challenges. Here a transactional supervisor could provide a new area of responsibility—perhaps asking her to design a new parent involvement program, or assume an administrative task.

For a transactional supervisor, staff morale and program goals are viewed as equally important, and each receives attention. Interactions with staff occur within the context of program needs. She views her role as someone who meets the staff's professional needs in order to empower them to be effective in their work with children and families. This supervisor shares control, but does not abdicate it. Neither boss nor team member, she can be thought of as team leader.

She will work in a consultative manner with staff, sharing decision-making so that staff share ownership of the program's success. She provides a clear framework for those decisions that need to be made, giving clear feedback to staff so they know her expectations and feel supported.

In the daily work of an early childhood setting, it is sometimes difficult for staff to know whether or not they have made a difference. When this is combined with a situation where staff have little control, job satisfaction suffers. On the other hand, when staff are empowered and have more control within clear parameters, job satisfaction increases, to the overall betterment of the program.

In general, research indicates that job satisfaction is associated with a democratic style of leadership; satisfaction is highest in small interaction-oriented staff groups. A collaborative team approach, where the supervisor is team leader, is usually best.

Women and Leadership: An Additional Consideration

Most of the literature dealing with leadership could not be called "gender-neutral." Traditionally, in most work environments the leader has been male, and the research dealing with leadership reflects this.

Early childhood education is a profession dominated by women—fully 98 per cent of the staff in Canadian early childhood settings are female. More recent publications (Baines et al. 1991; Gilligan 1982; Helgesen 1990) have examined the unique qualities of women in leadership roles, and provide interesting insights in a discussion of leadership styles.

Women' more typically display a capacity for caring and emotional contact. This is a particular strength they bring to their work with others. In a leadership role, women tend not to focus exclusively on task or person, but rather on the relationships between people and their work. Women leaders tend to view their staff in a more holistic manner, and this shapes the kind of decisions they make and how they make them. The transactional style is particularly suited to the typical capacities of women.

DECISION-MAKING IN A COLLABORATIVE ENVIRONMENT

Even within a collaborative setting, there are different ways of arriving at decisions.

- by consensus
- by majority vote
- by authority, on the basis of position and status
- by expert opinion, on the basis of specific knowledge.

Group decision-making which involves reaching consensus is preferable in most instances, but each method has its use depending on the particular circumstances. A good supervisor adapts her leadership style to fit her staff, and their stages of development. She will work with the staff and board of directors to find the approach that best fits the needs of the group.

Sharing the responsibility for decision-making with staff is essential in building a work environment characterized by trust and respect. The supervisor needs to ensure that staff are involved in decisions regarding resource allocation, program planning, parent involvement, policies and procedures, development of a philosophy statement, etc. She will need to structure time for the staff to meet and work as a group. In group decision-making, meetings may not always involve the entire staff. Some tasks may be assumed by ad hoc groups who then bring recommendations back to the larger group.

Working collaboratively is not without its challenges—in many ways, it is easier for a supervisor to make decisions without consultation. It is important therefore to examine the advantages and disadvantages of group decision-making.

Advantages

- When a group decides on something together, individual members are likely to be commited to implementing that decision. This improves productivity.
- "Two heads are better than one"—experienced staff will have valuable contributions, and the team leader has the opportunity to receive feedback when incorrect assumptions or information are aired.
- When the staff group works together, there is the opportunity to openly discuss different points of view and clarify ideas, and to draw on the strengths and resources of individual staff members.
- Collective decision-making can stimulate creative problem-solving techniques and result in more creative solutions.

Disadvantages

- Collaborative decision-making takes more time.
- The group itself can become something that individuals hide behind or within.
- Interpersonal conflicts may create obstacles to reaching joint agreement. Good communication skills are essential, and may not always be present.
- Effective group decision-making may not be possible if the group is too large.

Collaborative decision-making requires maturity. Members need to get outside their own individual needs and consider each other's perspectives. At the same time, a supervisor has to be aware of barriers that limit collaboration or make it impossible. Differences in power among group members, whether real or perceived, may prevent the group from functioning effectively. In a unionized setting, there may be difficulties when the supervisor is not a member of the bargaining unit. Some individuals may feel that their loyalties conflict.

Achieving Goal Consensus

The supervisor needs to first work with the staff and board of directors to develop a shared vision for the centre. She may help the board focus its vision of a successful centre.

The vision should represent a set of mission statements or guiding principles that form the foundation for the development of a philosophy statement. As discussed in Chapter 3, the philosophy statement is the blueprint for the work of early childhood educators. Commitment to a shared vision connects each individual to the centre. While it takes time, achieving consensus is the best method for producing a sound philosophy statement.

Some early childhood supervisors find it difficult to work collaboratively, because they feel it restricts their autonomy. But effective leadership should not require a choice between autonomy and collaboration. It is important to provide leadership by facilitating group work. This will require administrative support, such as ensuring staff have time made available. In-service for the team may be needed.

The results of working collaboratively are not always immediate, and everyone will at times experience frustration with the process, but the long-term benefits are worth the investment of time and resources.

Leadership Needs Leadership

A supervisor's job can be lonely. She has no peers in the program—she is always meeting the needs of others, but the amount of support she can receive back is limited.

She needs support too, from her own network of peers. This can be built through personal friendships, or involvement in professional and advocacy groups, and in professional development sessions. The board of directors can be a great source of support, providing the supervisor with both allies and resources in the work toward a common goal.

A good supervisor needs such a wide range of skills that she must learn to accept her own shortcomings—no one has equal skills in all areas. She must ensure her professional development needs are adequately looked after. Even so, time is limited and she can't do everything—a supervisor needs to be familiar with every aspect of the program, but she doesn't need to take part equally in everything. She has to know how to create time for herself.

Many supervisors belong to professional organizations which meet regularly. These can provide both professional support, through discussions and workshops, and by providing a place to make informal contacts.

ACTIVITIES

1. Write a paragraph describing a director interacting with her staff, trying to depict one of the leadership styles in the text. Exchange this with a classmate, and see if they can decide on which leadership style you intended.
2. Look at your own personal style and write a paragraph about what kind of leader you think you are, with another on the kind you would like to become.
3. Following the suggestion given in the chapter, think of three people you have encountered in your life who were in positions of leadership—how were they the

same, and how did they differ? How did they come to be in positions of leadership? Write a brief description of each one (you don't need to use their real names), and decide which leadership style they most closely resemble. Who of them was effective, who was not, and why?

4. What style of decision-making do you prefer and feel most comfortable with? Why?
5. Assess the leadership style needed by varous staff in your centre.
6. Using the assessment tools in the Appendix, taken from Jorde Bloomet al.'s *Blueprint for action*, review the leadership style of the supervisor at your centre.

FURTHER READING

Baines, Carol, Patricia Evans, and Sheila Neysmith (1991). *Women's caring: Feminist perspectives on social welfare.* Toronto: McClelland & Stewart.

Caruso, J. J., and M.T. Fawcett (1986). *Supervision in early childhood education: A developmental perspective.* New York: Teachers College Press.

Gilligan, Carol (1982). *In a different voice.* Boston: Harvard University Press.

Helgesen, S. (1990) *Female advantage: Women's ways of leadership.* New York: Doubleday.

Johnson, D. W., and F.P. Johnson (1991). *Joining together: Group theory and group skills.* Boston: Allyn and Bacon.

Jorde Bloom, P., M. Sheerer, and J. Britz (1991). *Blueprint for action: Achieving center-based change through staff development.* Mt. Rainier, MD: Gryphon House Inc.

Neugebauer, R. (1985). *Are you an effective leader?* Child Care Information Exchange, 45-50.

APPENDIX: LEADERSHIP STYLE

(This questionnaire is taken from Jorde Bloom, Sheerer and Britz's *Blueprint for action: Achieving center-based change through staff development.* It is reprinted here through the permission of New Horizons Educational Consultants (Part I) and Child Care Information Exchange (Part II). Part II was developed by Bonnie Neugebauer.

Rationale

The leadership style of the director of a child care centre is perhaps the most potent factor influencing organizational effectiveness. The director must create an environment based on mutual respect in which individuals work together to accomplish collective goals. The success of this endeavour rests in large part on the director's ability to balance organizational needs with individual needs. The research in this area suggests that leaders who head the most effective organizations tend to be those that apply a transactional leadership style—an ability to adjust their style to the demands of each situation so that both organizational needs and individual needs are met.

Part I of this assessment tool was adapted from the work of Blake and Mouton (1969), Getzels and Guba (1957), Giammatteo (1975), Hersey and Blanchard (1982), and Reddin (1970). It assesses three different leadership styles: the task-oriented style, the people-oriented style, and the transactional style. Part II was developed by Exchange Press (Neugebauer 1990). It allows staff to evaluate the director's overall administrative/management style.

Directions

Distribute the five-page "My Director. . ." questionnaire and a blank envelope to each individual who works at the centre more than ten hours per week. (If the director is male, some of the questions will need to be changed first to reflect masculine pronouns.) For more accurate results, it is advisable to distribute questionnaires to both teaching staff and support staff. Place a box labeled "Questionnaire Return Box" in your centre's office or staff room and ask respondents to deposit their completed surveys in this box. Assure staff of the confidentiality of their responses. It is suggested that the director also complete a survey of his/her perceived style. The results of this self-assessment may then be compared to the collective perceptions of the staff.

Scoring

The composite results of Part I summarize the staff's perceptions of the director's dominant leadership style. The following scoring sheet includes a brief description of the three leadership styles assessed by this questionnaire.

Scoring—Part I

To score Part I, tally the responses by noting with a mark each time staff checked a particular response:

1. _____	9. _____	17. _____
2. _____	10. _____	18. _____
3. _____	11. _____	19. _____
4. _____	12. _____	20. _____
5. _____	13. _____	21. _____
6. _____	14. _____	22. _____
7. _____	15. _____	23. _____
8. _____	16. _____	24. _____

Now total the marks for the following responses:

Task-oriented: 1, 6, 8, 10, 14, 17, 19, 22   Total _____
Achieving centre goals is most important in this leadership style. Strong concern for high performance and accomplishing tasks. Emphasis is on planning, directing, following procedures, and applying uniform standards and expectations for all. This director may be viewed as too structured, bureaucratic, and inflexible.

People-oriented: 2, 4, 7, 11, 15, 18, 20, 24   Total _____
Achieving harmonious group relations is foremost in this leadership style. Strong emphasis on maintaining comfortable, friendly, and satisfying working conditions. Allows staff to exercise control and be self-directed with minimal intrusion of centre-wide policies and procedures. Staff working in centres with this style of leadership may complain about the lack of order and co-ordination.

Transactional: 3, 5, 9, 12, 13, 16, 21, 23   Total _____
Achieving both centre goals and maintaining high morale is important in this leadership style. This director is flexible and fair, recognizing that different situations may require a different emphasis on centre-wide needs or individual needs.

Scoring—Part II

For Part II, add up the total score for each respondent. (Scores will range from 25 to 125.) Add together all respondents' scores and divide by the number of individuals returning questionnaires. This will yield an average score regarding the staff's evaluation of the director's performance in a wide range of administrative and supervisory behaviours.

On any assessment such as this where perceptions may vary considerably, it is important to note the range of scores (the lowest score and the highest score). Also, it is helpful to do an item analysis to discern those two or three items that staff rated the director lowest and those two or three items where the director consistently scored highest. This will provide the director specific feedback about those perceived areas where staff may feel he or she has the greatest skill and those areas in need of improvement.

QUESTIONNAIRE

"My Director. . ."

Dear Staff:
One of the hallmarks of an early childhood professional is the ability to reflect on one's performance. Your feedback about my leadership style is important in helping me improve and grow professionally. Please take a few minutes to complete this questionnaire. When you are finished, insert it in the attached plain envelope and put it in the "Questionnaire Return Box" in the office. There is no need for you to put your name on the questionnaire.
Thank you.

PART I. Place a check in front of the statement that most nearly reflects your director's leadership style in different situations. (Check only one response in each group).

With respect to planning, my director. . .

1. _____ does most of the planning herself by setting goals, objectives, and work schedules for staff to follow. She then works out procedures and responsibilities for staff to follow.

2. _____ does very little planning, either by herself or with the staff. She tells the staff she has confidence in them to carry out their jobs in a responsible way.

3. _____ gets staff members together to assess centre-wide problems and discuss ideas and strategies for improvement. Together they set up goals and objectives and establish individual responsibilities.

With respect to work assignments and the day-to-day operation of the centre, my director. . .

4. _____ checks with staff regularly to see if they are content and if they have the things they need. She does not see the necessity of precise job descriptions, preferring instead to let the staff determine the scope and nature of their jobs.

5. _____ is flexible in adapting job descriptions and changing work assignments as needed. Updates centre policies and procedures depending on the needs of the staff, parents, children, and board.

6. _____ tends to go by the book. Expects staff to adhere to written job descriptions. Follows policies and procedures precisely.

With respect to leadership philosophy, my director. . .

7. _____ tends to emphasize people's well-being, believing that happy workers will be productive workers.

8. _____ tends to emphasize hard work and a job well done. We are a results-oriented program.

9. _____ tends to emphasize both what we do and what we need as people.

During meetings, my director. . .

10. _____ keeps focused on the agenda and the topics that need to be covered.

11. _____ focuses on each individual's feelings and helps people express their emotional reactions to an issue.

12. _____ focuses on differing positions people take and how they deal with each other.

The primary goal of my director is. . .

13. _____ to meet the needs of parents and children while providing a healthy work climate for staff.

14. _____ to keep the centre running efficiently.

15. _____ to help staff find fulfillment.

In evaluating the staff's performance, my director. . .

16. _____ attempts to assess how each individual's performance has contributed to centre-wide achievement of goals.

17. _____ makes an assessment of each person's performance and effectiveness according to predetermined established criteria that are applied equally to all staff.

18. _____ allows people to set their own goals and determine performance standards.

My director believes the best way to motivate someone who is not performing up to his/her ability is to. . .

19. _____ point out to the individual the importance of the job to be done.

20. _____ try to get to know the individual better in an attempt to understand why the person is not realizing his/her potential.

21. _____ work with the individual to redefine job responsibilities to more effectively contribute to centre-wide goals.

My director believes it is her role to. . .

22. _____ make sure that staff members have a solid foundation of knowledge and skill that will help them accomplish centre goals.

23. _____ help people learn to work effectively in groups to accomplish group goals.

24. _____ help individuals become responsible for their own education and effectiveness, and take the first step toward realizing their potential.

What three words or phrases most accurately describe the leadership style of your director:

Part II. Circle the numeral that most nearly represents your assessment of your director in each of the areas described.

My director is. . .	strongly disagree			strongly agree	
. . .*knowledgeable*. She knows what is going on in the program for staff, children, parents, board, and administrators.	1	2	3	4	5
. . .*in control*. She has a handle on things and is actively and effectively in charge of the centre's programs and operations.	1	2	3	4	5
. . .*dedicated*. She demonstrates interest in learning more about her job from peers, professional groups, and reading material.	1	2	3	4	5
. . .*confident*. She has a sense of mission and a clear vision for the centre.	1	2	3	4	5
. . .*enthusiastic*. She has the energy to cope with the daily demands of her job.	1	2	3	4	5
. . .*an effective communicator*. She keeps us well informed about policies, procedures, activities, and schedules.	1	2	3	4	5
. . .*responsive*. When adults or children need her attention, she is able to focus on their needs.	1	2	3	4	5
. . .*available to parents*. She knows the families and encourages them to participate in the program.	1	2	3	4	5
. . .*open*. She encourages employees to participate in decision-making and welcomes their suggestions.	1	2	3	4	5
. . .*fair*. She investigates all sides of an issue and distributes criticism and praise with grace and equity.	1	2	3	4	5
. . .*predictable*. Expectations are clearly defined, and policies are routinely followed.	1	2	3	4	5
. . .*a trainer*. She encourages my professional growth by providing opportunities for on-going training and development.	1	2	3	4	5

My director is. . .	strongly disagree			strongly agree	
. . .a delegator. She uses authority with fairness and according to the staff's talents and time.	1	2	3	4	5
. . .prepared. She has a sense of priority about the centre and the requirements of her role.	1	2	3	4	5
. . .respectful. She understands people as individuals and shapes her expectations of them accordingly.	1	2	3	4	5
. . .understanding. She realizes that each of us has different interests, abilities, attitudes, and personalities.	1	2	3	4	5
. . .available. I am comfortable bringing my concerns, criticisms, problems and successes to her.	1	2	3	4	5
. . .efficient. She handles the day-to-day routines of the centre promptly and skillfully.	1	2	3	4	5
. . .supportive. She looks for opportunities to give feedback and offer praise.	1	2	3	4	5
. . .a motivator. She encourages each of us to give our best effort.	1	2	3	4	5
. . .realistic. She has a sense of humour and is able to keep things in perspective.	1	2	3	4	5
. . .an influence in the community. She is an advocate for children and quality care.	1	2	3	4	5
. . .genuine. She greets me warmly and demonstrates interest and concern. I know where I stand with her.	1	2	3	4	5
. . .resourceful. She knows where to go and what to do to get things done. She makes good use of community resources.	1	2	3	4	5

WORKING
COPY.

ENCED CAPACITIES BY AGE GROUP   Telephone: _____   Capacity: 34

ANTS   PRESCHOOL   24   AGES: 18mos-5y

TODDLERS   10   SR.KINDERGARTEN _____

SCHOOLAGE _____

upporting Documents to be attached to Budget-Submission

	Audit	don't need
	Financial Statement	does Dennis do this?
✓	II(e) Renovation Items ✓	
	IV(b) Replacement Items	
	IV(c) Equipment over $500.00 ✓	
	V Other	
	Vacation Policy ✓	
	Deposit Policy ✓	
	Fee Memo to Parents ✓	
	Staff Salary Sheet	? - positions & amounts of annual salar
	Employer Contribution to Benefits - copies of remittance	
	Mortgage -	
	Lease -	
	Copy of Signed Union Contract	
	Change of Officer of Board/Organization - coming from Meeting	

Financial Matters

This chapter will discuss the central importance of budgetting and financial planning under these headings:

◆ The importance of financial planning
◆ Different kinds of budgets
◆ An operating budget item by item—staff costs
◆ A budget item by item—non-staff expenditures
◆ A budget item by item—income
◆ Assessing the potential for outside funding.

THE IMPORTANCE OF FINANCIAL PLANNING

Child care in Canada faces an uncertain financial future. The federal government's restrictions on the Canada Assistance Plan (CAP) combine with cutbacks in individual provinces and uncertain municipal involvement to spell tough times for child care. As a young profession, we were just beginning to understand how to advocate for quality programs with stable funding, and we often lack both history and experience to fall back on. It has never been more important for all players in the child care arena to pull together, to set new financial directions for the future.

Students aspiring to work with young children may not see the need to learn about the financial planning and operation of a centre. Similarly, new staff and indeed some more experienced staff may not fully understand the overall financial picture, and how it can affect their work with children. As you work through this chapter, the importance of financial matters and how they involve staff should become clearer. The success of a centre depends not only on whether it meets its objectives and goals, but also on whether it does so in a financially responsible manner.

The statement of philosophy draws the blueprint or framework for a centre's financial planning. The budget reflects such considerations as services to be offered, programs to be included, ages of the children eligible for enrolment, and hours of operation.

In Chapter 6 we discussed the importance of developing a collaborative environment encouraging staff involvement. To be useful, this involvement requires a beginning understanding about what is involved in financial planning. Without an appreciation of the financial process, staff may decide this aspect of the operation is not their problem. When financial decisions are made that affect staffing, purchase of equipment, supplies, and other aspects of the program, knowledgeable staff will understand the reasons for these decisions. They are also more able to suggest alternatives and be creative in finding ways of easing budgetary restrictions. Difficult financial times require a team approach and a commitment to common goals, rather than staff feeling alienated by decisions they don't understand that were made in isolation from them.

Financial Organization

In any organization, be it large or small, it is essential to have one person who has overall responsibility for financial management. This guarantees that the financial operation stays on track. At the same time, a budget should reflect sensitive planning that responds to the goals of the staff, who are then committed to carrying them out.

The structure of an organization will determine who is responsible for various aspects of financial management, as well as the number of people who will contribute to budget development, implementation, monitoring, and year-end analysis. For example, most non-profit centres have boards of directors that are ultimately responsible for the development and final analysis of the budget. In order to make knowledgeable decisions when drawing up a budget, the directors will consult with the supervisor, who will in turn involve the staff. Once the budget is determined, the supervisor is then responsible for its implementation, monitoring expenditures and income accurately. When all goes smoothly, few problems exist. Should enrolment drop, supplies go over budget or unusual circumstances develop, the supervisor would inform the board and ask for direction. Ultimately, financial success or failure rests in the hands of the board.

In a for-profit setting, the supervisor may also be the owner, and therefore be ultimately responsible for every aspect of budget development, implementation and decision-making.

Budgets are based on the goals and objectives of the centre. Policies and procedures must be clearly articulated in order to ensure that they are covered by the financial plan. For example: one of a centre's goals is to meet the needs of working parents, and it becomes clear that those needs begin at 6:30 a.m. for many parents, rather than the 7:30 a.m. opening time. If it is decided to extend the hours, extra staff may be required, and this must be reflected in the budget planning.

The budget has to balance: that is, expenditures must not exceed income. A balanced budget is essential, regardless of how creative you may be in meeting your stated goals. Once a budget is established it drives every decision made and is the final determining factor in all aspects of program implementation.

DIFFERENT KINDS OF BUDGETS

For our purposes, there are three kinds of budget to consider.

Start-up budgets cover the human resources required to develop and carry out the plan of action. In some cases the purchase of land and initial capital investment are also included in the start-up costs.

Capital budgets cover the costs incurred for land, physical space, and equipment needed to open the centre. They also generally cover large capital items that are purchased from time to time in the operation of the centre.

Operating budgets cover the projected costs of operating the centre for a period of one year, including staff salaries and all ongoing expenses.

Start-up Budgets

For our purposes, start-up costs refer to the dollars needed to hire someone to do the initial planning for the centre. This would include:

- designing, or consulting with other professionals on the design of the physical spaces.
- identifying and making recommendations on the selection and purchase of equipment, furnishings, materials, and supplies for the entire centre.
- developing job descriptions and assisting in the hiring of the beginning staff.
- developing the beginning philosophy, and program goals and objectives, to be later refined and adapted by the program staff and management.
- developing the initial administrative forms and procedures.
- co-operating with other professionals to develop marketing strategies for the centre.
- reviewing the current child care legislation, applying for the licence, and ensuring that the centre meets all provincial and municipal requirements.

This person may be hired by a non-profit organization wanting to provide child care services to the community, or by a for-profit organization or individual who needs the expertise. Whatever the case, the main goal is to hire an expert who knows how to set up a successful quality child care centre, and can provide the "leg work."

Some organizations may prefer to hire the supervisor early, on a part- or full-time basis, in order to complete these tasks. Others may wish to contract with one or more consultants to do work and to provide more specialized skills in the different phases of the development. Whatever the decision, these human resource costs must be accounted for. Too often, the board or management group tries to take on these tasks, but lacks the expertise to do so. The frustration and loss of time incurred may cause tasks to fall between the cracks, resulting in poor decisions and expensive delays. A viable centre takes careful planning by professionals who have the knowledge and experience to design and implement a high quality program. Experienced guidance will ensure that the board or management team's time and areas of expertise are utilized effectively and efficiently.

Capital Budgets

Annual operating budgets usually include some capital equipment costs from year to year, in order to maintain and upgrade the quality of equipment. However, major capital items can be considered one-time expenditures, and include the following:

- land costs
- building costs
- additions to existing buildings
- renovation or alterations to existing buildings
- equipment and furnishings
- outdoor creative playgrounds
- fencing
- playground landscaping.

Land, building and renovation costs are very high. Financial assistance for non-profit organizations is available in some provinces to assist in this area.

Operating Budgets

The operating budget sets out anticipated costs over a period of a single year, referred to as a *fiscal year*. These costs are projected from the best information collected from other centres' experiences, ministry guidelines, the advice of consultants, and the centre's goals and objectives. Nevertheless, it is important to remember that these are projected costs for a new operation. Once the centre is established, a more realistic picture appears, as experience dictates more accurate costs. However, a budget has to start somewhere. Once the data has been collected from as many sources as possible, the first year budget is struck.

The budget becomes the centre's financial blueprint. Individual line item amounts may change somewhat as the year proceeds, but the final monthly income and expenditure totals cannot get off track. In other words, if income goes down, expenditures must also be cut back to ensure the continued financial viability of the centre. The balance each month of the expenditure and income columns acts as the financial barometer.

The operating budget must clearly reflect any changes or new directions in the centre, as stated in the philosophy and goals. This usually happens at the beginning of a new fiscal year. For example, if the philosophy supports continued professional development and ongoing in-service training for its staff, two things must happen.

- The philosophy must clearly contain this commitment in its stated goals for the staff. In addition, strategies need to be included to help staff meet these goals. These could include registration fees and replacement staff costs to allow full -

time staff to attend workshops and seminars or visit other centres; time to develop new curriculum areas by being replaced on schedule; reimbursement upon successful completion of approved courses; and so on.

- The budget must include a line item called "professional development" that indicates a clear financial commitment to support staff in their professional development goals. Without a budget, there is no true commitment for staff to reach these goals. The centre should not state goals for staff that are not financially viable.

Setting the operating budget takes planning and consultation. This may involve the board, supervisor, staff, and perhaps parents. Each has expertise to bring to the planning phase, and each has a role to play to a greater or lesser degree. Once the budget is prepared, final approval and ultimate responsibility rest with the organizing group, be it an incorporated non-profit board, a private owner, the executive of a parent co-operative, or a profit-making organization.

Expenditures and Income

Operating expenditures are usually grouped in one of three categories:

Fixed costs occur regardless of the number of children enrolled. They include such things as mortgage/rent, loan payments, utilities, telephone, and the like. They are fixed because there is little the centre can do to alter them.

Variable costs are tied to the number of children enrolled. They include food, materials, supplies, etc.

Semi-variable costs are directly related to the child/teacher ratio. For example, if the ratio is 8:1 and you have ten children in your group, you will still need two staff members. However, you can add six more children without increasing staff costs.

The other major category in a budget is *income*.

AN OPERATING BUDGET ITEM BY ITEM—STAFF COSTS

Salary expenditures take up more of the total costs than all other items put together— in some cases, as much as ninety per cent. Salaries for full- and part-time staff should be based on the policies and procedures established by the centre. Quality child care demands that all teaching staff be qualified, even if this is not a requirement of provincial or territorial regulations. Centres that want to attract and retain qualified staff must present an attractive salary and benefit package.

Historically, salaries in child care have been low and benefits minimal. The result has been high staff turnover, with the accompanying continuous recruitment and new staff orientation, stress on existing staff, and excessive paper work. The salaries in most centres strike a delicate balance between the income from fees and the need to attract and keep qualified professionals.

Although full-time staff are the major cost, part-time and supply staff must also be considered. For example, if the centre policy for paid sick days allows twelve days per year per staff member, the budget must include money to bring in supply staff to cover these days. The following formula would apply:

- Total number of staff × twelve days × 7.5 hours per day × the cost per hour. Salary policies must be consistent with budget figures—if your policy on paid sick leave changes, so will your budget allowance.

Other part-time employees include a cook, a janitor, and staff that may be needed to supplement the full-time staff hours. Provincial/territorial legislation will determine the ratios required for the ages of the children and the size of groups. The sample budget found at the end of the chapter will show you how to set up the full- and part-time salary items.

Each centre should develop a salary schedule with starting salaries, pay categories for qualification and experience, and proposed increments. This is the basis for hiring staff and finalizing salaries. If the centre is unionized, there will be a negotiated salary scale.

Fringe benefits

Contributions to Unemployment Insurance and Canada Pension for each staff member are mandatory and must be included in the budget. Contributions to Worker's Compensation are mandatory in most jurisdictions, and highly advisable in the rest. Other benefits such as medical insurance, dental plan, long- and short-term disability, life insurance, are optional but provide additional security for the staff. Overall costs for full-time benefits generally run at about twelve to eighteen per cent, while benefits for part-time staff average about twelve per cent.

Consultants

As the need occurs, specialists can supplement staff skills and meet the specific needs of some children. Skills needed on a per occasion basis might include a speech and language specialist, nutritionist, behavioural consultant, or an accountant. These contract services are similar to salaries, but they are usually not ongoing and don't require benefits.

Professional development and in-service training

An earlier example addressed the importance of having the goals of the centre reflected in the budget. A certain amount of money per staff number is usually the easiest and fairest way to come up with an initial budget amount. This total then can be negotiated between staff as circumstances present themselves, for workshops, conferences and such. A consultant or speaker may be invited to a staff meeting, to provide in-service training for the entire staff at once.

Calculating Staff Costs

Full-time salaries

Supervisor: Determined from the salary schedule
Teacher Category I: Number of teachers × salary as per schedule
Teacher Category II: Number of teachers × salary as per schedule
Teacher Category III: Number of teachers × salary as per schedule (and so on, depending on the categories in the salary schedule)

Full-time fringe benefits

These total between twelve and eighteen per cent of total full-time salaries, depending on personnel policies in your centre.

Part-time staff

Supply Staff: Number of sick days allowed per full-time staff member × number of staff × hours per day × amount per hour.

Part-time Staff: Requirements vary—for example, 24 hours per week × number of weeks × amount per hour.

Cook: Number of hours per week × number of weeks per year × amount per hour.

Janitor: Number of hours per week × number of weeks per year × amount per hour.

Secretary: Number of hours per week × number of weeks per year × amount per hour.

Part-time fringe benefits

These total between eight and twelve per cent of total part-time salaries, depending on personnel policies in your centre.

Consultants

Identify the specialties you may require—e.g., accountant. Then, consultant × number of days × amount per hour or per day, depending on the involvement necessary. As these people are hired by contractual arrangement, they do not receive benefits.

A BUDGET ITEM BY ITEM—NON-STAFF EXPENDITURES

Mortgage/rental and loan payments

Many centres make monthly payments for a mortgage or rent. These payments must be included in the operating budget. Some centres also have a monthly payment on a loan they have incured to cover capital equipment or renovations to an existing building.

Property taxes

These may be payable in some jurisdictions, depending on the auspice under which you operate.

Business taxes

These may be payable in some jurisdictions, depending on the auspice under which you operate.

Maintenance and repairs to building

New centres, and rented buildings where these services are included in the rent, have lower costs in this category. As a centre ages, there is increased wear and tear on the building, and costs go up.

Depreciation on building, equipment and furnishings

The specific circumstances regarding the category of depreciation will vary from centre to centre. An accountant can assist in determining the amounts to include in this category.

Utilities

These include heat, electricity, and water and sewage service. If the centre rents space, some or all of these costs may be included. More often they are separate costs, which can be estimated on a square metre basis. Estimates from other centres of similar size, plus a call to the public utilities, will help in developing the first year's costs.

For an existing centre, take last year's charges and add known or projected rate increases, plus a slight allowance for increased use. For example, this winter may be colder than last, and heating costs may rise.

Telephone

This is a fixed cost, and advice on the centre's needs will be available from the phone company. Long-distance costs can be approximated and spread over the twelve month operating budget.

Insurance

Insurance coverage becomes a fixed cost once a decision is made about what is included in the insurance package. Each centre must decide what is to be insured, and to what extent. Typically, supervisor, board and staff need to determine the level of insurance for the building, contents, outdoor equipment, and storage buildings. Liability insurance is required for children, employees and others while they are on the premises. If you transport children to and from the centre, or even on special occasions such as trips to museums or conservation areas, you will need additional insurance to cover it.

You are well advised to call several insurance companies to discuss your needs, and then compare prices and coverage. Costs may rise at intervals as determined by the insurer.

Grounds maintenance

Centre budgets often overlook the cost for garbage removal, grass cutting, snow removal, and general outdoor maintenance. A variety of creative ways can be found to cover these costs. When budgets are tight, high school students can be hired at reasonable rates to do the work, as opposed to contracting it out to professional services.

Food

Not all centres provide meals, but for those that do, the cost of providing a nutritious meal and two snacks per day will vary slightly. When presenting the budget, it is wise to show the formula you used to account for the costs. For example, a figure of $15,912 at the line item "budget for food" might seem high to the board. However, if you clarify this by including the formula you often get the opposite response from the board—they question how you can feed children for so little a day.

Example: The approximate cost for food for each child per day is between $1.05 and $1.25. In a centre with forty-five children and six staff, this would work out to: 51 children/staff × 52 weeks × 5 days per week × $1.20 per day = $15,912.00

Staff are included in food costs because they eat with the children as part of teaching self-help skills. The cost of the cook, of course, will be covered under salaries.

Educational equipment

The capital budget accounts for the initial purchases for educational equipment and toys. The operating budget must allow for additional and replacement items. A rough rule of thumb is to allow approximately $100 per child per year.

Teachers' resources

This part of the budget would include books and subscriptions, to keep staff up to date on developments in the field.

Educational supplies

Disposable materials such as paint, paste, paper, and general creative supplies and materials are included in this area. Allow approximately $25 per child per year.

First aid

This would cover the cost of first aid kits and supplies. Always make sure these supplies are up to date—when you need them is not the time to discover nobody replaced the bandages!

Housekeeping supplies

This would include items like toilet paper, paper towels, cleaning supplies, etc.

Kitchen equipment

Replacement and additional equipment is needed throughout the year to supplement initial kitchen capital purchases. Allow approximately $10 per child per year.

Office supplies and equipment

This category includes stationery, pens, computer paper and software, ribbons, and general office supplies. In a fairly new centre, major pieces of equipment such as an adding machine and a word processor are included in the initial capital costs, and should function for some time without problems. As time goes on, replacement and repairs must be budgetted for.

Photocopying may need to be a separate budget item.

Special programs

The cost of any special programs, such as dance or music, would be included here.

Field trips and travel

If the curriculum is developed to include visits to various places of interest, then the budget must include the cost of bus trips or whatever means of transport is used. Costs can easily be found out, one you have established the place and number of trips.

Advertising, postage, courier

An established centre may have few advertising costs or marketing expenses. These expenditures will vary from area to area depending on how well a needs analysis was carried out before setting the centre's location. Ongoing postage and occasional courier services are a common but not high expense item. The budget amount can be established based on the centre's estimates of mailings, while the marketing costs can be obtained from professionals in that area.

Bank charges

As banks keep raising their service charges, this is an item to consider. Try to keep operating funds in an interest-bearing account to offset these.

Audit and bookkeeping fees

You will need to budget for an annual audit, and perhaps for bookkeeping throughout the year.

Legal expenses

Some centres find it a good idea to budget for legal costs, although one hopes the need will not arise.

Bad debts and low enrolment

Careful income management should eliminate or minimize unpaid accounts. Nevertheless, it is wise to include 1 to 2% of the yearly income in this column, to act as the necessary cushion and assist in case of a drop in enrolment.

Miscellaneous

Licence fees, petty cash and other small items can be included in this column. This should be a small amount, because you want to know where your costs occur so that you can move them into specific categories. For example, petty cash expenditures should be just that—petty. Otherwise, they should be posted to the line item they fit under.

A BUDGET ITEM BY ITEM—INCOME

The line expenditures in a budget are balanced by the income side. Once expenditures have been determined, the sources of income are evaluated and the fees established. Fees from parents are commonly referred to as "fees for service"; income from subsidizing agencies or social services constitute the main sources of income for some centres. More recently, some provinces have instituted direct operating grants to centres. Donations make up a very small part of the income for the majority of centres. Whatever the case, total expenses incurred throughout the operating year cannot exceed the projected income from all available sources.

Let's suppose that the total income required for a centre is $290,000. The centre is licensed for forty-five children. The means of income is fees paid by the parents. We will allow three weeks for parents to withdraw their children from the centre during the holiday months of July and August without paying the fee. The formula to work out the income needed is as follows, assuming that all places can be filled:

$290,000 ÷ 45 children ÷ 11.25 months = $572.84 per month per child.

The actual fee charged should be higher than the exact formula amount, to allow some income over expenditures as a buffer or contingency fund. Accordingly, the fee charged in this centre would be a minimum of $580. Any money left at the end of the fiscal year is brought forward as income in the next budget year.

The registration fee charged should also be taken into account in the income column.

Calculating income

Registration Fee: A set fee × number of children in centre
Parent Fees: Number of children × number of months × the established monthly fee
Donations: Guaranteed commitments
Direct Grants: Amount based on the particular government formula
Total: Total of the above, plus any other categories applicable to your particular centre.

Balancing the budget

The total of the Income column and the Expenditure column should be expressed in terms of Income over Expenditures. A monthly flow chart can be established to record and monitor monthly costs and income to ensure the budget stays on track. An accountant or bookkeeper can assist with this process.

ASSESSING THE POTENTIAL FOR OUTSIDE FUNDING

Additional funding for child care services may be available through government and/or private sources. The first step in fundraising is to identify available sources of potential support. The following list identifies private sources of funding and fundraising information:

- At time of publication, the Child Care Initiatives Fund had committed all its funds. Its mandate has been to encourage and support the development of services that improve the quality of child care in Canada.
- Your local library may have the annual reports of the larger foundations and their funding patterns.
- Provincial and territorial ministries can provide information on current funding criteria.
- Service clubs such as Kiwanis, Rotary and Lions are located in most communities. They sometimes make one-time donations for items such as equipment or improvements to playgrounds.
- The Canadian Centre for Philanthropy (see Chapter 11, Appendix "A") distributes helpful publications and will do computer searches for a list of foundations which donate to child care services.

- Businesses can be approached to provide assistance. Some types of support include start-up funds, subsidies to employees to offset the cost of child care, salary enhancement grants, and the provision of space either free or at low cost.

Chapter 11, "Community, Resources and Advocacy" discusses outside funding, with a list of resources that can provide further information.

You will need to submit a formal, written proposal to request money from government sources, foundations and businesses. Preliminary personal contacts by telephone, letter or in person will tell you whether or not to submit a detailed proposal. Some funders have a preferred format for a proposal. The following describes a general format.

Cover Sheet or Title Page: A brief descriptive title for the proposed project, the name of the organization or individual submitting the proposal, and the submission date.

Executive Summary: A brief description of the need for the project based on data obtained from your needs assessment, your objectives and procedures, and the amount of money or type of assistance required. The information in this section should be concise, accurate and complete, because those reviewing the proposal may read only this section.

Table of Contents: Lists the sections of the proposal with corresponding page numbers.

Introduction: Includes background information about the submitting organization and the target user group, and illustrates the unique qualities of the proposed service.

Purpose: Outlines why the project is being embarked upon, highlighting the need for and importance of the proposed service.

Objectives: These are the substance of the proposal, because they must stem from the stated purpose and be reflected in the procedures. Your objectives must be stated clearly and in measurable terms, so they can be subjected to evaluation.

Procedure: Describes the specific service(s) to be provided to the user group. A description of staff may be included here.

Evaluation: Indicates how the service will be evaluated, to determine its success in carrying out its objectives.

Budgets: An accurate, itemized list of start-up and ongoing costs. Include contributions (space, equipment, volunteer help, etc.) and monetary commitments from other agencies.

Minor adjustments to the proposal may have to be made. Some tips for successful fundraising include making public acknowledgement of contributors and sending them frequent progress reports. If possible, show how the service is seeking additional funding sources and hopes to become self-sufficient.

ACTIVITIES

1. Make an appointment to visit a centre that is licensed for forty-five children. For the first activity find out exactly what line items the centre has included in its budget and why.
2. Name and describe any categories that need further explanation to justify their inclusion and amount in the budget.
3. Design your own complete budget for a centre for forty-five children.

FURTHER READING

Cherry, C., B. Harkness, and K. Kuzma (1987). *Nursery school and day care centre management guide*. Belmont, CA: Fearon.

Click, P., and D. Click (1990). *Administration of schools for young children*. Albany, NY: Delmar.

Morgan, G. (1982). *Managing the day care dollar*. Cambridge, MA: Steam Press.

Sciarra, D., and A. Dorsey (1990). *Developing and administering a child care centre*. Albany, NY: Delmar Publishers.

The Organizational Framework

This chapter looks at how child care centres are organized, and administrative procedures to maintain and control up-to-date information. Samples of various forms and policies can be found at the end. Chapter headings are:

◆ The organization of child care centres
◆ Organizing the flow of information.

THE ORGANIZATION OF CHILD CARE CENTRES

The way a centre is funded and managed will determine the organizational framework, affecting the level of parental involvement, government support and community input. Broadly speaking, there are three types of centre across Canada.

Non-profit centres

Also referred to as not-for-profit, these centres may be operated by a church, a parent or community group, an agency such as the "Y," an institution such as a university or college, or some other non-profit group that wishes to make child care available in the community. In some provinces, child care services are offered by the municipality and incorporated as non-profit.

A non-profit organization uses fees and other income to balance expenditures. Any excess would go back into the budget for the next fiscal year. The agency or group sponsoring such a centre will nominate a board of directors to manage its operations.

Commercial or for-profit centres/agencies

The free enterprise system is also involved in the operation of child care centres. Child care services can be provided as a profit-making business by sole owners, partnerships or corporations. The organization and its operations will be structured in such a way as to generate a profit for the owners. The director will be responsible to the owner, who will determine the organizational strucutre.

Proprietary agencies

In some cases a local business or government may provide a child care centre for their employees, or they may purchase space from a community centre, or else enter into a partnership with another business or local college on a collaborative basis. The organizational structure of the centre will be determined by the circumstances. For example, a business might decide to purchase child care spaces in either a non-profit or a for-profit centre for their employees. Or it might operate its own centre as part of its larger organization, in either for-profit or non-profit fashion.

Each of these basic types can offer the full variety of care. In the United States, the tendency seems to be towards providing child care in for-profit settings. In Canada, most provinces and territories seem to favour the non-profit approach.

Forming a Non-profit Corporation

A non-profit corporation is established when a group of people are committed to an identified goal. In order to arrange financing and seek a suitable location for a child care centre, the group may become incorporated in order to ensure recognition as a legal entity, continuity over time, and limited liability for its members.

Incorporation requires selecting a board of directors from among the members, and following the other established legal procedures. A lawyer's help will be necessary. Once incorporated, the non-profit corporation is well on its way to accomplishing the goals for which it was founded.

The board of directors

As the centre develops, the board's ongoing responsibilities include:

- administration of the centre
- management of finances
- program development
- human resources matters
- community relationships.

While the board determines a centre's overall direction, the supervisor is responsible for its day-to-day operation. The supervisor's responsibility must be clearly defined from the outset—it must be clear what kinds of issues she will address, and what issues belong to the board. A good relationship is critical.

The board is finally responsible for policy, but the supervisor, and when possible the staff, should be included in the process. Different studies have linked staff involvement in decision-making to job satisfaction and ultimately the quality of program offered in the centre. For example, supervisor and staff should be involved in the policies relating to curriculum and documentation of daily activities, in order to make sure that they are useful for planning, consistent with the centre philosophy, and helpful for parents.

Administrative Policies and Procedures

Developing, organizing and monitoring a centre's policies and procedures form one of the important tasks performed by the staff and supervisor in a well-run centre. They form the framework within which the daily life of the centre takes place. The level of involvement of parents, availability of resources and supports for staff, assignment of finances, leadership style of supervisor, are but a few of the variables affected.

The philosophy of the centre is at the heart of how policies and procedures are developed. For example, a philosophy that reflects cultural diversity would have policies that integrate this belief—in staffing, nutrition, diversified books and materials, and language considerations for children and parents.

Guidelines

Centres may also develop guidelines, in addition to policies and procedures. Guidelines help explain the policies with some examples, suggestions and alternatives that apply to various situations. For example, a guideline for student teachers first entering a field placement may suggest they not be intrusive, since children need time to become familiar with new people in the room.

Regulations

A centre's policies must incorporate provincial/territorial and municipal regulations. For example, your centre may want to develop a policy that parents park in a certain area for easy access in the morning. Then you discover the fire department doesn't allow parking in that area, because it is on the fire route path.

Once the regulations and their implications are clearly understood, policies to support and extend them may be established. A regulation on guiding children's behaviour may state that staff may not use corporal punishment, degrade, or in any way lower a child's self esteem. The centre would incorporate that regulation into their policy, extending it by adding how and why children's behaviour should be guided and directed, as well as the consequences for not following the philosophy.

Centres must adhere to laws such as employment standards acts, freedom of information legislation, and others that are dictated by the province or territory.

ORGANIZING THE FLOW OF INFORMATION

All written information we collect on children and their families should be collected and handled with the same level of consideration given to positive personal interactions. The forms, policies and procedures should reflect the philosophy and objectives of the centre. Since the brochure and other forms often give people their first impression of the centre, it is important to think carefully about what we want this impression to be.

Confidentiality

We early childhood educators are party to a lot of personal information about the children in our care and their families. We must always be sure to respect the confidential nature of this information. It is the responsibility of the centre and each staff member to become familiar with the freedom of information guidelines.

Caution must be exercised in this area, as there are greater legal complications than ever before. This topic should be reviewed as a regular agenda item for staff meetings, to ensure that each person has a clear understanding of the implications, professionally and legally, surrounding confidentiality.For example, it can happen that a staff member or student-teacher may share information with a parent about a child their child is playing with, intending to be helpful, but it is essential to examine the appropriateness and even the legality of this.

The need for confidentiality cannot be overstated. Written permission to disclose information must always be obtained from parents, and information should never be disclosed without such consent. Files and information must be housed in a safe and secure manner, with access allowed only to approved personnel.

Information about the Children

Application form

The initial application contains the information supervisor and staff need in order to enrol the child. However, many parents do not fill out more than the simplest questions on the application. There are several reasons for this. First, this may not be the only centre they are applying to. Second, they do not know who is going to read the information and how it may be used. Lastly, they may prefer to discuss the information directly with staff, rather than writing it on a form. Therefore, it is best to ask only questions you must know in order to continue the enrolment process, rather than complicate the application with questions that are not likely to be answered.

Provinces and territories generally specify the information that must be filed on each child enrolled in the centre. That should be the basis of forms to be completed by parents or guardians, but you will need further information to obtain the data you need to understand and plan for each child registered in the centre.

Consider the following when developing an application form:

- Review the human rights code, so you are clear on what you may and may not ask.
- Make the form easy to follow and simple to complete. Parents do not enjoy filling out long complicated forms, especially on the initial application.
- Be clear about why you are asking certain questions, and be prepared to explain the reason for them if asked by the parent. It is not good enough to say you didn't design the form and so don't know why the question was asked.
- Make sure the application reflects the belief that parents are important partners in your centre, and understand and know their child best.

Medical form

Whether legislated or not, the completion of a medical form is essential. Local health departments can provide centres with the forms a doctor needs to complete prior to the child's enrolment. Some centres send the medical form in the same mailing as the brochure and application form, in order to avoid a second mailing and red flag to the parents the need to fill it out. It often takes parents time to arrange an appointment with their family doctor, and having the form in hand helps speed up the process.

Developmental information form

The use of this form varies from centre to centre. It can provide a good beginning point for teacher and parents to begin a dialogue about the child. Parents know their children best, and the form is a good way to reinforce this. Helping teachers and parents work together is the blueprint for success for both child and centre, and what better way to begin this than to share information about the child's strengths, interests, activities, and needs? The form also provides information so staff can provide a program based on the child's individual needs.

This form should be completed just prior to the child's admission into the centre. This is particularly important for infants and toddlers, since their development is so rapid.

Individual instructions for children

Whether required by legislation or not, it is good centre policy to have parents provide written instructions for feeding and caring for young children. This should be done when children enter the program, or when any major changes in diet or procedure occur.

Daily information sheets

The daily information sheet is particularly important with infants. The first part of the page should include information provided by parents regarding details of sleeping and eating during the last twelve hours. The second part allows staff to record similar information, so that parents know how their child's day has gone. In addition, activities and developmental milestones are recorded, since children change and grow at such a quick pace at that age. The form can also help ease the discomfort parents can experience when first using group care for their infant.

Information for Parents

The centre brochure

The centre brochure gives parents a strong first impression about the centre's philosophy, objectives, program, and services. You want this impression to be a positive one. The brochure should be uncluttered, and contain only the information parents need to know in order to understand the philosophy and objectives of the centre. More detailed information takes away from the initial presentation and can follow later.

The brochure should contain:

- the centre's name, address and phone number
- its licensing body
- a summary of the philosophy and main objectives
- staff qualifications
- the age range of children accepted
- an overview of the program
- a brief description of the facilities
- fees (you may want to have an insert with the fees, since they will probably change more frequently than your printed brochure)
- the process for enrolment
- a statement or two about what makes this centre special.

Pictures with captions that reflect the philosophy enhance the appearance of the brochure and often capture the essence of the centre. After you design your brochure, field test it with parents and with other early childhood educators. This will help make sure it is clear, attractive, and includes all necessary information

Financial policy

The centre should have a clear financial policy. This should include the registration fee, schedule of payments, notice necessary for withdrawal, and any other policies outlining the financial responsibility of parents. For example, some centres allow parents to take several holiday weeks, while their place is reserved and no fee is payable. Others require a portion of the fee to be paid to hold the place. It is important for parents to understand that fees may be due regardless of the number of days the child attends, inclement weather or statutory holidays. Whatever the centre's policy about fees, a clear explanation is necessary so parents understand the commitments they are making when they enrol their child.

Health and safety policies

The health and safety policy of the centre is designed to protect the safety of all the children and adults. Parents need to plan for alternative care in the case of their child's illness. Once again, it is important that parents understand the reasons for this policy. In addition, accidents may happen in the centre that necessitate parental decisions and medical care. Each centre should spell out the procedure so that everyone concerned is fully aware of the process to be followed should an accident occur. Local and area evacuations may also occur, and a plan of action should be available for both parents and staff to follow. In areas where heavy snow is a frequent occurrence, plans for morning or early closing may also be important.

`In addition, the centre needs to have very specific procedures to ensure the health and safety of the children in its care. Chapter 5 contains a discussion of specific steps to take, with a suggested checklist.

Return after serious illness form

This form is to be completed by the family doctor after a child has had a serious illness, childhood disease or accident. It is important that the child not return to the centre until well enough to join the other children safely. In some cases it may be possible for the child to return, but with activity limitations. These limitations should be explained by the doctor. Several copies of this form should be given to the parents upon enrolment, and the purpose for it explained.

Administration of medication at school

Each centre must develop policies and procedures for the administration of prescription and non-prescription medications. The licensing authority in each province or territory may dictate its own requirements here, and some prohibit the administration of non-prescribed medication. More and more children are requiring the administration of medication such as insulin, asthma medication and antibiotics. This puts increased responsibility on staff, requiring a clear procedure to ensure safety and proper record keeping.

Centres that feel unable to handle these needs must make their position clear to all parents and prospective parents at the time of the admission interview, so that children needing regular medication are not accepted into care.

Permission for field trips

The point here is to guarantee that parents are informed about any activity that occurs off the centre property, and to ensure they are fully apprised about where their child will be at any time. This process can be handled in several ways. One form can be used to grant permission to go on any field trip arranged by the centre. Another way is to give parents the option of which field trips they would like their child to participate in.

Additional forms required

Some centres are involved in research that requires permission from parents, while other centres may be engaged in videotaping for special events, or for study by student teachers in college lab school situations. Parents are generally co-operative and want to have their children involved in such interesting ventures, but it is critical to gain permission first.

Other information for parents

Once parents have decided to enrol their child, they will need other information about the operation of the centre. A handbook for parents may be designed that includes the following specifics:

- recommended clothing
- how children's behaviour is guided
- specific information about the staff in the centre
- information on when and how to reach their child's teacher
- specific information about their child's program
- parking, describing location and safety considerations

- the policy on bringing toys from home
- arrival and departure procedures
- parental involvement
- newsletters
- information on nutrition
- car pooling
- special visitors
- special procedures for various age groups
- transitional objects from home.

This information will vary depending on the centre. The main goal is to help parents understand as much as possible about the centre and its overall operation, and the reason why the information is being asked. Although personal one-to-one communication is essential, some information can more readily be communicated in the handbook.

Information Provided by Staff

Staff need to review the application form, medical information and other forms completed by parents. The forms discussed in this next category are completed by staff.

Intake interview

This form provides a guideline for staff to follow when meeting with the child for the first time. The information gathered in this first meeting helps the teacher plan to make the child's initial experience at school a success. In addition, general information about the child's interests, abilities and overall developmental level may be assessed.

Generally, information recorded includes:

- response to visiting centre
- response to interviewer
- activities preferred during visit
- special information from parents about play habits
- mastery of language
- co-ordination
- parents' reaction to school.

Checklist for initial interviews

This checklist provides a second guide for staff in the initial interview, making sure all necessary information is covered with each family, and acting as a support system for new staff while they become comfortable with each area to be discussed with parents.

The checklist could include:

- description of the program for parents
- completion of all forms
- information on the child's beginning days in the centre

- arrival and departure procedures
- information boards, newsletters, parental involvement
- discussions on behaviour management
- question time for parents.

Guide for subsequent parent interviews

Based on the stated goals of the centre, this interview guide is completed by staff prior to a parent interview. It includes categories where staff can list specific information they need from parents in order to better understand and plan for the child. In addition, it provides areas for staff to record information about the child that they want to share with the parents. It assists the teacher in outlining each developmental area and identifying the child's strengths in each of these areas. This planning enables the teacher to enter an interview with the confidence that the important aspects of the child's development and involvement in the program are not overlooked.

Accident form

Careful consideration to safety does eliminate many unnecessary accidents. However, children move quickly and often unsteadily, with the result that some mishaps do occur. The accident form records such incidents when they occur, and describes the situation to the parents. It is always wise to show the form to parents and have them sign it, so the information is not misunderstood.

Child guidance policy

Each centre should have a procedure outlining the guidance policy to be followed by every staff member. In this procedure, the process of guiding children's behaviour should be outlined, including general principles accepted by all staff and parents. The policy should also spell out those behaviours by staff that are clearly unacceptable.

Child abuse policy and procedures

It is important to know and understand the legal requirements for staff in cases of suspected child abuse. The centre should provide the staff with as much information on this subject as possible. A format to record information in the case of alleged abuse should also be in place.

Serious occurrence

Depending on your province or territory's licensing agency, a serious occurrence may be defined as a child breaking a bone, an incident serious enough to require hospitalization, an alleged case of child abuse by a staff member, and so on. A serious occurence policy describing how to report and record such an incident should be in place in every centre. This will ensure that each staff member understands and follows prescribed practices and procedures. Whether this policy is required by the licensing body or not, it is important to clearly record such incidents for parents, medical personnel that might become involved, insurance purposes, and so on. In some provinces it is mandatory to phone the government licensing agency to report a serious occurrence.

Emergency information

An up-to-date list of emergency telephone numbers should be posted in several obvious locations and at the telephones. This list should include fire department, nearest hospital, ambulance service, poison control centre, police department, and taxi service. Some centres may have specific services that they use regularly that need to be included on this list.

Allergy lists and information

The kitchen and playrooms should contain lists of the children with allergies and medical conditions that need constant referencing. Every precaution should be taken to ensure that children are protected from foods or materials that cause reactions. Staff should be provided with detailed information on any condition of a child in their care and what to do in case of a reaction or emergency.

Severe allergies to many common foods are widespread, and child care staff need to be rigorous and sensitive in their commitment to keeping children safe.

Filing and use of forms

The information contained in the child's file is good only if it is used, and useful to the staff. Continue to review the need for information collected, and make sure it is useful and up to date. Some means of ensuring that all the information on each child is correctly filed should be developed for each centre. Whatever administrative system is developed, it should be easy for staff to use, protected for confidentiality, and well-organized.

ACTIVITIES

1. Visit two different child care centres and ask if you can have copies of several policies and procedures prepared for use for children and parents. Compare the two sets of information and make a list of the strengths and weaknesses of each form, policies and procedure.
2. Design a brochure for a centre for children ages four months to five years of age. Describe why you included the information you did, and how you feel it makes your centre appealing to parents.
3. Outline in detail the financial policy for a centre.
4. Make a list of ways that you could make parents feel an integral part of your centre. Now take that list and incorporate your ideas into the centre's policies and procedures.
5. Encourage students to collect copies of key policies at each of their field placement experiences. Use these to compare with the ideas developed in this chapter.

APPENDIX

FIGURE 9-1 EXAMPLE OF AN APPLICATION FORM

1. Child's name _____

   F ____ M ____ Date of birth _____ Telephone no. _____

   Address _____

   City _____ Postal Code _____

---

2. Mother's name _____

   Place of business _____ Telephone no. _____

   Address _____

---

3. Father's name _____

   Place of business _____ Telephone no. _____

   Address _____

---

4. Family doctor _____

   Address _____

   Telephone no. _____ Child's health card number _____

---

5. Please name two people that could be called in an emergency if you cannot be reached.

   1st name: _____ Relationship _____

   Address _____ Telephone no. _____

   2nd name _____ Relationship _____

   Address _____ Telephone no. _____

FIGURE 9-1 Continued

6. Commencement date _____ Centre _____

   Period preferred: Full days _____ Half days   am   pm

   1/2 Day Kindergarten Program   am _____ pm _____

   School age: Before school _____ Hot lunch _____ After school _____ .

   Arrival time _____ With whom? _____

   Departure time _____ With whom? _____

7. Describe previous/present child care arrangements: _____

   _____

   _____

   _____

8. Would you tell us a little about your child? (use n/a if appropriate)
   a) Physical abilities, health (any allergies, toilet abilities and method of letting you
      know s/he needs to use toilet):

      _____

      _____

      _____

   b) Personality characteristics (shy, outgoing, any fears):

      _____

      _____

      _____

   c) Eating habits (strong likes and dislikes):

      _____

      _____

      _____

FIGURE 9-1 Continued

d) Sleeping habits (special toys, blanket, etc.)

_____

_____

_____

e) Is there anything else you can think of that would help us to know and understand your child better?

_____

_____

9. Other children in the family:

Name _____ Age _____ Sex _____

Name _____ Age _____ Sex _____

Name _____ Age _____ Sex _____

Other people living in household:

_____

_____

Please Note
* Children will be released to the parent (s) who register their children in the Centre
* CHILDREN WILL NOT BE RELEASED TO ANYONE NOT LISTED ON THE FORM UNLESS THE CENTRE IS ADVISED OF THE CHANGE OF PERSON (INCLUDING TAXI SERVICE).
* Fees (see Fee Schedule)
* A registration fee of _____ is required with this application. This fee is not refunded.
* The monthly fee is due regardless of the number of days in the month, absenteeism due to illness or inclement weather, plus school and statutory holidays. Payments are due the first day of each month.
* If for some reason it becomes necessary to withdraw your child, a minimum notice of ONE MONTH is required or one month's fee in lieu of notice.
* It is important that parents read and understand the Health and Emergency Policy, and the Financial Policy.

Date _____ Signed _____
(Parent or Guardian)

FIGURE 9-2 PERMISSION FOR GIVING MEDICINE

PERMISSION FOR GIVING MEDICINE

Date: _____

I hereby give my permission for _____
"name of child"

to be given _____ of _____ at _____
         "amount of medicine"   "type"   "time(s) of day"

_____
"date (or dates) medicine to be given"

                                       _____
                                              Parent's signature

---

For school use only   Administered by _____

FIGURE 9-3 SAMPLE RETURN TO DAY CARE CENTRE FORM

RETURN TO CHILD DAY CARE CENTRE FORM

Parents:

This form is to be completed by family physician after your child has a serious illness, childhood disease, or accident.

TO: EARLY CHILDHOOD EDUCATION CENTRE

Date: _____

I have examined _____, and find him/her recovered
                           "Child's Name"

well enough to return to the Early Childhood Education Centre, taking part in all activities

with these limitations: _____

                                   Signed: _____
                                         (Physician's Signature)

FIGURE 9-4 ACCIDENT FORM

ACCIDENT FORM

Date: _____

Name: _____

Time: _____

Type of injury (please describe result of accident)

_____

_____

First aid administered (please describe)

_____

_____

Administered by: _____

Were the parents informed? _____   _____
                                                    Parent's signature

How did the accident occur? (please describe in detail)

_____

_____

_____

_____

_____

Your name: _____

Note: This form is to be completed as soon as possible after any accident.
       Parents to be informed by the teachers only.

FIGURE 9-5 INFANT-TODDLER PROGRAM DAILY INFORMATION SHEET

DAILY INFORMATION SHEET

NAME: _____ ARRIVAL TIME: _____

DATE: _____ DEPARTURE TIME: _____

1. When did your child eat or drink last? Time: _____

    Type and amount of food: _____

2. Did your child sleep well last night?_____ If not, please describe: _____

    What time did your child get up this morning? _____

    How is your child feeling this morning? _____

3. If your child has had a bowel movement this morning please describe: _____

4. Is there any other information that will help us take better care of your child?

    _____

THE FOLLOWING TO BE COMPLETED BY STAFF			
FOOD	AM	NOON	PM
Refused Ate Little Ate Moderately Ate Well			
Comments:			
BOTTLES	AM	NOON	PM
Formula Milk Juice Water			
Comments:			

FIGURE 9-5 Continued

BOWEL MOVEMENTS	AM	PM
Normal/Formed Soft/Loose Diarrhea		
Comments:		
SLEEP	ASLEEP BY:	AWAKE BY:
AM PM		
ACTIVITIES AND DEVELOPMENTAL MILESTONES:		

FIGURE 9-6 SAMPLE MEDICAL RECORD

EARLY CHILDHOOD EDUCATION CENTRE

NAME _____ NICKNAME _____ BIRTH DATE _____

PARENT OR GUARDIAN _____ PHONE (Home) _____

MOTHER'S PHONE (Work) _____ FATHER'S PHONE (Work) _____

DOCTOR _____ TELEPHONE _____

(Approx.
IMMUNIZATION RECORD Dates)   CHILDHOOD DISEASES   MEDICAL EXAMINATION

Quad (Primary Series)   Chickenpox _____   General Appearance _____

Dose 1 _____   Measles (Rubella) _____   Height _____ Weight ____

Dose 2 _____   Mumps _____   Hearing _____ Vision _____

Dose 3 _____   Measles _____   Chest _____ Abdomen ____

1. Quad Booster _____   Others _____   Skin _____ Extremities ____

2. Quad Booster _____   Allergies _____

Mumps _____   _____

Measles _____   _____

TB Skin Test _____

Haemophilus Influenzae Type B (HIB) _____

Please add any other information that would be helpful for us in meeting this child's needs.

CHILD'S HEALTH CARD NUMBER

M.D. _____

DATE _____

FIGURE 9-7 SAMPLE INTERVIEW FORM

GUIDE FOR PARENT INTERVIEWS
EARLY CHILDHOOD EDUCATION CENTRE

Based upon the stated goals of our centre, this guide is based upon the observed characteristics of each child.

NAME OF CHILD: _____ D.O.B.: _____

DATE OF COMPLETION OF FORM: _____

DATE OF INTERVIEW: _____

INTERVIEW: _____

PARENT (S): _____

SPECIFIC INFORMATION TO BE REQUESTED FROM PARENTS:

_____

_____

_____

_____

ADDITIONAL INFORMATION RESULTING FROM INTERVIEW:

_____

_____

_____

_____

_____

_____

_____

_____

_____

_____

_____

FIGURE 9-7 Continued

SELF-CONCEPT	
Assertion of needs	
Pride in accomplishments	
Need/Response to approval	
Persistence in achievements	

Reaction to limits _____

GENERAL COMMENTS: _____

_____

EMOTIONAL	
Demonstration of awareness of emotions	
Emotions freely expressed	
Acceptance of assistance	

Expression of emotions _____

Most commonly expressed emotions _____

Response to conflict _____

GENERAL COMMENTS: _____

_____

COMMUNICATION	
Understands and responds to teacher's direction	
Understands and responds to peer direction	
Comprehension of spoken words	

FIGURE 9-7 Continued

Clear verbal expression	
Uses language to seek assistance	
Uses language to share information or ideas	
Age-appropriate sentence structure	
Enjoys literary experiences	
Interest in written language	
GENERAL COMMENTS: _____ _____	

SOCIAL	
Awareness of others	
Enjoys interacting with peers	
Plays with variety of children	
Relationship with adults	
Relationship with peers	
Problem-solving skills	

Quality of play with peers _____

GENERAL COMMENTS: _____

_____

CHOICE MAKING	
Makes choices	
Follows through on choices made	
Direction needed	

FIGURE 9-7 Continued

Chooses a range of activities	
GENERAL COMMENTS: _____ _____	
CREATIVE EXPRESSION	
Interest in creative art activities	
Interest in dramatic play	
Interest in musical activities	
Interest in creative movement	
Chooses own materials	
Preference of activities _____ GENERAL COMMENTS: _____ _____	
GROSS MOTOR	
Outdoors: Skilled use of equipment	
Enjoyable time	
Favourite activity _____ _____	
Indoors: Skilled use of equipment	
Enjoyable time	
Favourite activity _____ Activities not attempted _____ GENERAL COMMENTS: _____ _____	

FIGURE 9-7 Continued

FINE MOTOR	
General competence	
Eye-hand co-ordination and manual dexterity	
Favourite activity _____	
GENERAL COMMENTS: _____	
SELF-HELP	
Independent dressing	
Independent toileting	
GENERAL COMMENTS: _____ _____	
EATING HABITS	
Enjoys snack/lunch	
Self-help skills	
General likes or dislikes _____ GENERAL COMMENTS: _____ _____	
SLEEPING HABITS	
Able to relax	
Awareness of others	
Length of sleep _____ GENERAL COMMENTS: _____ _____	

FIGURE 9-8 INITIAL INTERVIEW FORM

INITIAL INTERVIEW FORM

YOUR NAME _____

CHILD'S NAME _____ NICKNAME _____

PARENT (GUARDIANS) WHO COME IN WITH CHILD _____

_____

---

1. Child's response to visiting centre:

   a) undisturbed   ( )   d) extremely active ( )

   b) anxious to stay close to parent ( )   e) whining   ( )

   c) cried   ( )   f) other (please specify) _____

2. General appearance: a) well-groomed ( )

                            b) healthy   ( )

3. Relationship to interviewer:

   a) co-operative ( )   e) aggressive   ( )

   b) hostile   ( )   f) dependent   ( )

   c) fearful   ( )   g) demands full attention ( )

   d) shy   ( )   h) friendly   ( )

4. Activity preference throughout interview: _____

5. Relationship with parent during interview

   a) warm   ( )   d) understanding ( )

   b) hostile   ( )   e) hanging on to ( )

   c) demanding ( )

6. Special information from parents:

   a) play with other children _____

   b) relationship with siblings _____

   c) allergies _____

   d) physical problems (e.g., sight, hearing, etc.) _____

   e) parent's special request or concern _____

      _____

      _____

   f) physical markings or characteristics _____

      _____

FIGURE 9-8 Continued

7. How do you feel child will manage at the preschool centre:

Initially shy but soon feel comfortable ( ) Other (please specify) _____

Frightened ( ) _____

Ready to enter immediately ( ) _____

Separation difficulty ( ) _____

8. General Description:

a) active ( )

b) sedentary ( )

c) very quiet ( )

d) quick ( )

e) other _____

9. Co-ordination: large muscle - good ( ) fair ( ) poor ( )

small muscle - good ( ) fair ( ) poor ( )

10. Language mastery: vocabulary   above average ( ) average ( ) poor ( )

11. Expresses self in: a) words ( )

b) phrases ( )

c) short sentences ( )

d) longer sentences ( )

12. Enunciation: a) clear ( ) d) impediment ( )

b) baby talk ( ) e) other (please specify) _____

c) mumbles ( ) _____

_____

13. Parent's reaction to school: a) co-operative ( ) d) somewhat hostile ( )

b) eager ( ) e) other (please specify)

c) apprehensive ( ) _____

_____

Starting date agreed upon: _____

Teacher responsible for child: _____

Any additional comments you wish to make: _____

_____

_____

_____

FIGURE 9-9 INTAKE INTERVIEW CHECKLIST

INTAKE INTERVIEW CHECKLIST

1. DESCRIPTION OF THE PROGRAM
- developmentally appropriate
- based upon the needs and interests of children
- themes used as a point of departure and focus for all developmental areas
- staff and student teachers
- schedule established but flexible—describe child's day

I/T –sensorimotor

---

2. FORMS
- explain and sign –video
                    –permission to leave premises
- check for signatures – application
                    –2 policies
                    –registration fee paid
- give to parents –medical form–tell parents a doctor's signature is required
- explain drug administration
                    –original container
                    –medicine form
                    –medicine cabinet and fridge
                    –permission to return forms
                    –general information forms–highlights
- complete initial interview form–ask relevant questions
- confirm start date

I/T –daily info sheet   I –feeding schedule

3. ARRIVAL AND DEPARTURE
- rooms open–early morning arrivals
- separation anxiety-say goodbye–use of obs. booth
- remind parents to sign children in and out–daily forms
                    –clipboards

---

4. GENERAL INFORMATION
I/T | PRESCHOOL
- daily info box
- drawer/security items
- diaper storage
- sanitary procedure

PRESCHOOL
- signin/out clipboards
- curriculum charts
- high-low cubbie
- security items
- parent information boards

FIGURE 9-9 Continued

5. TOUR
- orange room, infant room, toddler room, muscle room, green room, blue room, creative room, observation booths, playgrounds, kitchen, parent bulletin board, menu posted, office-slot for cheque, (preschool) medicine forms/cabinet, resource centre

6. DISCIPLINE
- children helped to take responsibility for their own actions
- problem solving/child's active role
- positive approach
- stop undesired behaviour
- biting

7. SUMMARY
- ask parents if they have any questions
- clear on first-day procedure
- arrangements made for –name on cubbies, lunch plan, bed plan
                         –post necessary allergy information
- complete file and return to team leader

FIGURE 9-10 GUIDE FOR INFANT/TODDLER PARENT INTERVIEWS

GUIDE FOR PARENT INTERVIEWS
EARLY CHILDHOOD EDUCATION CENTRE

Based upon the stated goals of our centre, this guide is based upon the observed characteristics of each child.

NAME OF CHILD: _____ D.O.B.: _____

DATE OF COMPLETION OF FORM: _____

DATE OF INTERVIEW: _____

INTERVIEWER: _____

PARENT (S): _____

SPECIFIC INFORMATION TO BE REQUESTED FROM PARENT:

_____

_____

_____

_____

ADDITIONAL INFORMATION RESULTING FROM INTERVIEW:

_____

_____

_____

_____

(use back if more space needed)

OVERALL RESPONSE TO PROGRAM

LEVEL OF ENJOYMENT, APPROACH, COMFORTABILITY.

_____

_____

_____

_____

FIGURE 9-10 Continued

GOAL & GUIDELINE CONSIDERATIONS HABITS AND ROUTINES

Sleeping patterns _____

_____

Eating patterns _____

_____

Toileting patterns _____

_____

ACTIVITY TIME

Favourite activities _____

Gross motor _____

Fine motor _____

Response to sensory/creative stimuli _____

_____

Cognitive _____

Response to outdoors _____

_____

SOCIAL

Awareness of others/recognition of familiar people _____

_____

Method of communication/interaction _____

_____

Interactions with adults of particular enjoyment (i.e., songs; body games; peek-a-boo)

_____

Attachment to particular children _____

_____

Response to group activities _____

_____

FIGURE 9-10 Continued

Method of play _____

_____

EMOTIONAL

Emotions expressed/method of expression _____

_____

Ability to make needs known/method of making needs known _____

_____

Stressful situations _____

_____

Reaction to change _____

_____

Acceptance of comfort _____

_____

Attachment relationships with adults _____

_____

SELF-CONCEPT

Demonstrates awareness of self (i.e., recognition of: name; self in mirror; possessions; etc.)

_____

Awareness of body parts _____

_____

Self-help motivation/abilities (i.e., feedings; dressing) _____

_____

Response to positive reinforcement/approval _____

_____

Response to limits _____

_____

Level of persistence _____

_____

FIGURE 9-11 HEALTH AND EMERGENCY PROCEDURES

EARLY CHILDHOOD EDUCATION CENTRE
HEALTH AND EMERGENCY PROCEDURES

1. If your child should become ill while at school, the staff will call you at the numbers listed on the application to come and pick him/her up. The staff will make the decision to call you based on the best interest of both your child and the health of the other children in the centre. For this reason it is important that your business numbers and the people listed on the application as alternative emergency numbers be kept up to date.

2. If your child should have a minor accident while at school, the staff will call you to come and decide on medical treatment. If the injury is deemed serious by the centre nurse and/or doctor, an ambulance will be called and we will meet you at the hospital.

   We will use _____ Hospital if you are from the area or

   _____ if you are from _____.

3. Should it become necessary to evacuate the Early Childhood Education Centre, children

   would be safely moved to _____.

   Arrangements have been made for us to use the _____

   on a twelve-month basis. Parents would be notified should it become necessary to use the

   alternative facility. The phone number at _____ is _____.

4. Should a major area accident occur and we were required to immediately evacuate the

   entire _____ area, the children would be safely transported by the centre

   to the _____ telephone _____. Facilities are available to

   accommodate the children until they can be picked up by parents.

   The above procedures are designed to keep parents informed and reduce concerns should unusual incidents occur.

   I have read and understood the Health and Emergency Procedures.

   Date: _____   Signed: _____
                                                    (Parent or Guardian)

FIGURE 9-12 FINANCIAL POLICY

EARLY CHILDHOOD EDUCATION CENTRE
FINANCIAL POLICY

1. A registration fee of $10 is required with an application for enrolment. This fee is not refunded.

2. Fees are due at the beginning of each month. The Early Childhood Education Centre is operated on a non-profit basis and fees are our main source of income. Therefore it is important that fees are paid at the beginning of each month.

3. The monthly fee is due regardless of the number of days in the month, absenteeism due to illness or inclement weather, plus school and statutory holidays. The centre closes for two professional development days a year, one day in November and Easter Monday. In addition the Half Day Nursery School Program is closed during Winter Break Week,

   usually _____. The centre closes the week between Christmas and New Year's Day.

4. Parents withdrawing their child(ren) for summer holidays will not be required to pay the fee for up to two weeks during the months of July and August only. A minimum of two weeks notice for holiday time is required. Beyond the two-week period fees are charged in order to reserve your child's space.

5. If, for some reason, it becomes necessary to withdraw your child, a minimum notice of one month is required, or one month's fee in lieu of that notice.

6. Parents may apply to the _____ child care office to seek assistance with all or part of the fee to send their child to the Early Childhood Education Centre.

Date: _____   Signed: _____
                                                                   (Parent or Guardian)

Families and Early Childhood Programs— A Vital Partnership

What place do early childhood settings have in the lives of families? Although working with parents is an integral part of what we do, we often find our role in this area lacks definition. This chapter addresses the partnership between families and early childhood settings.

◆ Why involve parents?
◆ The role of the supervisor.

WHY INVOLVE PARENTS?

In order to think about the relationship between parents and early childhood educators, it is useful to look at the early childhood setting as a *service*, a *support*, a *resource*, and a *partner*.

A service

The last two decades have seen a dramatic increase in the number of mothers who work outside the home. Now, two out of every five Canadian workers are women. The service provided by early childhood settings responds to the resulting need for child care.

A support

The child care setting provides an important support for young families. This is a relatively new role for early childhood educators. Some caution that it potentially diminishes the rights and responsibilities of parents, but such involvement can enhance family life and reduce the strain of everyday parenting.

Canadian families are in a process of transition. Significant social pressures are profoundly affecting the lives of young children and their families. Higher divorce rates and increasing economic pressures have resulted in more single parent families and mothers working outside of their homes. These changing family structures have led to greater demands being put on early childhood educators, who now must perform many of the roles that were once the responsibility of the extended family. Caregivers may find themselves in the position of discussing personal issues, as they provide the family with needed support.

A resource

Alice Honig (1979) talks about parents' rights to have access to tools that can help them fulfil their roles as parents. The early childhood setting is in a unique position to provide these tools. Through parent education programs, caregivers can play a significant role in providing information to enable parents to be more effective.

Informal discussions, surveys and brainstorming sessions can help parents identify their specific needs and interests. Parent education programs can then be organized in response. These programs can take many forms, including workshops, parent meetings and self-help groups.

This sounds like a straightforward proposition—it isn't. First, the needs of families are as diverse as the needs of individual children, representing a range of values, beliefs and customs. Secondly, training programs focus on preparing students to work with children, so early childhood educators may lack experience related to working with parents. Additional opportunities for professional development in this area must be provided.

There is no "one way" to parent. It is a real challenge to provide information among many valid models. Early childhood educators must adopt an eclectic approach, selecting strategies that best meet the unique needs of each family.

A partner

Parents and early childhood educators need to see each other as partners in the care and education of children. Parents have the final responsibility, but the centre where a child spends many hours a day for five days a week has a great effect on that child's development. In the best interests of the child, each partner must collaborate with the other.

The Benefits of Parental Involvement

When parents are involved in the education and care of their young child, everyone wins. An examination of some of the potential outcomes indicates that parental involvement is indeed powerful.

Parents and children come as a package. "As children enter the classroom, their families also come with them" (Lightfoot 1978). By working together, parents and early childhood educators can ensure that settings provide the best possible care for young children. A collaborative effort utilizes the skills and knowledge of both partners, enhancing the program and standards for care.

As Doherty (1991) shows, there is a correlation between parent involvement and quality care. At present, early childhood educators primarily define their roles in terms of their work with young children. But if we work with the child alone, we fail to acknowledge the depth of influence and involvement of parents with their children. We must implement strategies which involve parents in the care and education of their young children. Parent involvement is fundamental to ensuring that children's needs are met.

There is increasing evidence that parental involvement is the key to sustaining the gains achieved in early intervention programs for children believed to be at risk. It follows that parental participation enhances children's experiences in all early childhood settings.

Many parents experience a sense of guilt when they place their child in an early childhood setting (many don't, of course). By empowering parents and affirming the central role they play in the care and education of their children, early childhood educators can relieve some of the anxiety parents feel here. At the same time, involvement enables parents to exert some influence over the setting to which they entrust the care of their child.

For the child, parent involvement helps form a bridge between home and child care. Transition from one to the other is often not easy, and the presence of parents in the setting helps to reassure the child of the connections. In addition, there is substantial evidence that parental involvement affects children's cognitive development.

Participation gives parents opportunities to interact with and observe early childhood educators, along with other parents and children in the setting. These interactions can enhance their understanding of child development and early childhood programs. Some parents will develop new skills from this, thus contributing to their self-confidence and sense of competence.

Educators benefit when interactions with parents provide some new understanding about a child, enabling them to meet their needs more effectively. Parent participation can also result in a greater variety of activities at the centre, reflecting the talents and skills of individual parents.

Finally, it is the parents' right to be involved in the education of their child. They did not abdicate their rights to influence their child's development when they enrolled him or her in the early childhood setting. On the contrary, they expressed their nurturing role through their choice of a setting which provides quality care, and this role can be further enhanced by involvement in that setting.

Obstacles to Parental Involvement

Philosophical commitment to working with families is not enough to ensure parental involvement. If parental involvement is so powerful, why is it so difficult to establish?

Early childhood educators may interpret lack of parental participation as lack of interest. Is this true? Closer examination reveals a number of obstacles on the way to meeting a commitment to work with families.

Parents are busy people with many demands on their time and energy—work, family members, continued studies, and the like. However, time is not the only obstacle to involvement. Parents may not realize they have something to offer to the early childhood setting, or they may hesitate because they don't know what to do. This hesitation may result in their feeling uncomfortable and unable to contribute.

Barriers to parental involvement may also originate within the early childhood setting:

- Staff may not fully understand the value of parent participation. Often staff are not themselves parents, and they may have difficulty fully comprehending the importance—or the difficulties—of parent involvement.
- Some educators may secretly believe that mothers should not work and leave their children in the care of others. In her work, Galinsky (1990) found it is not uncommon for early childhood educators to hold this view. Such a belief could create a barrier interfering with their readiness to work with parents.
- Staff may lack the skills needed to work effectively with parents. Early childhood programs have not usually made learning to work with families a priority.
- The educator may be threatened when parents perform some of the tasks she or he usually does in the early childhood setting.
- Some may view the parent's presence as an intrusion and may choose to work in isolation.
- Parent involvement requires additional preparation on the part of staff, who may already feel overburdened by existing demands on their time.

Ways for Parents to Get Involved

Involvement can take many forms, ranging from informal conversations to parent membership on the board of directors. Different possibilities include:

- parent meetings
- newsletters
- open house evenings
- special parent programs, including support groups, self-help groups and special interest groups
- volunteering, fundraising, membership on the board of directors or advisory group
- informal visits to the setting
- surveys of parent skills, talents, needs, interests
- parent-teacher conferences
- toy-lending libraries
- coffee hours, muffin mornings, potluck dinners.

THE ROLE OF THE SUPERVISOR

What is usually lacking is not the commitment to working with parents, but rather the communication systems to make the partnership work. The development of these systems is one of the supervisor's most important responsibilities. Good communication links the child's two worlds, and is critical in order that staff and parents may work as partners.

Effective communication takes work. Staff may encounter problems in trying to communicate with parents at either end of their work day, when both parties may be tired or pressed for time. This can be mistakenly interpreted as a lack of interest. While parents will confirm that these pressures play a role, they also report they are uncomfortable in their initial contacts with staff, or that they don't know what to ask. Thus supervisor and staff must take responsibility for initiating contact and sharing information with parents.

First impressions are important. A parent's first contact with an early childhood setting sets the stage for future involvement, or lack of it. For example, when a parent first calls a centre, a staff representative should be prepared to provide whatever information is required to make the parent feel welcome.

The unfamiliar setting, and sometimes guilt about entrusting their child to another's care, may make parents feel uneasy prior to their first visit. Supervisor and staff must help parents feel more comfortable. In some communities, this may include strategies for responding to parents' multicultural backgrounds and special needs. By describing the setting and the program, and emphasizing the importance of the parents' role, staff will make the parent more aware of what to expect and how to behave in the setting.

During the first visit by parents, the supervisor should plan for an informal tour, a classroom observation and an interview. Some programs may wish to provide a checklist or questionnaire to assist parents in focusing their observations and questions. At the end of the visit, it is important to discuss the parents' reactions and impressions, and to answer any questions. Parents should also be encouraged to visit other centres, to make sure the one they've chosen is the right one for their child.

Separating from home is difficult, particularly for very young children, but it can be less disturbing when parents and early childhood educators work together. Separation is difficult for parents too. Supervisors and staff can support them by acknowledging this difficulty, and encouraging them to discuss their responses. Some centres may prefer that parents leave shortly after their arrival if the child seems overly upset during the first few days of adjustment. Other centres will encourage parents to stay until their child is calm. Whatever the preference, the staff need to discuss their expectations with parents beforehand, so that both are consistent in their response.

Communication Strategies

The supervisor needs to provide leadership, by working with staff and board to define the centre's level of commitment to working with families, and articulating policies to reflect this commitment. Such policies could enable parents to visit the setting without an appointment, or stay with their children during their first days in the centre. Policies like these send a clear "Welcome!" message to parents.

The supervisor can work with staff to develop strategies for involving parents, and a plan for assessing these strategies' effectiveness. Part of this approach is to work with staff to explore their attitudes about working with parents, and provide related staff training needs. Parental involvement will meet with resistance if staff do not have attitudes and skills which facilitate parent integration.

An orientation program for parents needs to be developed for the centre. This program might include a review of centre philosophy and goals, an informational tour, an opportunity to meet the teachers, discussion of the fee schedule, and an overview of policies and procedures. This is also a good opportunity for the administrator to learn about the child, and discuss any special requirements, needs or concerns.

Parents should be involved in decision-making. A parent advisory committee can provide feedback and recommendations to the centre, and advocate for parents and their involvement in the setting. Parents can also serve as advocates in the community at large.

Specific communication strategies might include some of the following:

- Surveys could be used to gather information about parents' skills, talents, needs, and interests. This can be used to create a card file or computer file with information about tasks that parents can be involved in. Information gained in the survey can help ensure the program is responsive to the cultural needs of each family. An example of such a survey is given in the Appendix.

- A notice board could be reserved for parent information. Information displayed on this could include written statements with guidelines for interacting with children, or articles and news of centre and community interest. Parents could be asked to post their own information. Daily information can also be shared using message centres, mailboxes, journals or conversations, and parent-teacher conferences to discuss a child's progress.

- Newsletters could be put together containing children's work, parent contributions, anecdotes, plans for future activities, and other information related to the operation of the centre. It is important to keep a positive tone in these communications.

- A parents' space could be set aside, containing comfortable seating, coffee, reading materials and resources, pictures of children, posters, etc. As an adjunct, coffee hours could be arranged for parents to chat informally with one another, staff and even children.

- An open house with slides or a video could illustrate the centre's program or philosophy.

- The family could be visited in their home, or phoned to share their child's accomplishment.

As early childhood educators, we need to move beyond a verbal commitment to designing mechanisms to involve parents in the education of their young children. Once the role of families in early childhood settings has been defined, we need action plans to give life to our definitions. Good intentions are not enough.

ACTIVITIES

1. Design a parent survey that will identify needs, interests and talents. Such a questionnaire could also solicit feedback about the effectiveness of the early childhood setting. Once completed, what will you do with the information to encourage parental involvement in an early childhood setting?

2. Draw a diagram of an early childhood setting, and modify the space to incorporate a space for parents. The design should take into account traffic patterns and noise levels, and should be situated in such a way that it invites parents to make use of it.

3. Survey your community and identify potential resources and support systems for families with young children.

4. How could you evaluate the effectiveness of different strategies designed to encourage parental involvement? Identify several mechanisms.

5. Design a questionnaire or activity that will help staff assess their values and beliefs about parenting and/or their attitudes to parent involvement at their centre.

FURTHER READING

Bjorklund, G., and C. Burger (1987, January). "Making conferences work for parents, teachers and children." *Young Children*, 26-31.

Canada Department of Health and Welfare (1987). *National strategy on child care.* Ottawa, Ontario: Health and Welfare Canada.

Denholm, C., R. Ferguson, and A. Pence (1987). *Professional child and youth care: The Canadian perspective.* Vancouver: University of British Columbia Press.

Feeney, S., D. Christensen, and E. Moracvik (1987). *Who am I in the lives of children?* (3rd ed.). Columbus, OH: Merrill.

Galinsky, E. (1988). "Parents and teacher-caregivers: Sources of tension, sources of support." *Young Children*, 4-12.

Galinsky, E. (1978). *Easing parents through beginnings and endings.* Child Care Information Exchange.

Honig, A. *Parental involvement in early childhood education.* (Rev. ed.). Washington, DC: National Association for the Education of Young Children.

Joffe, C. (1979). *Friendly intruders: Childcare professionals and family life.* Berkeley: University of California Press.

Lightfoot, S. (1978). *Worlds apart: Relationships between families and schools.* New York: Basic Books.

Manburg, A. (1985). "Parent involvement: A look at practices that work." *Exchange*, 9-11.

APPENDIX: A SAMPLE PARENT INVOLVEMENT PHONE QUESTIONNAIRE

Hi. My name is _____ and I am doing a survey for

_____ Child Care Centre.

We are interested in using parents as resource people to broaden the learning of the children. I was just wondering if you could give me three or four minutes of your time.

1. a) Would your workplace or place of study be willing to have a small group of

    approximately 10-12 children of _____ ages for a brief tour or visit?

    Yes ( ) Go to 1(b)   Maybe ( ) Go to 1(b)

    No ( ) Go to 2   Don't go to work or school ( ) Go to 2

   b) How interesting do you think this would be for children of this age group?

    Very interesting ( )   Fairly interesting ( )   Not very interesting ( )

2. Do you have any hobbies or interests you could share with the children in a classroom visit?

    Sports ( )   Presentations ( )

    Arts/crafts ( )   Cultural activities ( )

    Music/dance ( )   No ( )

    Collections ( )   Other _____

3. a) If you are willing to say, which ethnic or cultural groups did your ancestors belong to?

    _____

   b) Is there an aspect of your heritage you might share with the children in the way of food, dance, music, or costumes?

    Yes ( )   No ( )

   c) Are other languages besides English spoken in your home?

    None ( )   Other languages _____

4. Would you be able to contribute in other ways?

    Donating materials ( )   Sewing cushions ( )

    Donating story books/toys ( )   Making story tapes ( )

    Baking/buying snack ingredients ( ) No ( )

    Making games/toys ( )   Other

5. Would you be interested in getting involved in fundraising for the child care centre?

Yes ( )   No ( )   Maybe ( )

6. Do you have any other ideas or suggestions for a way in which you could participate in the child care centre?

No ( )

7. When might you have extra time available to participate further in the child care centre?

Mornings ( )   No time ( )

Afternoons ( )   Other ( ) _____

Evenings ( )

8. a) Is there another parent or guardian in your household who would be available to answer our questions?

Yes ( ) Go to 8(b)

No ( ) Go to next question

b) What would be the best time to contact them by telephone?

Mornings ( )

Afternoons ( )

Evenings ( )

Classifying Section

9. [DO NOT ASK] The respondent is

Male ( )

Female ( )

10. Can I have your name, for the centre's reference?

Respondent's name _____ Phone _____

Parent/Guardian of _____

Name refused ( )

Interviewer's name _____ Date _____

(This questionnaire was developed by Sarah Allan and Adrienne McRuvie, of Ryerson Polytechnic University.)

11

Community, Resources and Advocacy

As early childhood educators, we have a wider public responsibility: to work to provide necessary services, and to speak out to gain the critical mass of support needed for a national high quality child care system. This chapter examines this public responsibility.

- ◆ Developing new programs within the community
- ◆ Ensuring a variety of programs
- ◆ Community partners and outside funding
- ◆ Public education and advocacy.

Many Canadians feel there is a crisis in child care today. Too many Canadian families find regulated child care unavailable, unaffordable, or both. Quality is sometimes poor; existing services are often unresponsive to different needs. While some parents prefer informal arrangements, a number of studies have shown that many parents who would prefer regulated care cannot find it available.

Mothers still bear the primary responsibility for child care arrangements. Employers have not responded adequately to the changing needs of families. In most parts of the country, services are almost non-existent for parents working shifts and irregular hours, or for those needing part-time, seasonal and emergency care. Services for infants and school-age children are even less available than those for children of other ages. The special needs of children with disabilities, multicultural and aboriginal children are often ignored. In some places, long waiting lists for subsidized spaces exist alongside full-fee vacancies in established programs.

This is a long list full of challenges. Many Canadians have little understanding of the crucial issues in child care, and it is up to us in the child care community to increase public awareness. It is important to recognize that we can exert an influence.

DEVELOPING NEW PROGRAMS WITHIN THE COMMUNITY

The strong unmet need for regulated child care means that many new programs will have to be opened. Many advocates believe a doubling of total spaces by 1995 will not be enough. A increase in the number of licensed subsidized spaces needs to be planned for. Existing programs may choose to expand their capacity or broaden the types of services they offer, or both. Practitioners, governments, parents, and interested community representatives will need to work together to realize this expanded system.

Creating new programs in a community is an exciting challenge requiring abundant creativity and energy. Community groups must work in partnership to co-ordinate local programs for children, making sure that individual, cultural and regional needs are met. Services to consider include licensed programs such as family home day care and group child care centres, support services for parents and caregivers, toy lending libraries, drop-in centres, parenting workshops, and information and referral services. Flexible and innovative models need to be developed for rural and isolated communities, parent relief and emergency care.

Steps in Establishing a New Program

When embarking on a new venture, time spent planning is always saved in the long run. It is important to do your homework, researching government policies and assessing existing services. If you feel the project has potential for outside funding, then you need to talk with those funders to determine their priorities, before you develop your proposals to them. Potential funders may be able to provide you with helpful information about service design and the development of a realistic time frame. Visiting other child care programs is also highly beneficial at this point, providing the opportunity to explore a variety of models and approaches. Above all, your motivation and enthusiasm for developing a relevant, high quality child care service is essential and infectious. When you believe in what you are doing, others will too.

These are the steps in developing the plan for a new program:

- Create the vision
- Assess community needs
- Review the legal requirements
- Ensure a variety of programs
- Identify potential partners in your community
- Assess the potential for outside funding.

Creating the Vision

A new program must meet a need in the community, and there must be some driving force to realize the vision. This driving force is often an individual, often an early childhood educator with a strong desire to develop a child care service. It may also be a group of parents or community professionals who have an interest in responding to needs for child care in their neighbourhood, or it could be a community agency whose members wish to expand their current services to include some form of child care.

Whoever the original motivators are, they must be prepared to carry out all the preliminary tasks for the new program until a supervisor is hired. Some groups find it beneficial to work with a consultant experienced in developing child care programs. There will be no revenue until children are actually attending, so there is usually no reimbursement for the time and energy invested in the planning stages. In some instances, the group may secure a start-up grant.

This is the creative stage of planning, a time to envision the full potential of the program. The dream will be refined by what families want and the available resources. Additional services can be phased in over time as more funds are received.

Assessing Community Needs

The first step in realizing your vision is to assess the need for child care in your community. What programs currently exist, and what services are wanted by families? Here are questions to ask the child care programs that are already functioning in your community:

- what services are available
- age groups served, and hours of operation
- current enrollment
- waiting lists
- utilization patterns
- plans for expansion
- fees
- staff salary range

The answers will help you determine the current availability of child care, while information about local fees and salaries will serve as reference points in determining a preliminary financial plan.

You will need to determine the number of families and children who will use your planned service, and the type of service they want. It is important to gather your information directly from potential users, and do it before you seek a location, or do any financial forecasting or program planning.

Some planning information may be available through local municipal offices, or the community may have recently conducted similar surveys. Before beginning your own survey, you need to define your objectives, to determine what kind of information you need. The development and use of a survey to determine community need involves six basic steps.

1. Define the objectives.

Be clear about why you are doing a survey. You want to ensure that your planned program meets real community needs.

Determine who will be surveyed: for example, parents of children attending the local elementary schools. Determine how many parents will be surveyed—this is called the sample size. Determine how you are going to collect information.

2. Prepare the questions.

Construct questions to fit your objectives, making sure each question solicits useful responses that can be compared and tabulated. If you gather information you don't need, just because it seems interesting, the survey will take longer to complete, and you run the risk of reducing participation. Always remember to ask yourself:

- Why am I asking this?
- What will it tell me?
- What will I do with the information?

Arrange the questions in a logical order, each leading to the next. Test out the completed survey on a sample group, to make sure instructions are clear and the questions are being interpreted the way you intended them. You may need to revise the survey after the test.

Here is what is usually considered in a survey:

- Number of families and children
- Socio-economic status or family income
- Ages of children to be served
- Location of program
- Types of service families require and prefer.

A sample questionnaire is provided in Appendix B.

3. Gather the information.

You will need to determine how you will collect the data. Possible methods include questionnaires, telephone surveys, use of key informants, and small group meetings. Personal interviews are the most costly and time-consuming of the suggested methods, but they often provide the best results. Telephone interviews are also useful for asking in-depth questions, although they too can be time-consuming. Phone to arrange appointments with individuals who have been difficult to contact. Train the individuals conducting the interviews, so that questions are asked and recorded in a standardized manner—you will need to compare the results.

Mailed questionnaires are less expensive, but usually have a lower rate of return. To assist participants in returning their completed questionnaires, provide a stamped, self-addressed envelope. A reminder phone call should follow up the mailing. Sending out letters to potential families also serves as an effective way to promote the program.

4. Canvass the community.

Inform local community and service organizations of plans for the child care service. This helps market the service to professionals who work with potential users. Home and school associations, child care resource centres, public health, and social services departments also may be able to assist with the selection of neighbourhoods and work places for distributing questionnaires.

5. Evaluate the findings.

You will need to analyze the information you collect, and put it into a suitable format for presentation. Elaborate statistics are often not necessary; reporting total numbers and percentages may suffice. Keep in mind who will be reviewing the results when the findings are completed. Sharing the information with a committee or government body may affect the method of presentation: for example, graphic illustrations or detailed statistics may be required.

6. Take action.

The information gathered and analyzed will hopefully confirm that the proposed service will be a welcome addition to the community. On occasion, a survey will show that the original plan needs to be substantially revised, or even that it is not a viable project.

Reviewing the Legal Requirements

Across Canada, the care of groups of children is subject to regulatory control, in the jurisdiction of each territory and province. Standards vary greatly across Canada and are difficult to compare, since each province employs different criteria to define categories of care. Anyone planning to open a child care program should be in touch with his or her provincial/territorial consultant, who will provide the appropriate licensing requirements. In addition, municipalities usually have building, zoning, and health requirements. Chapter 2, "The Role of Government," provides an overview of Canadian legislation and a list of provincial licensing offices.

ENSURING A VARIETY OF PROGRAMS

Facilities may offer a combination of full-, half- and part-time programs. Some programs, usually half-day programs, provide services to children with special needs.The type of program being developed should relate to the assessed need identified by representatives of the community. Other factors that may affect program design are the philosophy, goals and objectives of the group initiating the program, and the sources of funds available.

Infant-Toddler Care

Quality group programs for infants and toddlers are costly. Small ratios and group sizes demand high parent fees in order to cover increased staff and special program costs. The proper care for infants and toddlers is physically hard work and requires special equipment, a highly child-proof environment and a meticulous approach to health and caregiving practices. Many parents prefer home-based settings for this age group.

Preschoolers

Preschoolers, children aged three to six, are the best served sector. The majority of licensed group spaces are used by this group and family caregivers tend to prefer caring for children of this age.

School-Age Children

Kindergarten-age children attend school for part of a day or a week. The availability of public kindergarten programs varies across Canada. In some areas, junior kinder-gartens offered through the school system are meeting the needs traditionally served by nursery schools.

Part-time care for school-age children is offered in some communities in the local school, community centres or the "Y." Some of these programs adhere to standards set by provincial and territorial governments. Combinations of child care arrangements can be shaped to meet parents' overall needs.

Some caregivers are reluctant to provide care for school-age children, because of the part-day nature of the care, and complicated scheduling around the school calendar. Parents are often forced to leave their children in before- and after-school "self care"—so-called "latch key" children. Another problem for school-age children arises because of the need for co-ordination among the different parties responsible for their care: parents, school and child care provider.

Exceptional Care

Children with special needs, including physical and mental disabilities and exceptional health care needs, usually benefit from attending an integrated quality child care program. Integration with "typical" peers provides such children with irreplaceable opportunities to develop and enhance their social and adaptive behaviours.

A child care centre requires additional resources to accommodate the needs of such children. Inclusive programs would provide consultative and health-related supports, as well as environments that facilitate both physical and social integration. A family focus and meaningful parent involvement are critical. All the challenges that face parents seeking care are increased for the parents of children with special needs. The framework for the development of an accessible, affordable, quality continuum of child care options should include the "...fundamental principles of access, equity, opportunity, and inclusion..." (Guralnick 1990).

Aboriginal Children

Cultural integrity is a major consideration for aboriginal families, whether child care programs are provided on or off reserve. Child care models must be consistent with aboriginal cultural values. Native families will feel more inclined to enrol their children in programs that clearly value their involvement. The most effective way of ensuring cultural integration is to increase the number of aboriginal staff.

Inclusive Programs

As Beach (1992) states, all children should be welcomed as individuals regardless of ability or disability, cultural background, family income, or where their parents work. Children require caring adults who meet not only their physical needs, but are concerned for their intellectual, social and emotional growth as well. Inclusive programs welcome cultural, racial and linguistic diversity. Inclusive programs are not targeted to a particular segment of the population, for programs that are targeted create inequalities in service provision. Consideration should be given to hiring, training and educating caregivers who will foster appreciation of different child-rearing and nurturing styles, as well as attitudes and values from other cultures.

Group Care Programs

Group care refers to centre-based care for children ranging from newborn to twelve years, including nursery school and school-age care. The day care centre is generally the first image that comes to mind. Most group centres tend to serve children aged three to five years. Many parents choose group care because of increased opportunities for socialization with children of a similar age, the child-centred environment, and the reliability that comes from having back-ups when a staff member is ill or moves.

Group facilities vary in terms of resources, toys and outside areas, but all must meet minimum standards defined by each province or territory. Care is usually offered on weekdays, typically from 7 a.m. to 6 p.m. Some centres provide part-time programs, although these are in short supply in Canada.

Many centres have an arrangement whereby fees to low-income families are subsidized by the government. Child care centres are licensed by each province and territory. As most provinces and territories require some level of training for teachers in group care, the caregivers in these programs are more likely to have some training in child care and child development. In many cases, these required qualifications only apply to the lead caregiver.

The costs for centre care are generally higher than home child care. It can be difficult to obtain a space, particularly for an infant. The location is not always convenient, and transportation can present a problem for some families. The quality of care and programming will depend very much on the particular staff involved, the leadership of the supervisor in the centre and the resources available to the program.

Part-time programs are geared to provide a half-day educational experience for children from 2 1/2 to 5 years of age. The options include nursery schools, preschools, Montessori programs, kindergartens, play groups, and some group care programs.

Family Child Care

Parents working or studying either part- or full-time need care for their children. Existing centres are rarely structured to accommodate irregular working hours or care for children who are sick, and this presents difficulties for many parents. Homemaker parents also require child care while they shop, study, perform community or volunteer activities, are involved in recreational activities, recuperate from an illness, or care for another family member. Family child care generally offers more flexible hours than child care centres, and it is also attractive because of the home environment and the small number of children being cared for. Some parents choose home care because all their children, of varying ages, can be looked after in one location.

Family child care can be licensed or informal. If parents are to be provided with quality options, support must be available to both. Family child care should not be viewed as a smaller version of group care, but rather as a different kind of care provided in a home environment.

Depending on the relevant legislation, in licensed care the provider may care for up to nine children in her own home. The fees may be subsidized by the government. In some provinces, private homes are supervised by agencies licensed by the government. The agency is responsible for recruiting, screening, training, and monitoring the home care providers. In other jurisdictions, the family home care providers are licensed directly by the provincial or territorial government, and receive occasional inspection visits. Currently no jurisdiction in Canada requires providers to obtain any formal training in child care or child development.

Informal care arrangements are the norm for the majority of Canadian children. This care can be provided in the child's or caregiver's home, by a relative, neighbour, friend, or babysitter. According to *The report of the Task Force on Child Care*(1986), the caregiver is usually not related to the child.

Parents want a variety of options and they are concerned with the quality of care. Cost, location and availability are often the key reasons parents choose family child care. A number of studies have shown that more parents would prefer regulated care than currently use it (Beach 1992).

COMMUNITY PARTNERS AND OUTSIDE FUNDING

Identifying Potential Partners in Your Community

High quality child care requires strong partnerships among representatives of the child care community, parents, schools, employers, and all levels of government. These partnerships can help make child care services more available, accessible, affordable, and generally better. Co-operative efforts between employers and child care experts, or with the school system, already exist and serve as models.

Potential partners for a new centre in your community include:

- non-profit child care programs sponsored by community organizations such as churches, businesses, societies, colleges, or charities
- parent-run co-operatives
- programs operated by a municipality
- employer-sponsored or supported child care programs at or near the workplace.

The board of directors of a child care centre should reflect these partnerships. Parent representation is vital—it is essential that parents are at the core of decision-making about the program.

When forming a new program, identify what types of skills are needed on the board of directors. You will need someone with financial planning skills, such as an accountant or manager. An expert in the developmental needs of children could be represented by a faculty member from the local college or university. This individual may also facilitate student placements in the program. A lawyer can be helpful, particularly at the early stages, when the program undergoes the process of incorporation. There should be someone with expertise in health issues, such as a public health nurse or pediatrician. A supervisor/director from another child care program in the community can add firsthand knowledge of the issues faced by the program, such as setting appropriate fees and developing schedules. Someone with expertise in personnel issues is essential.

This is not an exhaustive list. At various times members will be required with particular skills, such as fundraising, public relations and construction.

Assessing the Potential for Outside Funding

Securing funds to start and maintain an early childhood program is a challenging task. Administrators may find themselves either carrying the full responsibility for fundraising, or developing ways to meet the budget. In some situations board members or prospective parents may be willing to help find funding sources. Obtaining start-up capital is more difficult than funding an operating program. When parent fees are the only source of income, initial capital must be obtained through loans, donations or grants. Funding for child care services may be available through government and/or private sources.

A few early childhood programs are subsidized by local charities, church groups or United Way funds. Groups such as community organizations, school boards and work places sometimes provide in-kind contributions such as free rent, janitorial services, coverage of utility bills, or administrative help.

The first step in fundraising is to identify available sources of potential support.

- Local libraries may have the annual reports of the larger foundations, and their funding patterns.

- In some provinces, government grants may be available for non-profit child care programs. Some are targeted to help cover initial capital and start-up expenses, while others are intended to support ongoing costs of operation. Provincial and territorial ministries can provide information on current funding and criteria. Again, there is a list on such offices in Chapter 2. There may be waiting lists.

- Local service clubs such as Kiwanis, Rotary and Lions sometimes make one-time donations for items such as equipment or improvements to playgrounds.

- The Canadian Centre for Philanthropy (see Appendix A) distributes helpful publications and will do computer searches for a list of foundations which donate to child care services.

- Businesses can be approached to provide assistance. Some types of support include start-up funds, subsidies to employees to offset the cost of child care, salary enhancement grants, and free or low-cost space.

It will be necessary to submit a formal written proposal to request money from government sources, foundations and businesses. Preliminary personal contacts by telephone, letter or in person may indicate whether or not to submit a detailed proposal. Some funders have a preferred format for a proposal. Additional information is provided in Chapter 8, "Financial Matters."

PUBLIC EDUCATION AND ADVOCACY

There are many misconceptions about child care and the needs of Canadian families. Some continue to believe that the "traditional family" of two parents, two children and a mother at home is typical. A few continue to think a mother's working will harm her children. Some Canadians question why their tax dollars should be spent on child care, and why these services are so expensive. Some people believe that children do not learn much when they are young, so the training of caregivers is unnecessary.

A concerted public and government education effort will be needed to achieve a comprehensive, high quality child care system in Canada. This effort is hampered by non-standardized nomenclature in the field. For example, there is no consensus yet on what we should call ourselves: *early childhood educators, child care workers, caregivers*, or—? Some groups have evolved a glossary of terms, but they are not accepted at the national level. The debate about terminology remains a priority area for the next decade.

The public's image of child care needs clarification and improvement. The report *Caring for a living* (CCCF & CDCAA, 1993) found that only sixteen per cent of child care staff surveyed felt they were respected by the general public. It identified promoting more respect for child care workers as a priority second only to providing better salaries.

Too often the link between inadequate salaries, the resulting quality of care and the cost of that care is poorly understood. As discussed in Chapter 1, training in child development is linked to higher quality. Caregivers with appropriate education should receive adequate wages.

Some early childhood educators don't believe they have a role in public education and advocacy, while others feel powerless to do anything. But there are a number of ways to be involved. Caldwell (1987) identifies three types of advocacy—personal, professional and informational.

Personal advocacy can be as straightforward as helping your neighbours understand what you do at your job. When they refer to an early childhood educator as a "babysitter," gently but firmly correct them. Encourage friends to think about why child care costs as much as it does, and how it helps them in their own jobs. Enlighten them on how the early years are a critically important time for learning. Correct assumptions that child care is a custodial service for the poor by making clear that child care is a service used by families of all income groups.

Personal advocacy is generally carried out on one's own time. Some employers, such as public institutions, do not allow advocacy efforts by employees. In such situations, make it clear that you are speaking as a citizen, not as a public employee.

Professional advocacy is more appropriately labelled *lobbying*. Like personal advocacy, its aim is to benefit your profession and the children and parents it serves. There are many groups which advocate for quality early childhood programs. It is important to work toward greater public understanding and support for high quality child care, by broadening the base of support to include other groups such as pediatricians and the business community.

Caldwell entitles her third category *informational advocacy*. This refers to attempts to raise public awareness about the importance of the period of early childhood, and the capacity of high quality programs to strengthen families and provide opportunities for optimal growth and development. To be an effective advocate, all one requires is firsthand knowledge of the issues facing children, families and staff.

Some effective messages to communicate include:

- Child care is not just an issue for women. Both men and women feel the stress of work and family responsibilities.
- Child care services need to be expanded. The gap between supply and demand is significant. Local agencies report long waiting lists for many child care programs. Parents have great difficulty finding care for their infants, toddlers, and school-age children.
- Teacher-caregivers will no longer continue to work for low wages. There is a growing shortage of qualified child care staff in Canada.
- The training of teacher-caregivers is a major determinant of how well children do in child care. Research studies found that one of the most important components of high quality programs was the ongoing training of the staff. In programs where the caregivers had training in early childhood education, the children behaved more positively, were more co-operative, and were more involved in the program.
- Child care is not only a concern of the individual family. It affects business and society as a whole. Employers are becoming increasingly aware of the problems which arise when families are unable to make adequate child care arrangements.

There are a number of ways early childhood educators can convey these messages. It is essential to get more accurate images of the field of child care to the public and government. This requires personal efforts using professional supports.

Membership in a professional organization provides an effective channel for communication with the public and government. Local, provincial and national groups are usually involved in public education and advocacy efforts, and it is beneficial to be aware of the objectives of these groups and to work with them. Some organizations have local branches. National organizations are listed at the end of this chapter in Appendix A. For provincial and local child care organizations, the Canadian Child Care Federation publishes a directory. This publication is a useful tool for contacting others who are concerned with quality child care.

Each practitioner can participate in a number of public education strategies, either through membership in a professional organization or through their work at an individual centre. You can:

- share information and anecdotes with others about your experiences in the program and its significance in the community.
- speak to service clubs and the local media.
- arrange visits to your program from decision makers.
- write letters to the editor of your local newspaper.
- write for professional newsletters or journals.
- write for popular magazines.
- provide leadership at workshops or conferences.
- prepare a deputation to policy-makers on an issue affecting children, families or staff in your program.
- participate in lobbies.

Some individuals you might talk with about your program could include legislators, members of the business community, politicians, media representatives, parents, and other professionals. They are often interested in knowing the number of children you serve and their ages. Describe your program, explaining the service it provides children and families. Take the opportunity to explain the support you require in order to improve the service for children and their families. It is useful to have photographs of the children engaged in positive activities. Encourage prearranged visits to the program. Include parents and staff in presentations.

Starting Points

The following points will assist your thinking about the kinds of information you could provide through public education endeavours:

- Think about the availability of child care in your community. Are there waiting lists for infant care? Is part-time care available for school-age children?
- Is funding available to assist families with the cost of child care? What percentage of a family's total income is needed for child care?
- What are the average salaries of early childhood educators in your community?
- Are there enough training opportunities for child care staff in your community?
- Are salary levels affecting staff retention and the quality of programs? Are salary levels attracting appropriate candidates to the field?
- Do parents have access to information about child care services?
- Are provincial/territorial licensing standards adequate?
- Is there support for child care from your business community?
- Is there a need for care for the children of parents who work shifts? Is there care for children who are sick?

It is important to recognize that we early childhood educators can and do make a difference in improving the quality of programs for young children and their families. Only by working diligently together can we hope to change public attitudes toward child care and early education. This change is required to get the critical mass of support needed to provide a comprehensive, high quality child care system that responds to the diverse needs of Canadian families.

ACTIVITIES

1. Identify an organization in your community that is working for better child care. Make arrangements to attend a meeting, subscribe to a newsletter or interview staff about the goals of the organization.
2. Take out a membership in a professional organization.
3. Attend a conference of a child care organization.
4. Identify three potential funders of a pilot child care service in your community.
5. In small groups, develop a brief presentation on why child care is important for children, parents and employers.
6. Approach a new child care centre and find out the details of how they were able to get started. Compare their experiences with the suggestions in this chapter on steps to follow for new programs.

FURTHER READING

Hendrick, J. (1993) *The whole child, second Canadian edition*; Chapter 22, "Canadian Trends in Early Childhood Education" and Chapter 23, "Canadian Child Care Dilemma: Stategies for Change." Toronto: Maxwell Macmillan Canada.

APPENDIX A: NATIONAL ORGANIZATIONS

The Canadian Centre for Philanthropy
1329 Bay Street, 2nd floor
Toronto, Ontario
M5R 2C4
Phone: (416) 515-0764

Canadian Child Care Federation (CCCF)
120 Holland Avenue
Ottawa, Ontario K1Y 0X6
Phone (613) 729-5289

Child Care Advocacy Association of Canada (CCAAC)
323 Chapel Street, 3rd floor
Ottawa, Ontario K1N 7Z2
Phone (613) 594-3196

Canadian Association for Young Children (CAYC)
5417 Rannock Avenue
Winnipeg, Manitoba R3R 0N3

For a complete listing of additional child care organizations, including provincial /territorial, see the directory published by the CCCF.

APPENDIX B: SAMPLE CHILD CARE SURVEY QUESTIONNAIRE

The establishment of a child care facility in this community is being explored. Your help is needed in this crucial developmental stage. Please complete this survey. The information you provide will remain confidential.

1. My current family status is

    _____ single   _____ one parent   _____ two parent

2. I have children under 6 years living with me.

    _____ I do not have any children 6 years of age living with me, but am expecting children within 3 years.

    _____ I do not have children under 6 years of age living with me and am not expecting to within 3 years.

3. Please indicate the age category of your children:

    _____ Newborn to less than 6 months   _____ 18 months to less than 36 months

    _____ 6 months to less than 18 months   _____ 36 months to six years

4. How satisfied are you with your present child care arrangements?

    _____ Very satisfied   _____ Somewhat dissatisfied

    _____ Somewhat satisfied   _____ Very dissatisfied

5. If you could have your choice of child care arrangements, what would you prefer? Circle one only.

    _____ Child care in my own home   _____ Group child care centre

    _____ Out-of-home caregiver   _____ Other (please describe)

6. What are your usual child care hour needs?

    From _____ to _____

7. When would you require child care?

    _____ Weekends, evenings and/or nights?

    _____ Regularly

    _____ Occasionally

    _____ Never

Your response to this survey is appreciated. Please take a few minutes to share any comments or suggestions you might have regarding child care services. Further comments

BIBLIOGRAPHY

Abbott-Shim, M., and A. Sibley (1986). *Child care inventory*. Atlanta, GA: Humanics.

Almy, M. (1975). *The early childhood educator at work*. New York: McGraw Hill.

Association for Early Childhood Education, Ontario (1988). *High quality child care statement*. Toronto, Ontario.

Ayles, T., and S. Becker-Griffin. (1990). *An A-Z handbook for boards of directors of non-profit community-based child care programs*. Toronto: Umbrella Central Day Care Services/Child Care Initiatives Fund, Health and Welfare Canada.

Ayles, T., and S. Becker-Griffin. (1990). *Daily operations manual with supplement on finance management*. Toronto: Umbrella Central Day Care Services/Child Care Initiatives Fund, Health and Welfare Canada.

Baines, Carol, Patricia Evans, and Sheila Neysmith. *Women's caring: Feminist perspectives on social welfare*. Toronto: McClelland & Stewart, 1991.

B.C. Task Force on Child Care (1991). *Showing we care: a child care strategy for the 90s*. British Columbia.

Beach, J. (1992). *A child care agenda for the 90s: Putting the pieces together—A comprehensive system of child care*. Toronto: Ontario Coalition for Better Child Care/Canadian Advocacy Association.

Belsky, J. (1980). "Future directions for day care research: an ecological analysis." *Child Care Quarterly II*, pp. 82–99.

Berger, E. H. (1981). *Parents as partners in education*. St. Louis, MO: Mosby.

Berlew, D. (1982). *Effective leaders make others feel stronger*. Child Care Information Exchange.

Bertrand, J. (1991). "George Brown College guide to work place child care," in *Health Care Facilities Manual*. Toronto.

Bertrand, J. (1992). *A child care agenda for the 90s: Putting the pieces together—caring for the children*. Toronto: Ontario Coalition for Better Child Care/Ottawa: Canadian Advocacy Association.

Bjorklund, G., and C. Burger (1987). "Making conferences work for parents, teachers and children." *Young Children*, 26–31.

Blenkin, G.M., and A.V. Kelly (eds). (1988). *Early childhood education: A developmental curriculum*. London, England: Paul Chapman Publishing Ltd.

Bloom, P. Jorde, M. Sheerer, and J. Britz (1991). *Blueprint for action: Achieving centre-based change through staff development*. Mt. Rainier, MD.: Gryphon House Inc.

Bloom, P. Jorde (1986). "The administrator's role in the innovation decision process." *Child Care Quarterly*, 15 (2), 182–197.

Bloom, P. Jorde (1986). *Improving the quality of work life: A guide for enhancing the organizational climate in the early childhood setting*. Evanston, IL: National College of Education.

Bloom, P. Jorde (1988). *A great place to work: Improving conditions for staff in young children's programs*. Washington, DC: National Association for the Education of Young Children.

Boutte, G.S., D. Keepler, V. Tyler, and B. Terry (1992). "Effective techniques for involving 'difficult' parents." *Young Children*, 19–22.

Bredekamp, D. (ed.) (1986). *Developmentally appropriate practice*. Washington, DC: NAEYC.

Bredekamp, S. (ed.) (1987). *Developmentally appropriate practice in early childhood programs serving children from birth through age 8*. Washington, D.C.: National Association for the Education of Young Children.

Bronfenbrenner, J. (1979). *The ecology of human development*. Cambridge, MA: Harvard University Press.

Brown, J. (ed.). (1982). *Curriculum planning for young children*. Washington, DC: National Association for the Education of Young Children.

Bryant, B., M. Harris, and D. Newton (1980). *Children and minders*. Ypsilanti, MI: High Scope Press.

Caldwell, B. (1984). "What is quality care?" *Young Children* 39 (3), pp. 3–8.

Caldwell, B. (1987, March). "Advocacy is everybody's business." *Child Care Information Exchange*, 29–32.

Canada, Ministry of Health and Welfare. (1987). *Sharing the responsibility—Federal response to the report of the special committee on child care*. Ottawa: Queen's Printer.

Canada Mortgage and Housing Corporation (1978). *Play spaces for preschoolers* (advisory document prepared by P. Hill, S. Esbensen, and W. Rock). Ottawa: CMHC.

Canadian Child Care Federation (1991). *Definition of high quality child care*. Ottawa.

Canadian Child Care Federation (1991). *Issues in post-secondary education for quality early childhood education care: a discussion paper*. Ottawa: Canadian Child Care Federation.

Canadian Child (Day) Care Federation (1991). *National statement on quality child care*. Ottawa: Canadian Child (Day) Care Federation.

Canadian Child Care Federation (1992). *Directory of Canadian child care organizations*. Ottawa: Canadian Child care Federation.

Canadian Day Care Advocacy Association (1985). *Child Care Facts*. Ottawa: Canadian Day Care Advocacy Association.

Canadian Day Care Advocacy Association and the Canadian Child (Day) Care Federation (A joint project). *Caring for a living: A study on wages and working conditions in Canadian child care*. Ottawa: Karto Communications, 1993.

Canadian Pediatric Society. *Well beings: a guide to promote the physical health, safety and emotional well-being of children in child care centres and family day care homes*. Toronto, 1992: Creative Premises Ltd.

Canadian Standards Association (1990). *A Guideline on Children's Playspaces and Equipment*. (CAN/CSA-Z614-M90).

Carter, M., and E. Jones (1990, September). *The teacher as observer: The director as role model*. Children care information exchange.

Caruso, J., and M. Fawcett (1986). *Supervision in early childhood education: A developmental perspective*. New York: Columbia University: Teacher's College Press.

Chandler, K. (1987). *Survey of accreditation initiatives in Canada*. Canadian Child Day Care Federation.

Chandler, K. (1988). "Accreditation: one route to professionalism." Presentation at the annual conference of the Alberta Association for Young Children.

Chandler, K., and P. Hileman (1986). "Professionalism in early childhood education." *Association for early childhood education newsletter*.

Cherry, C., B. Harkness, and K. Kuzma (1987). *Nursery school and day care center management guide*. Belmont, CA: Fearon.

The Child Care Employee Project (1990). *Taking matters into our own hands: A guide to unionizing in the child care field*. Berkeley, CA: 1990.

Chud, Gyda, et al. (1985) *Early childhood education for a multicultural society: A handbook for educators*. Vancouver: Pacific Educational Press.

Click, P., and D. Click (1990). *Administration of schools for young children*. Albany, NY: Delmar.

Coletta, A. (1982). *Working together: A guide to parent involvement*. Atlanta, GA: Humanics.

Cooke, K., et al. (1986). *Report of the task force on child care*. Ottawa; Supply and Services.

Decker, C. A., and J.R. Decker. (1987). *Planning and administering early programs*. Columbus, OH: Merrill.

Denholm, C., R. Ferguson, and A. Pence (1987). *Professional child and youth care: The Canadian perspective*. Vancouver: University of British Columbia Press.

Derman-Sparks, Louise, and the A.B.C. Task Force (1989). *Anti-bias curriculum: Tools for empowering young children*. Washington, D.C.: National Association for the Education of Young Children.

Doherty, G. (1991). *Quality matters in child care*. Huntsville, Ontario: Jesmond Publishing.

Eiselen, S.S. (1992). *The human side of child care administration—a how-to manual*. Washington, DC: National Association for the Education of Young Children.

Esbensen, S.B. (1984). *Hidden hazards on playgrounds for children*. Hull, Quebec: Université du Québec à Hull.

Esbensen, S.B. (1987) *The early childhood education playground: An outdoor classroom*. Ypsilanti, MI: High Scope Press.

Evans, E. D. (1975). *Contemporary influences in early childhood education*. New York: Holt, Rinehart & Winston.

Feeney, S., and R. Chun. (1985). "Research in review: effective teachers of young children." *Young Children*, 41 (1).

Feeney, S., and R. Chun. (1987, May). "Ethical case studies for reader response." *Young Children*.

Feeney, S., D. Christensen, and E. Moracvik (1987). *Who am I in the lives of children?* (3rd ed.). Columbus, OH: Merrill.

Friendly, M. (1988). *Child care information sheets*. Toronto: Centre for Urban and Community Studies.

Frost, J.L. (1992). *Play and playscapes*. New York: Delmar.

Galinsky, E. (1978) *Easing parents through beginnings and endings*. Child Care Information Exchange.

Galinsky, E., and D. Friedman (1986). *Investing in quality child care: A report for AT&T*. Short Hill, NJ: Bank Street College of Education.

Galinsky, E. (1988) "Parents and teacher-caregivers: Sources of tension, sources of support." *Young Children*, 4–12.

Galinsky, E. (1990, July). "Why are some parent/teacher partnerships clouded with difficulties?" *Young Children*, 2–3, 38–39.

Gilligan, Carol. *In a different voice*. Boston: Harvard University Press, 1982.

Glickman, C. D. (1985). *Supervision of instruction: a developmental approach*. Boston: Allyn and Bacon.

Goelman, H., and Pence, A. (1985). "Towards the ecology of day care in Canada: a research agenda for the 1980's." *Canadian Journal of Education*.

Goffin, S., and J. Lombardi (1988). *Speaking out: Early childhood advocacy*. Washington: NAEYC.

Government of Alberta. (1987). *Day Care Regulation 14*. Edmonton: Publication Services.

Government of Alberta. (1988). *The Social Care Facilities Licensing Act*. Edmonton: Publication Services.

Government of Alberta. (1990). *Day Care Regulation—Alberta Regulation 333/90*. Edmonton: Publication Services.

Government of British Columbia (1989). *Community Care Facility Act—Child Care Regulation*. Regulation 319/89. Victoria: Queen's Printer for British Columbia.

Government of British Columbia. (1979). *Community Care Facility Act*. Chapter 57. Victoria: Queen's Printer for British Columbia.

Government of British Columbia. (1979). *Guaranteed Available Income for Need Act*. R. S. Chapter 158. Victoria: Queen's Printer for British Columbia.

Government of Manitoba (1987). *The Community Child Day Care Standards Act—Child Day Care Regulation*. Winnipeg: Queen's Printer for Manitoba.

Government of Manitoba. (1986). *Manitoba Regulation 62/86*. Winnipeg: Queen' s Printer.

Government of Manitoba. (1987). *The Community Child Day Care Standards Act—Child Day Care Regulation*. Winnipeg: Queen' s Printer for Manitoba.

Government of New Brunswick (1983). *Child and Family Services and Family Relations Act*. Fredericton: Queen's Printer for New Brunswick.

Government of New Brunswick. (1983). *Child and Family Services and Family Relations Act*. Fredericton: Queen' s Printer for New Brunswick.

Government of New Brunswick. (1983). *Family Services Act*. Chap. C - 2.1, Part II Community placement resources. Fredericton: Queen' s Printer for New Brunswick.

Government of New Brunswick. (1985). *Day Care Facilities Standards*. Fredericton: Queen' s Printer for New Brunswick.

Government of New Brunswick. (Consolidated to June 30, 1985). *Family Services Act Regulations 8385;* under *Family Services Act. O. C. 83-457*. Fredericton: Queen' s Printer for New Brunswick.

Government of Newfoundland (1982). *Newfoundland Regulations 219/82: Day Care and Homemaker Services Regulations, 1982*.

Government of Newfoundland. (1982). *The Day Care and Homemaker Services Regulations*. Newfoundland Regulations 219/82, 1982 (under *The Day Care and Homemaker Services Act, 1975*). St. John's: Queen's Printer for Newfoundland.

Government of Newfoundland. (1990). *The Day Care and Homemaker Services Act*. St. John's: Queen's Printer for Newfoundland.

Government of Nova Scotia (1989). *Day Care Act and Regulations: Chapter 120 of the Revised Statutes, 1989*. Halifax: Queen's Printer for Nova Scotia.

Government of Ontario (1987). *Initial steps in starting a day nursery in Ontario*. Toronto: Ministry of Community and Social Services.

Government of Ontario. (1985). *Day nurseries: Highlights of the legislation*. Toronto: Ministry of Community and Social Services.

Government of Ontario. (1987). *New directions*. Toronto: Ministry of Community and Social Services.

Government of Ontario. (1988). *Day nurseries manual*. Toronto: Queen's Printer of Ontario.

Government of Ontario. (1988). *The Ontario study of relevance of education and issue of dropouts*. Toronto: Queen' s Printer for Ontario.

Government of Ontario. (1990). *Day Nurseries Act* (Revised Statutes of Ontario, 1980. Chapter 11). Toronto: Queen' s Printer for Ontario.

Government of Ontario. (1990). *Ontario Regulation 760/83*.
(Under the *Day nurseries act.*).

Government of Prince Edward Island. (1987). *Guiding principles for the development of child care services*. Charlottetown: Acting Queen' s Printer.

Government of Prince Edward Island. (1988). *Prince Edward Island's Child Care Facilities Act Regulations*. R. S. P. E. I. Cap. C-5. (including any amendments to December 31, 1990). Charlottetown: Acting Queen' s Printer.

Government of Quebec (1987). *Regulations Respecting Day Care Centres*. Quebec City: Editeur Officiel du Québec.

Government of Quebec. (1992). *Loi sur les services de garde à l'enfance L. R. Q., chapitre S-4.1 1979* (incluant les modifications apportees jusqu'au 1er octobre 1992) A jour au 1er décembre 1992. (*An act respecting child care.*) Quebec City: Editeur Officiel du Québec.

Government of Quebec. (1993). *Reglement sur les services de garde en garderie, dernière modification*: 17 octobre 1991, à jour au 16 février 1993. (*Regulations respecting child care centres.*) Quebec City: Editeur Officiel du Québec.

Government of Saskatchewan (1990). *An Act to Promote the Growth and Development of Children and to Support the Provision of Child Care Services to Saskatchewan Families*. Regina: Queen's Printer for Saskatchewan.

Government of Saskatchewan. (1989). *The Child Care Act*. Chapter C-7.3. Regina: Saskatchewan Social Services.

Government of Saskatchewan. (1990). *The Child Care Regulations 948/90*. Chapter C-7.3 REG. 1 Section 27. Regina: Saskatchewan Social Services.

Government of the Northwest Territories. (1987), *Child Day Care Standards Regulations*. Yellowknife: Queen' s Printer.

Government of the Northwest Territories. (1988). *Northwest Territories Child Day Care Act*. Yellowknife: Queen' s Printer.

Government of the Yukon (1990). *Child Care Centre Program Regulations, O.C. 1990/115*. Whitehorse: Commissioner of the Yukon.

Government of the Yukon. (1990). *Child Care Act*. Bill 77. (Statutes of the Yukon). Whitehorse: Commissioner of the Yukon.

Government of the Yukon. (1990). *Child Care Subsidy Regulations*. Order-in-Council, 1990/116. (Pursuant to section 40 of the Child care act.) Whitehorse: Commissioner of the Yukon.

Government of the Yukon. (1990). *Family Day Home Program Regulations*. Order-in-Council, 1990/117. (Pursuant to section 40 of the Child Care Act.) Whitehorse: Commissioner of the Yukon.

Green, Barbara (Chair). (1991). *Canada's children: Investing in our future—report on the standing committee on health and welfare, social affairs, seniors and the status of women*. Ottawa: Queen's Printer.

Greenberg, P. (1989, May). "Parents as partners in young children's development and education: A new American fad? Why does it matter?" *Young Children*, 61-75.

Greenman, J., and R. Fugua (1984). *Making day care better: Training, evaluation and the process of change*. New York: Teacher's College Press.

Guralnick, M. (1990). "Major accomplishments and future directions in early childhood mainstreaming," in *Topics in Early Childhood Special Education* Vol. 10, No. 2: p.1–7.

Halpern, R. (1987, September). "Major social and demographic trends affecting young families: Implications for early childhood care and education." *Young Children*, 34-40.

Harms, T., and R. Clifford (1980) *The early childhood environment rating scale*. New York: Teacher's College Press.

Harms, T., and R.M. Clifford. (1989), *Family home day care environment rating scale*. New York: Teacher's College Press.

Harms, T., D. Cryer, and R.M. Clifford. (1990). *The Infant/toddler environment rating scale*. New York: Teachers College Press.

Health and Welfare Canada. (1992). *The child benefit—A white paper on Canada's new integrated child tax benefit*. Ottawa: Queen's Printer.

Helgesen, S. *Female advantage: Women's ways of leadership*. New York: Doubleday, 1990.

Hersey, P., and K. Blanchard (1977). *Management of organizational behavior: Utilizing human resources*. Englewood Cliffs, New Jersey: Prentice-Hall.

Hildebrand, V. (1993). *Management of child development centers*. New York: Macmillan.

Honig, A. *Parental involvement in early childhood education*. (rev. ed.). Washington, DC: National Association for the Education of Young Children.

Hunsaker, P., and A. Alessandra (1980). *The art of managing people*. New York: Simon and Schuster.

Hurst, Lynda. (1992). *A death blow for day care—How Tories reneged on their promise to set up a national system*. Toronto: Toronto Star (March 15, 1992).

Janmohamed, Zeenat. (1992). *Making the connections—Child care in Metropolitan Toronto*. Toronto: Metro Toronto Coalition for Better Child Care.

Joffe, C. (1979). *Friendly intruders: Childcare professionals and family life*. Berkeley: University of California Press.

Johnson, D. W., and F.P. Johnson (1991). *Joining together: Group theory and group skills*. Boston: Allyn and Bacon.

Johnson, D. W., and R. Johnson (1989). *Cooperation and competition: Theory and research*. Edina, MN: Interaction Book Company.

Jones, E., and L. Derman-Sparks (1992, January). "Meeting the challenge of diversity." *Young Children.*

Katz, L. (1972). "Developmental stages of preschool teachers." *Elementary School Journal*, 73, 50–55.

Katz, L., and E. Ward (1978). *Ethical behaviour in early childhood education.* Washington, DC: NAEYC.

Kilbride, Kenise. (1990). *Multicultural early childhood education: A resource kit.* Toronto: Ryerson Press.

Kipnis, K. (1987). "How to discuss professional ethics." *Young Children.*

Kritchevsky, S., E. Prescott, and L. Walling (1983). *Planning environments for young children: Physical space.* Washington, D.C.: National Association for the Education of Young Children.

Kurtz, R. (1991, January-February). *Stabilizer, catalyst, troubleshooter, or visionary— Which are you?* Child Care Information Exchange, 27–31.

Kyle, I., and D. Lero (1985). *Day care quality: its definition and implementation.* Ottawa: Task Force on Child Care.

Lemire, Denise. (1993). *Services de garde au Québec.* Ottawa: Federation canadienne des services de garde à l'enfance.

Lero, D. S., and Kyle, I. (1985). *Day care quality: Its definition and implementation.* Paper submitted to the Task Force on Child Care.

Lightfoot, S. (1978). *Worlds apart: Relationships between families and schools.* New York: Basic Books.

Lovell, P., and Harms, T. (1985). "How can playgrounds be improved? A rating scale." *Young Children* 40 (3): 3-8

Manburg, A. (1985, January). "Parent involvement: A look at practices that work." Child Care Information Exchange.

Manitoba Community Services Child Day Care (1986). *Competency based assessment: Policy and procedures.* Winnipeg, MB.

Martin, S. (1987). *Sharing the responsibility: Report of the special committee on child care.* Ottawa: Queen's Printer.

Maxwell, Anne. (1993). *Child care in Alberta.* Ottawa: Canadian Child Care Federation.

Ministry of Culture and Recreation, Ontario. (1982). *A guide to creative playground equipment.* Toronto: Government of Ontario.

Mitchell, M. (1987). *Caring for Canada's children—Special report on the crisis in child care.* Ottawa: Queen's Printer.

Morgan, G. (1982). *Managing the day care dollar.* Cambridge, MA: Steam Press.

Morgan, G. (1984). "Change through regulation," in J. Greenman and R. Fugua, eds. *Making daycare better: training, evaluation and the process of change.* New York: Teachers' College Press.

Murphy-Hupé, Jennifer. *Child care in British Columbia*. Ottawa: Canadian Child Care Federation.

Murphy-Hupé, Jennifer. *Child care in Manitoba*. Ottawa: Canadian Child Care Federation.

Murphy-Hupé, Jennifer. (1992). *Child care in New Brunswick*. Ottawa: Canadian Child Care Federation.

Murphy-Hupé, Jennifer. (1992). *Child care in Ontario*. Ottawa: Canadian Child Day Care Federation.

Murphy-Hupé, Jennifer. (1993). *Child care in the Yukon*. Ottawa: Canadian Child Care Federation.

Murphy-Hupé, Jennifer. (1993). *Child care in the Northwest Territories*. Ottawa: Canadian Child Care Federation.

Murphy-Hupé, Jennifer. *Child Care in Newfoundland*. Ottawa: Canadian Child Care Federation.

Murphy-Hupé, Jennifer. *Child care in Nova Scotia*. Ottawa: Canadian Child Care Federation.

Murphy-Hupé, Jennifer. *Child care in Prince Edward Island*. Ottawa: Canadian Child Day Care Federation.

Murphy-Hupé, Jennifer. *Child care in Saskatchewan*. Ottawa: Canadian Child care Federation.

National Academy of Early Childhood Programs. (1985). *Guide to accreditation by the National Academy of Early Childhood Programs: Self-study, validation, accreditation*. Washington, DC: National Association for the Education of Young Children.

National Association for the Education of Young Children. *Position statement on licencing and other forms of regulation of early childhood programs in centres and family day care* (535). Washington, DC: National Association for the Education of Young Children.

National Association for the Education of Young Children. (1984). *Accreditation criteria and procedures of the national academy of early childhood programs*. Washington, DC: NAEYC.

National Association for the Education of Young Children. (1986). "Position statement on developmentally appropriate practice in early childhood education programs serving children from birth to age 8." *Young Children*, 41(6), 3.

National Association for the Education of Young Children. (1987). *NAEYC position statement on licensing and other forms of regulation of early childhood programs in centres and family day care*. Washington, DC: NAEYC.

National Council of Welfare. (1988). *Child care: A better alternative*. Ottawa: Minister of Supply and Services Canada.

National Council of Welfare. (1992). *The 1992 budget and child benefits*. Ottawa: Minister of Supply and Services, Canada.

National Day Care Information Centre (1987). *National strategy on child care.* Ottawa: Health and Welfare Canada.

National Day Care Information Centre (1991). *Status of day care in Canada.* Ottawa: Health and Welfare Canada.

National Day Care Information Centre. (1986). *Provincial day care requirements— Nutritional requirements, space requirements, minimum staff/child ratios.* Ottawa: Health and Welfare Canada.

National Day Care Information Centre. (1986). *Provincial funding of day care services.* Ottawa: Health and Welfare Canada.

National Day Care Information Centre. (1987, December). *National strategy on child care.* Ottawa: Health and Welfare Canada.

National Day Care Information Centre. (1988). *Child care initiatives fund.* Ottawa: Health and Welfare Canada.

National Day Care Information Centre. (1991). *Status of day care in Canada.* Ottawa: Health and Welfare Canada.

Nedler, S. E., and O.D. McAfee (1979). *Working with parents.* Belmont, CA: Wadsworth.

Neugebauer, B. (1990, September-October). *Are you listening?* Child Care Information Exchange, 62.

Neugebauer, R. (1985, November). *Are you an effective leader?* Child Care Information Exchange, 45–50.

Olenick, M. (1986). *The relationship between quality and cost in child care programs* (7). Los Angeles, CA: Brief reports on current research compiled by the Bush Program in Child and Family Policy.

Oloman, Mab. (1992). *A child care agenda for the 90s: Putting the pieces together— child care funding.* Toronto: Ontario Coalition for Better Child Care/Canadian Day Care Advocacy Association.

Ontario Coalition for Better Day Care. (1986). *Child care challenge: Organizing in Ontario.* Toronto: Ontario Coalition for Better Day Care.

Parkay, F., and S. Damico (1989, Spring). "Empowering teachers for change through faculty-driven school improvement." *Journal of Staff Development,* 10(2) 8–14.

Pence, A., H. Goelman, and D. Lero (1993). *Where are the children: an analysis of child care arrangements used while parents work and study.* Ottawa: Statistics Canada.

Pence, Alan. (1992). *Canadian child care in context: Perspectives from the provinces and territories.* Ottawa: Statistics Canada.

Peters, D. (1988). "The child development associate credential and the educationally disenfranchised," in *Professionalism and the early childhood practitioner.* Columbia University: Teacher's College Press.

Phillips, D. (ed.) (1987). *Quality in child care programs: What does research tell us?* Washington, DC: NAEYC.

Radomski, M. (1986, July). "Professionalization of early childhood educators: How far have we progressed?" *Young Children.*

Read, K., and J. Patterson. (1993). *The nursery school and kindergarten—A human relationships laboratory.* New York: Holt, Rinehart & Winston.

Ruopp, R., H. Travers, F. Glantz, and C. Coelen (1979). *Children at the centre: Final report of the national day care study (vol. I).* Cambridge, MA: Abt Associates.

Schom-Moffat, Patti. (1992). *Caring for a lving: National study on wages and working conditions in Canadian child care.* Ottawa: Canadian Child Care Federation and Canadian Day Care Advocacy Association.

Schwartz, S., and H. Robison (1982). *Designing curriculum for early childhood.* Boston, MA: Allyn and Bacon.

Schweinhart, L., and D. Weikart (eds.) (1985). *Quality in early childhood programs: Four perspectives.* Ypsilanti, MI: High Scope Early Childhood Policy Papers.

Sciarra, D., and A. Dorsey (1990). *Developing and administering a child care centre.* Albany, NY: Delmar Publishers.

Seaver, J., and C. Cartwright (1986). *Child care administration.* Belmont, CA: Wadsworth.

Seefeldt, C. (1980). *Teaching young children.* Englewood Cliffs, NJ: Prentice-Hall.

Seshagiri, Lynne. (1993). *Child care in Canada—Highlights of the 1992/1993 background papers.* Ottawa: Canadian Child Care Federation.

Sissons, Brenda, and Heather McDowall Black. (1992). *Choosing with care— The Canadian parent's practical guide to quality child care for infants and toddlers.* Toronto: Addison-Wesley Publishers Limited.

Spodek, B. (1970, October). "What are the sources of early childhood curriculum?" *Young Children.*

Spodek, B., O. Saracho, and D. Peters (eds.) (1988). *Professionalism and the early childhood practitioner.* Columbia University: Teacher's College Press.

Spodek, B., O. Saracho, and D. Peters (eds.) (1990). *Early childhood teacher preparation.* Columbia University: Teacher's College Press.

Stengel, S. (1982). "The preschool curriculum." In D. Streets (Ed.), *Administering day care and preschool programs* (pp. 27–69). Boston, MA: Allyn and Bacon.

Stevens, Jr., J. H., and E.W. King. (1976). *Administering early childhood education programs.* Boston: Little, Brown.

Taylor, B.J. (1993). *Early childhood program management—People and procedures.* New York: Merrill.

The Roeher Institute (1992). *Quality child care for all: A guide to integration.* North York, Ontario: The Roeher Institute.

Townson, M. (1986). *The costs and benefits of a national child care system for Canada*. Halifax: DPA Group Inc.

VanderVen, K.D. (1988). "Pathways to professional effectiveness for early childhood educators," in B. Spodek, O. Saracho and D. Peters, *Professionalism and the early childhood practitioner* (pp. 137–160). New York: Teacher's College Press.

Wach, T.D. and G. Gruen (1982) *Early experiences and human development*. New York: Plenum.

Walsh, P. (1988). *Early childhood playground: Planning an outside learning environment*. Melbourne, Australia: Martin Educational, in association with Robert Andersen and Associates.

Whitebrook, M., C. Howes, and D. Phillips (1990). *Who cares? Child care teachers and the quality of child care in America. Final report of the National Child Care Staffing Study*. Oakland, CA: Child Care Employee Project.

Whitebrook, M., C. Howes, R. Darrah, and J. Friedman (1982). "Caring for the caregivers: Staff burnout in child care" in *Current topics in early childhood education*, vol. 4. Norward, NJ: Ablex Publishers.

Willer, B. (1987). *The growing crisis in childcare: Quality, compensation and affordability in early childhood programs*. Washington, DC: NAEYC.

INDEX